Travel Tales: Women Alone — The #MeToo of Travel!

True Travel Tales, Volume 3

Michael Brein

Published by Michael Brein, 2018.

TRAVEL TALES: WOMEN ALONE — THE #METOO OF TRAVEL!

First edition. March 2, 2018.

Copyright © 2018 Michael Brein.

ISBN: 978-1886590533

Written by Michael Brein.

Also by Michael Brein

True Travel Tales
Travel Tales: Michael's Own Top 25
Travel Tales: Michael's Own Best 150
Travel Tales: Women Alone — The #MeToo of Travel!

Watch for more at www.michaelbrein.com.

You wouldn't believe the incredible strories people have told me about their travels!

Introduction

Michael Brein

These are the true travel tales of solo women travelers being sexually harassed and assaulted in their travels around the world and what some of them were able to do about it!

They are shouting *"Me Too!"* to you through these pages!

No human being should be subjected to the despicable, disgusting and degrading behaviors that these women have had to put up with at the hands of men who should be relegated to the dregs of humanity!

For my *True Travel Tales* series, I have interviewed nearly 2,000 world travelers. And I have weaved the best of their 10,000 fantastic travel tales into a psychology of travel as revealed by these very telling stories. These are travelers I've met on airplanes, trains, buses, ships, tours, safaris, and in hotels, campgrounds, cafes, and pubs.

These courageous travelers have shared often their most personal and private travel experiences, some good and wonderful and others horrific and life-threatening, which I, in turn, share with you now through this series in general and this book in particular.

Travel Tales: Women Alone is Volume 3 of the *True Travel Tales* series and deals with safety and security of the woman solo traveler. It is about how to travel safely throughout the world.

Unfortunately, travel today finds us in a world of growing terror threats, the imposition of severe and strict cultural and religious restrictions on women's rights and freedoms, as well as decreasing tolerance for cultural and religious differences and diversity around the world.

For women traveling alone, having to deal with sexual hassles and assaults is daunting in the least. For women alone, travel mostly is exciting and relatively safe, but for many women, traveling in some countries, particularly in North Africa and the Middle East, can often be traumatic and downright dangerous.

I have tales of women constantly being bothered and harassed. And, sad to say, some women have even disappeared from marketplaces, never to be seen again.

To be a woman and to travel alone in such forbidding and foreboding places is not for the faint of heart. Many young women are naively unaware and must be exceedingly careful in their interactions with men overseas.

Just because men are well-dressed and speak your language does not necessarily mean that they can be trusted.

Every woman traveling abroad needs to know about and prepare herself for dealing with such things. Again, while travel is mostly adventurous, exciting and safe, it can also be foreboding and downright dangerous at times, and one must be prudent.

Forgive me for pulling no punches: but, if I were you, I'd think very carefully about traveling to some parts of the world as a woman ALONE!

Women have shared hundreds of travel stories with me about how they have had to fend off — yes, even *fight off* at times — the unwanted advances of men, ranging from verbal harassment, unwanted touching, exposure, and, yes, even rape and disappearance!

I have had young women relating to me, "Yes, I should have known better; I should have seen the signs."

The stories in this book emphasize how women alone have gotten themselves into dangerous situations in the first place, how they coped and sometimes managed to escape and survive, and what they might have done differently in retrospect if they had to re-experience these harassments and assaults all over again.

Every effort is made to uncover the clues and cues to dangerous situations and to provide, where feasible, possible ways to avoid these scary and horrific experiences in the first place.

Finally, a series of *"Travel Tips"* are offered throughout this book in support of experiencing travel in the most safe and secure manner possible.

And to those brave and courageous women who have forged their paths in travel and endured the suffering of sexual harassment and assault to bring to you useful knowledge and valuable information that can help you to avoid that which they have had to suffer through, we say, *"Thank you"* for shouting out to the world in your own special ways, *"Me Too!"*

DISCLAIMER

Please know that some stories in the *True Travel Tales* series may be graphic, unpleasant, and disturbing. This book is aimed towards a mature adult audience. Yet, some material ought to be communicated in a clear and responsible manner to younger and relatively inexperienced travelers who could benefit by knowing how to travel more safely and securely.

No story in the series is meant to depict any country, people, race, culture or religion in a negative light. Good and bad things can and do happen anywhere and to anyone.

Finally, some stories may appear in other books depending on the countries and subject matter covered.

What's in Your Wallet?

Ellen Good

Paris, France, the 1970s. After having gotten lost in the Paris Metro, I finally got to the youth hostel at 11:30 PM, and it was still open, thank God! They gave me a room all to myself since I was obviously the last person to arrive.

At 3 o'clock in the morning, this light flashes on. Of course, I was sound asleep, and not realizing at the time that it was in the middle of the night, this guy asks me, "Where is your plastic card?"

I wake up and he goes, "Do you have your plastic card?"

Then, half asleep I go, "Yeah," and begin looking through my things. "What plastic card?" I ask.

He then goes, "The one that says you can stay here."

So, I look through my things again and tell him that I have it.

He goes, "Well, this is your thing that tells you can have breakfast and lunch."

I say that I knew that.

He offers, "Would you like a cigarette?"

"No."

"Would you like something to drink?"

"No."

"I'm just working. Would you like to talk for a while?"

"No."

"How about a kiss then?"

"NO!"

And then he goes, "I need a kiss before I can leave."

I tell him, "Kiss the outside of a door then!"

Finally, he leaves. I slept with a knife on my wrist for the rest of the night.

Multiple Harassments

Alicia Alexander

Havana, Cuba, the early 2000s. Using your own expression of having described yourself as being a 'small female,' has that come into play during any of your other travels?

Havana

I am Alicia Alexander (an assumed name). That I was a girl of small stature might have been a factor in my being harassed multiple times during my travels. I feel that it definitely has come into play in a number of countries that I traveled in. Maybe that made me more vulnerable to being a potential target; who can say for sure? But it might have been a factor.

Could you perhaps give a couple examples of this?

I was in Cuba. I decided to walk around Havana and sightsee. I came across some men who were carriage drivers. They were saying, "Oh, come up on the carriage and take pictures!"

I did. And when I got back down, one of them started to walk with me. I didn't really know what to think of it, but since I wanted to learn more about life in Havana, I kind of humored him for a little while.

And so, we walked a ways, and then it became clear that it was getting to be very uncomfortable for me.

Okay, please be more explicit.

Well, he tried to have me go up into this room in an abandoned building, and I said no. And I just kept on walking.

Then, I walked into a church where there were a lot of people there, hoping to shake him. And I felt pretty safe there thinking that was a good thing to do. But no such luck! He followed me right in there, and then he did something that was very inappropriate.

What did he do?

Well, he basically flashed me.

Right there in the church?

Yep, right in the *CHURCH!*

So, what did you think then?

I was completely shocked, especially since it was in a church, and even then, while there were other people around, even though they weren't directly looking and didn't see anything.

And here I was thinking, *Well, this is more of a safe situation — a safe place for me to be!*

But, it couldn't be further from the truth! So, anyway, I threw down the flower that he had given me earlier and just started running.

Meanwhile, it's nighttime in Havana, and I sort of know my way back to the hotel, but I'm not really sure. It was scary. On the way back, you know, I had some people kind of calling out to me, whether it was because they could tell I was American and wanted money, or if it was for whatever other reason. I just ignored them.

Well, you must have looked a bit distressed, right?

Right.

But I made it back okay. Definitely, that was one of several instances where I've been followed in different countries

Paris

Paris, France, the early 2000s. It happened in Italy and France as well. One time it was in Paris, and I was trying to run away from this guy who kept bothering me. I didn't really want to run back to my hostel because I didn't want him to know where I was staying.

But you know, I also didn't know where else to go, and so, at first, I tried to pretend that I didn't speak French and didn't understand what he was saying to me. And then, you know, after a while, I decided to get where there were other people around him and yelled very loudly in French for all to hear. "Leave me alone! Get away from me! Go away!"

Did that work?

Yes, it worked!

Making a scene in a public place to embarrass the assailant!

Right, that helps!

Venice

Venice, Italy, the early 2000s. And then one other time I wasn't quite as tenacious. I was in Venice, and the same kind of thing happened — somebody was following me and not really leaving me alone. I think with him it was more just a matter of ignoring him for a long time. Finally, he gave up.

Okay, so what works for getting rid of these people?

I think part of it might depend on the country, but getting to where there are other people is certainly helpful. And creating a public scene seems to work. Also, what probably works best, when you really need more support in such situations, is to try to connect with other tourists or other English-speaking people. Let them know that you're in an uncomfortable situation and that you need their help or you need somebody else to be with you briefly.

Let's go back to the Cuban incident and reexamine that. In retrospect, did you see cues that you could have perhaps picked up on earlier?

Yeah, definitely. Looking back on it, there are definitely things that I would have done differently. And, I think I had a false impression about Cuba, not realizing that in Cuba, machismo thrives there, too, as well as all over Latin America.

I felt that there were things I could have done differently. But at the same time, I also felt that even if I were walking around the streets by myself, this person could have forced me into that room in the abandoned building instead of letting it go when I simply said no.

So, looking back on all these experiences, it kind of makes me feel like I'm not sure that I would want to travel all by myself anymore, which is very discouraging because I think it's ultimately really the best way to travel.

Well, now you say that you might have done some things differently; can you be more specific?

Just not trusting people as much — which is kind of sad to not be able to trust people — but yeah, I'm thinking that walking with someone in the daytime in a populated city is probably relatively safe. But you know, it can become unsafe very easily.

Yes, I guess I kind of wanted to meet friends, but you kind of have to do that with other women travelers than with local men.

If I were to ask you how do you know you can trust someone, is there anything that comes to mind in a situation like that? How do you know you can trust a man?

Well, I don't know, quite honestly. It could be the same situation with a male American that you meet in a hostel, you know. So, anyone that you travel with, you really have to be cautious about. I guess the only thing really is that you have to be able to trust your instincts. I don't know, quite honestly.

Sounds as though you kind of have done the right things. Although you took a few risks, you didn't really get yourself totally into a situation that you couldn't get out of.

So, you know you were doing it right. And let's face it: you've got to take some risks to really get the full benefits of travel.

In the Mosque?

Amy Christine Godard

North Africa, Morocco, 2000. We were touring the oldest part of the city in the *medina* (the market). There was a mosque in there. This Moroccan guy pulls us from off the street. He's talking English to us, and he is saying, "You must go in and visit the mosque, and it's a women's mosque! Where women can go in."

So, how'd you feel about that?

Of course, I was curious. It was interesting. I wanted to learn as much about the culture as I could. Since my German boyfriend, Henning, was with me, I felt safe. And so, we went into the mosque together. There was a woman in there by the entrance with a basket in front of her, presumably used to charge and collect a fee. The man said to pay the woman to go in and to get a tour of the mosque.

It was about how much?

I think it was the equivalent of about two American dollars. So, we hand her the money and we enter the mosque. She walks us around and gives us a brief tour. And this guy's still with us, of course; he is following us around in the mosque.

And then, for some reason — maybe the 'tour' was finished — she now leaves us. And, now it's apparently his turn; he now asks us for some money for himself.

What crosses your mind at that point?

Well, we, of course, think it is a little ridiculous for us to have to pay again, sort of a scam. But, since it wasn't a lot of money, we think it's not that big a deal. So, we decide to give him a little money, anyway, and we hand him the money.

Next, out of the blue, he then embraces Henning and gives him a hug. How odd and out of place that seems.

And, if that is not enough, he now comes up to me and does the same thing to me: he embraces me, too, but *WHOA!* — He *ALSO* gropes me. (Laughs embarrassedly).

In the *MOSQUE?* Of all places! Who'd a thunk!

It's not very holy to do that, is it?

And I am like ... my jaw drops! I am so surprised by this. I just cannot believe it!

What did you do?

Well, he basically plays it as if I didn't notice it at all. As if maybe it is accidental on his part and apparently just below some kind of a threshold of noticeability, under the radar, so-to-speak, maybe.

So, I look right at him and say to him with great emphasis... *"In the MOSQUE?"*

That's what I say to him, "In the Mosque?"

And he just kind of just scuttles off with his two dinars and his cheap little thrill.

I just I say to Henning, "Let's leave! NOW!"

I then tell Henning, "This man just does not know enough about women. You just don't grab a woman like that!"

But they evidently DO! Don't they? And they do it in other countries, too, like in Turkey.

I mean, I just felt violated, but it's funny; it was like I wasn't too upset because I couldn't really go any further with it. It seemed pretty basic, and almost like he just might have or could have accidentally done it, or tried to make it seem accidental, as if just below some sort of a threshold. Believe me, I wish it could be interpreted that way.

But, I certainly knew better, that it was <u>NO</u> accident — that he had, of course, done it on purpose.

So, you knew that he knew that you knew... that kind of thing?

Absolutely.

In the end, he definitely appeared to be wary, if not a little embarrassed afterwards.

He was embarrassed?

He appeared to be a little embarrassed.

Because of what you said maybe — *"In the MOSQUE?"*

No doubt!

We kind of just walked out of there in total disbelief and just continued to walk along.

He kind of scammed you, too, didn't he? As if there was some method to his madness, huh?

Yes, he scammed us on a couple of accounts.

I thought at first that he maybe had some sort of connection with the mosque. That perhaps he was somebody who had his wife go to the mosque or something like that. Or had something to do with the mosque in some way.

Do you think that is the normal charge, and that the two-dinar price you paid to go in was typical in that culture?

Yeah, I think the entrance charge to the mosque or for the tour was fairly normal — what they did as part of their culture. But the part where the man asked us for money for himself, no doubt, was a bit of a scam. That was, undoubtedly, something that just about anyone could try to charge you, whatever they wanted to, to get you to go in or to be a guide of some sort, or to give you a tour. It was probably whatever they could get away with.

Little kids tried all the time to get you to let them be your 'guides' for a fee and lead you around. So, it's no surprise that the adults would try to get money from you as well — to rip you off, or not quite that. And there are about a million and one ways they can do that to you, you know. They certainly learn how to do it in their lifetimes!

Did anybody else try one of these other million and one ways to get money from you?

Oh, yeah... definitely. They tried.

For example, when you walk through the medina, you know, they literally grab you and pull you into their shops.

And I'd just go, "No, no, no!"

All the time, literally; they'd just grab you and pull you in.

It's overwhelming and really different from our culture. The men would just look and see your clothes. They'd see that you're a Western-looking woman, so they'd think: number one — that you have plenty of money; and number two — that you are loose as well.

I think it's really different to see all the older Moroccan women totally covered up. They were wearing all black; they all had their whole bodies covered. And it was very hot outside and probably horribly uncomfortable for them.

A lot of the younger women, however, weren't so all covered up, and some of them even wore more modern clothes as well.

It's how they treat you. They treat you like it's okay to try to get something from you, and it's very known that they are trying to get your money. And the shop people speak enough languages to get you to buy something. After a while you just need to get out of there; it's so stifling and overwhelming.

Cautionary Tales:
Ignominy in Bari

Pamela K. Stewart

Bari, Italy, 1973. I was 17, blonde, wearing shorts and toting a back-pack. I had been getting mildly harassed through much of Italy, but it was mostly, you know, of the "hey baby, what's cooking" variety. Essentially harmless, but discomforting nonetheless.

But, then when I got to Bari, which is on the Adriatic Coast and is a major train hub, things got entirely different. I was coming from Venice on my way to Greece. So, I stopped in Bari in order to catch the train to Brindisi, in the heel of Italy, from where you depart for Greece by ship.

As I was walking along the streets in Bari, just minding my own business, men would come up to me and do horrendous things like grab my breasts or even put their hands in between my legs just as they were passing by and they just kept on going. Each time it happened I was so surprised that I just sort of froze in place, and by the time I recovered, they were gone — you know like... poof! There was very little I could do about it.

So, what do you do? In retrospect, what would you do now?

I have no idea, really. I talked to other people. One girl said that when something like that happened to her — she had been eating an ice cream cone at the time — she just mashed it in the guy's face, whereupon he got very threatening and almost beat her up.

Maybe that was not such a good idea.

And, oh, one thing that seems to work is to walk with nuns, believe it or not! I've talked to some girls who had friends, who just happened to be nuns, and they walked around with them, and nothing of that sordid kind of thing ever happened to them.

Walking with boys or men you would think might be a good idea, but it doesn't seem to always work. I was talking to some guys who had a woman with them. To protect her, they would even walk with her between them, and the Italian guys would try to go through them to get to her, so these guys were actually quite glad when she left, even though they really liked her company. It just was too much of a hassle for them to have to deal with.

Another girl said that she had been traveling with a large dog, which definitely seemed to be of help.

Another thing I heard was that if you look Italian and look like you are a school girl or something, or you are walking around with your daddy, that seemed to work. But lots of luck; that doesn't help foreign girl tourists much, does it?

On a sad note, I did run into a girl on a train in Spain, who had accompanied her girlfriend to Morocco, and the girlfriend disappeared in Morocco, never to be heard from again. I don't remember the girl's name, but I do recall her telling me that they had either been doing drugs in Morocco or were involved somehow with people who were doing drugs or looking for drugs, something like that. It seems like it was drug-related, anyway.

I don't remember any more details of the story, but they had been walking around, and somehow the girl got kidnapped. The friend got really weirded out by it and did make it out of Morocco okay.

She said she tried to go to the police, but they were unable to do much of anything about it. As far as I know, they had never found her friend again.

Ignominy in Jerusalem

Pamela K. Stewart

Jerusalem, Israel, 1974. I was in one of the towers along the wall in the old part of East Jerusalem. It had been roped off because they were doing renovations. But this obliging fellow there said he'd let me go up and see the view from the tower.

Did you have any cautionary feelings?

He seemed okay. I mean, he seemed like he was a tour guide or something and was just doing me a favor by letting me go up.

He accompanied me. We went up, and he was perfectly nice until we got to the top, and then he started trying to corner me in one of the alcoves. There was obviously nobody else in there because it was roped off and they were doing renovations, so I just kind of decided that this is not a good place to be. I quickly ducked under his arm and ran for the exit and escaped out of there. I was faster than he was, thank God! Boy, was I lucky!

Good. So, what would you advise?

Either take a friend or don't go at all.

Near Ignominy in Algeria

Pamela K. Stewart

Djanet, Algiers, Algeria. This is where they have the famous cave paintings. People come there to see the paintings. And this time, I did manage to heed my own cautionary advice (of taking a friend along when things look iffy).

I got invited to a dinner by a Bedouin at his house.

We were all there on the truck, and they were trying to ask us which trip option we wanted to go on. There were a couple of different trips that you could take through the caves to see the paintings, but they couldn't tell us about our options since everybody spoke only French or Arabic there.

However, since I spoke a little bit of French, I went over to one of the nearby local tour agencies to find out more details, and this one fellow was very obliging. And so, in my broken French, I was able to learn a little bit more about our options. He offered to give me a book in English, giving really good information about the caves by a fellow who had come there and made a study of the caves, if only I would come to dinner. *Fair enough,* I was thinking,

Was this conditional?

Uh, well, yeah. Kind of.

Well, it was at his house, so, naturally, of course, I would have had to come to his house to get it, right?

So, how did you feel about that?

Well, being not a little suspicious, I thought, *Well, gee, I'd really like that book.*

So, what to do? I immediately ran out to the truck and grabbed one of the guys off the truck and said, "We're going to dinner!" (Laughs)

And with that, we went to dinner, and the Bedouin did give me the book, and it was fine.

Do you think if you had been alone with him, it would have been different?

Well, I did manage to find out! (Laughs)

As a matter of fact, I did go alone with him into the desert the next night! (What WAS I thinking?) And predictably, he DID try to ravish me in the dunes, but I managed to fend him off, and he finally left me alone. I guess I should have heeded my own cautionary advice, huh?

Ignominy in Istanbul

Michael Brein

———————◆———————

Istanbul, Turkey, 1974. When you experience people at their worst — so much so — that it causes the Turks, in this instance, to earn my story the well-deserved title of 'Ignominy in Istanbul.' While you certainly cannot fault the Turks as a whole, for surely, they cannot all be like this... And, surely, they must detest such behavior themselves as well...

And although you, yourself, are not the direct victim of such truly heinous behavior... You still feel, no less, the accompanying negativity and pain caused by this despicable behavior, just as if you, yourself, were just as much the 'victim' as the poor Western woman who has had to bear the direct brunt of this aggressive attack and suffer the disgrace of it all.

For you, too, being a non-Turk, just as much share the brunt of the negativity that accompanies such behavior. And you, being a man, cannot help but feel the humiliation and disgrace, the embarrassment, the disgust, and the demeaning feelings that Western women must assuredly suffer when they become the direct 'victims' of such aggression.

I can only hope that this does not happen so much today, if at all. I haven't been back to Turkey in over 35 years. So, I'd like to think that times and attitudes have changed.

So, what is this all about? I'll give you a scenario, which I have observed a few times in my street wanderings in Istanbul. It happened to one group of us walking together, and I saw it happen at least a couple more times to others.

You are casually walking along, taking in the sights and the street life, with not a worry in the world, when all of a sudden, seemingly out of nowhere, one or two young men appear and 'strafe' a young woman, grabbing her about the breasts, laughing, and then bolting off as if it was 'open season' on young Western women in this way.

It was also as if it was just good sport that these men were engaging in — the thrill of the chase and seeing whether they can get away with it. I'm sure they 'competed' with one another in these exploits.

To call them 'scoundrels' is patently inappropriate, for in the West we would label this as sexual assault. It is much more serious than that and nothing less than symbolic rape. They would not behave this way towards their sisters, their mothers, as well as other Turkish women.

I maintain that the men suffer from this effrontery as much as their women do because it is directed against Europeans (and other Westerners). Oh yeah, the men of the victims will make an effort to chase down and catch the perpetrators but rarely succeed. And what if they do? What then? There are usually two or more of them in collusion together increasing the risks of confrontation.

I venture to say that, today, if a Turkish policeman saw this happening, he would likely try to apprehend the perpetrators. Nevertheless, I would like to know for sure.

Ignominy in the Near East

Jeannie Kelley

North Africa and the Middle East, the 1970s. As to walking down the streets, what can you say about being touched by people?

Surprisingly, it wasn't always just the men who were the offenders. Oh, yeah, of course, walking down the street, the men would sometimes try and touch you, but you'd move very quickly aside.

You were always aware when you'd walk down the street. There would be the better-dressed men in suits. Then you'd usually be all right. You could walk past them. They might make comments, but they would never try to touch you because it brings them down in front of the poorer people and also their friends.

But sometimes walking past the young children, that's another matter altogether. The children are sometimes the worst. They'll try and touch you on occasion, too. And groups of teenage boys can also be horror stories as well.

WOMEN on Women!

But in Cairo, we went into the bazaar and it would be the *WOMEN* who tried to touch my girlfriend and me, and it was the men who pulled the women away! The women tried to touch us between the legs and on our busts, and it was the men who pulled the women away.

In Tehran, I found the same thing walking down the street. The women tried to touch us. The men tried to touch us, too, but the women were worse.

All we could do to get away was go into a shop, a cake shop or some sort of shop, and buy something and stay in there for a while and then try to hail a taxi.

When we were in Tehran, we found that the taxis wouldn't stop. Although, if the taxis did stop, once they saw us, that we're European people, they'd often just speed off. A lot of taxis just wouldn't stop for us. They'd see we were in trouble because the people were annoying us and so many people were coming around us, I guess they just didn't want to be bothered and they'd speed off.

I think the place where I've been hassled the most is Tehran. If you are a woman, you are always better off going there with a fellow or a couple of fellows.

Why were the women touching you?

A lot of the women are bisexual and homosexual, I guess, and to see another nationality, another race of woman, and that we had trousers on... they'd just assume it.

I wouldn't go into town with shorts on either. If we had trousers on, they could obviously see we were something else aside from what they were used to and they would try to touch us.

That's the way they are.

A sexual thing?

I don't know whether it was that so much. They'd often be laughing or wanting to touch us, or feigning so, and as we went past them, they'd want to touch us, grab us in the bust, and sometimes even between our legs.

Same in the bazaar in Cairo. Exactly the same thing. And, again, strangely, it would be the fellows that helped us. Shoved the women away, just pushed them away. They were adult women. Maybe in their 20s laughing and touching us.

Really?

Most of the people I've been with — a lot of the girls I've been with at the time — have had the wrong attitude. They'd go into hysterics or they'd just keep on going. But if you keep a very blunt face and show anger, it'd usually frighten them. They never picked on me. It was my friend; she tried to be friendly. They think it's just a come-on, some of them, when you are simply just trying to be friendly.

Groped on a Bus

Elisa Wirkala

Guatemala, 2005. I was on a five-week trip traveling with a friend around Mexico, Belize, and Guatemala. We were traveling cross-country from Belize to Antigua, Guatemala and then to Xela in Guatemala, which is the nickname for Chichicastenango, the famous market town.

We had been on the bus for maybe 15 hours traveling from Belize, but we were with just Guatemalans; there were no other tourists on the bus. When we started out we were the only two people on the bus.

So, we decided to take seats across the aisle from each other and kind of stretch out. And then a few hours later an old woman decided to sit next to me, and that was fine. I fell asleep again. Several hours later I kind of half wake up and I feel this man's hand on my leg. I was kind of in a dream state, and I finally snapped out of it, and there was this huge man, especially for Guatemala standards — 300 pounds — sitting next to me, blocking the aisle.

Now, what's your first thought when you experienced this?

Uh oh! How do I get out of here? What's going on here?

He's pretending to be asleep, but his hand is obviously in my lap.

And what is that experience like to wake up with that happening?

Oh, it's terrible; it's just terrible!

It's a really disgusting feeling waking up to that; it's a horrible feeling. I hope to never repeat it. And, it really left me scared, and I felt very violated. Very violated.

So, what were your options? What did you do?

It took me a couple of seconds. The first thing I did was bat his hand away. And he moved his hand and kind of pretended to just kind of roll over and continue sleeping. It was obvious he was NOT sleeping.

And, it took me a second to just make sure that he wasn't really sleeping. I thought, *Was he really sleeping? Was it really just an accident that he did that? No, it couldn't have been!*

So, I jumped out of my seat yelled at him and I told him to get out of my way in order to get past him.

Did you have your stuff?

Yes, I had my stuff. I just had my purse with me. My bag was above me, anyway.

So, I kind of just jumped over him at that point. My friend was right on the other side of the aisle.

Did she see what happened?

No. She was asleep, but she still had her seat. She didn't let anybody sit next to her, and she's a lot feistier than I am.

Did any other people see this happening on the bus?

Nobody saw it, but as I jumped up, I saw that the bus was full of almost just men, which was another scary thing.

Did you get any looks from these men?

Well, not yet, but we sure got looks a few minutes later. (Laughs)

I threw myself from my seat past this man and into my friend's empty seat next to her. And she woke up looking like she was just about to hit me, you know, thinking I was a Guatemalan man or something.

Had she had similar experiences with Guatemalan men?

Yes, with Latinos. Since both of our mothers are South American, we have had plenty of experience with men like that.

Having mothers that are South American, were you both pretty good in Spanish?

Yeah, we were, luckily. (Laughs)

So, my friend asked me, "What's wrong, Lisa? What's wrong?"

I said, "This man... I just woke up and he was touching me. And I just don't know what to do I'm so mad!"

She just has me sit down and tells me, "It's okay."

And then about 30 seconds later she says, "You know, I have to go to the bathroom. Can you excuse me, please?"

So, I say, "Okay, sure."

She gets up, crosses the aisle and goes straight for that man's seat. And she sits down next to him, makes him move over his stuff, takes his bag, and slams it in his lap and sits down right next to him.

Now, this is a 120-pound very pretty American-looking girl that sat down and started saying things to him really quietly. And, I could tell from her expression that she was just totally pissed. And his expression — I'll never forget that — he looked shocked and he looked scared, like he didn't know what he was going to do with this little girl.

Was she speaking perfect Spanish?

She was peaking very funny Ecuadorian street kid Spanish, the Spanish she speaks with her mother.

Her mother was Ecuadorian?

Yeah.

Finally, a minute or two later, she comes back to my seat and sits down. And I say, "Jackie, what did you do? What did you say to that guy."

And, just as I say that, the guy gets up, grabs his stuff, goes to the bus driver, has the bus stop, and he gets out. And keep in mind, this is in the middle of the mountains in Guatemala — seemingly in the middle of nowhere — just countryside and fields all around — no towns, nothing. He just gets off the bus!

This little 120-pound friend of yours just scared the shit out of him, huh?

Yeah. Scared the shit out of him!

And he just got off the bus? What did she say to him?

She said she told him — playing the Catholic card on him knowing that Latin Americans are very Catholic, and because she is from a family that was very Catholic, herself — that God was watching him, and that God knows what he was doing, that he was going to burn in hell, and that if he ever did anything like that again, she was going to hunt him down and kill him.

And so, he apparently decided to just walk the rest of the way, I guess.

And after that, the other Guatemalan men on the bus wouldn't even look in our direction. Apparently, some of them had overheard the conversation, and they just wouldn't even look.

That is a great way to deal with that, but maybe it's not always the best way to deal with it. I mean, it won't always work out the way people think. But she certainly knew what she was doing, huh?

Yeah; she's a real tough girl, really tough.

.

Groped on the Paris Metro

Susan Stroh

Paris, France. 1973. I was in Paris and I was on the Metro in a first-class train section at rush hour, which they had in those days, and some guy groped me.

Well, what do you mean? Were there a lot of people around you?

It was packed. We were like sardines in a can.

What did you feel happening?

I felt someone, you know, fondling my behind. (Laughs) That was it.

What did you do about it?

I just looked at him, and then, you know, I just squealed?

And that was it!

What was his reaction?

Nothing. Nothing.

And, in the late 1970s, it happened to me again. This time it happened to me in the San Francisco East Bay Terminal. I was standing on a platform by a railing, and somebody reached up under my skirt apparently while coming up a ramp that was adjacent to where I was standing.

How did that happen? What was your reaction?

Well, it happened so fast, he was gone! I didn't stand like that ever again!

How were you standing?

I guess I was leaning against one of those open railings, you know, along a ramp that came up from another level. And some guy just stuck his hand right up my skirt while he passed by.

Did he manage to reach anywhere?

Definitely! I felt it! (Laughs)

And, you never saw who it was?

No, by the time I looked back he was already gone!

It was after work, about 5:30 PM, rush hour.

Groped on the Madrid Metro

C.R. Chaney

Madrid, Spain. 1965. My wife and I were in Madrid riding the Metro on our way to a bullfight. The Metro car was packed like a can of sardines. My wife, a very attractive young lady, managed to be surrounded by a crowd of men who unbelievably surged up against her, groped her, and even dry humped her. It was disgusting; it was vile!

And I could not get to them; if I could have, I would have wailed on them.

She and I were virtually helpless to do anything about it. I couldn't get close enough to her to be of any help whatsoever. There was absolutely nothing that either she or I could have done about it. I figure if I could have, I would have most certainly at least punched their lights out, if I had had any opportunity to do so.

Afterwards, what was your and her reactions to this?

She really didn't like it; she was quite angry.

And the frustrating thing was that there was just absolutely nothing that she or anyone could have done about it.

Nothing. The Metro car was so packed, you could hardly move.

These guys, you say they were Spanish. Could they have been Gypsies?

I think they were more or less just Caucasian Spaniards. They weren't dark and swarthy like the Gypsies, like the flamenco guys you see.

In retrospect, would there have been another way to deal with the situation?

If it were up to me, I'd have done what I could, but I'd probably wind up doing some time in a Madrid jail for it.

Now, you watched all this. What was going through your mind?

Insane rage and jealousy.

Did they surround her on all sides?

Yes. Like a bunch of bees converging on a honey jar.

Now, these guys could very easily have doubled as pickpockets under other circumstances, don't you think?

I'm sure of that. I think so.

Maybe they would have done that as well.

Fortunately, she didn't have any pockets at the time.

You talked about this afterwards. Did it take a while for things to calm down?

Yes, it took a while to calm down. We were both upset about it.

And these guys simply vanished at the next stop. Suddenly they were out the door and just gone! So, there was nothing to do about it even after the fact.

A Stab in the Dark!

Vittoria Abercrombie

━━━━━◉━━━━━

Naples, Italy, the late 1980s, on the Metro. When in Rome, maybe it's a good idea to do what the Romans do. Or maybe it's not. But everyone roots for the underdog. And if something works, maybe it's a good idea to adopt it.

A favorite friend of mine is a tough, hearty Italian woman who has been known to be able to take care of herself. She's a no-nonsense woman who told me about the times she was traveling and commuting on public transit in southern Italy.

Her commute at the time was taking long rides every day including buses and subways and such — a combination — that often would find her on very crowded Metro cars, where everyone was crammed and scrunched in together. It was so crowded most of the time that there were absolutely no seats, and she had to hold her own in a sea of people.

You know, where everyone is withdrawn, motionless, and doing whatever he or she can do to minimize bodily contact as well as eye contact in order to keep things, well — in check.

In those days, much more than now, Vittoria discovered that Italian men did feel quite free to get very close to you and invade your person, and sometimes they would very overtly express themselves in a very physical and sexual way.

Basically, there were two methods of operating. One was a touch with the hand. All of a sudden you would feel a wandering hand where it wasn't supposed to be, sort of grabbing and whatnot. And, of course, the other one would be literally to rub themselves on your body somewhere.

And, the trouble is, you never quite knew exactly who it was. It was all very anonymous and sneaky. And it was all very mysterious because you would be trapped in wall-to-wall bodies. And, by the time you turned around to look and see who was doing this, and to see how the physical positioning of people would allow for this to happen, you would be facing three or four stoic-looking men, all staring ahead with placid-looking faces, all standing quietly, innocently and motionless around you.

But, operating blindly, however, nonetheless, you would always know where it was that you were being violated on your body and sort of have a sense of the direction from whence it came.

What was that feeling of violation like? How did you feel?

Anger, you know. Anger and intolerance! And there was always the feeling of being a victim because you were trapped in the situation and were sort of making a scene. And, of course, actually I think, because it happened to me so often, that you didn't just blow up. I mean, it was almost a fact of life. You knew it was going to happen. And once it happened, you would be put in a position of thinking, *Damn... Here we go again! Somebody's taking liberties with me that they shouldn't.*

It happened to lots of women; it was part of life then.

Did this happen to you more than once? How many times do you think this happened to you?

Oh, yeah! It happened *A LOT!* I don't know, probably, in the course of a year, it would happen maybe a couple of times a week, even. What's more, it happened most often in the mornings. I suppose it may have had something to do with males' hormone levels, too. (Laughs)

You had an interesting way of handling this then, didn't you?

I did. Because, I didn't, basically, particularly like to be angry all the time in those situations. I'm not an explosive person, so I was trying to find a solution to the problem rather than exacerbating the situation and making it worse. Creating a scene was not my style.

What I did was I started bringing along a rather long hatpin tucked under the lapel of my coat. Anytime I was feeling the proximity of someone that was too close, so, you know, without having to turn around, my solution was to simply, quietly, and without much fanfare pull the hatpin out from under the lapel of my coat, and I would simply prick them with the hatpin. Pure and simple. It was not a particularly nice or elegant way of doing it, but it was effective — it worked without fail, and it worked *ALL* the time!

And, I had a built-in surprise factor on my side, because nobody, I think, would ever suspect that by my touching my lapel, I was, in fact, extracting a lethal weapon of sorts from it. (Laughs)

I really didn't quite know what I was doing, basically. Sometimes, I was hitting the person on the hand or the thigh, or wherever, of whoever was intruding in my privacy. So, who knows?

What usually happened after you'd do this?

Well, there was always a very muffled kind of sound that would come from somewhere behind me usually. And, of course, their action would instantly cease. And sometimes there would even be a shuffling of bodies — a hasty retreat by the person who was perpetrating the violation. And basically, it was a relief to me that it would end.

Nobody got any serious injury from it?

No. Nobody got seriously injured. And, basically, nobody around me really even knew what was going on, except, of course, the person doing the dastardly deed. There was no scene. There was no screaming. Nothing. Just muffled sounds or shuffling about.

It was a perfect solution.

Vittoria's husband, Andy: The thing was, because you said the transportation was so crowded, that before you did the hatpin trick, that if you were to turn around to accost somebody or to talk to somebody who had done this, you wouldn't know who to talk to, because there would have been three or four people back there. So, when you'd take the pin and go back just behind you not looking, are you always sure you were hitting the perpetrator and not some poor innocent victim, huh?

No, because you can feel... If you've got a hand... Of course, you would know this, because there would be a guy...

And, you never got the wrong guy, did you?

You couldn't help it. I mean, they were very naked and obvious about it. And maybe it was a woman's intuition, part of it, anyway.

And they would have protested, anyone who was the wrong man?
Absolutely.

Did you ever see any red faces among the men back there? You could have hit the wrong person in the wrong place, huh?

To tell you the truth, I never even bothered to turn around. At that point, I could have cared less. As far as I was concerned, they were poking me in the wrong place. (Laughs)

It seems that the typical scenario was just this:

Well, a sneaky man must just have happened to grope Vittoria right there and then on the spot, probably thinking that he was being quite clever and could get away with it.

Now, most of us would be hard put to try to ascertain who did it. But not Vittoria. She was not one to be messed with. This pervert had groped the wrong woman.

Not to be deterred, Vittoria, once she pretty much determined who it was, she very carefully, stealthily, and painstakingly removed her long hat-pin (which she fortuitously just happened to have under the lapel of her coat) and then — can you possibly believe it? — she then proceeded to stab the culprit right in the thigh!

And then she would very predictably hear a tightly muffled and barely audible — and VERY suppressed — painful groan, and she would know right away that she got her man!

At least the pervert lived to travel the Metro yet another day. Unfortunately, we'll never know whether or not this lesson ever stuck! (Pun intended!).

Escalation

Ellen Good

———◆———

Paris, France, the 1970s. I came into Paris by train. I had planned for three weeks to meet a friend of mine at the Paris train station, 'Paris Nord', between 4 and 6 in the afternoon. We had set this up weeks in advance.

But there had been a suicide on the train tracks and my train was late, finally arriving about 7:30 PM in the evening. My friend and I had not been in contact for weeks and had no plans in case of foul-ups. So, I went to the cafe and she wasn't there.

This was a Friday afternoon. I had no French money and no hotel room. (The plan was that she was going to arrive there earlier and arrange a hotel room for us.) Everything was closed, so I couldn't get any French money. I didn't know where I was going. I had no idea where the hotel was, let alone if there was a room anywhere for me. So, all I could do was wait at the station hoping she would come.

I was literally walking circles around the train station hoping I would run into her. No information booths were open. A guy comes up to me and asked me if I had a place to stay in Paris.

At first, he spoke French to me, which I didn't understand, and then he switched to English.

I said that I didn't have a place to stay. I was pretty desperate. I didn't know where I was going to stay.

He asked me, "Well, would you like to stay with me? I'll pay."

He gives me this funny little smile, and I go, "No thanks."

He reaches over, "Oh, I need a kiss then."

He reaches over to give me a kiss, and I began to move up the escalator. I was really mad at this time, so I pushed him back down the escalator, and he fell into his friend's arms. I felt great.

They stood there with their eyes bugged out. Another show of feminine brutality!

Hair on Fire

'Heather and Liz'

Istanbul, Turkey, the 1960s. **Heather:** Once we left Istanbul it seems like there was always someone to take care of us.

My friend, Liz, was a blonde and people really noticed her. My hair was long and black and didn't look much different than the Turks, so I didn't get too much hassle. But she got her butt pinched a lot; I think she attracted people to us.

Well, Liz's hair is long and kind of a strawberry blonde color and has lots of shine to it, and when the sunlight would hit it, they thought it was on fire. They said it looked like fire, and they would actually come up and stare and touch it. They very cautiously took their hands to touch it to see if it was hot and if it was on fire. It was just a very strange experience for them.

I also wore in those days hot pants and mini-skirts, and things like that were in, so when you're running around in a country where it's 93, 95, 96 degrees, you're not wearing very much clothing.

They don't dress like that over there. They're all covered with brown from their necks to their ankles, so they were staring at Liz constantly because her legs were exposed or else she'd have short skirts or something.

Liz: Once, when I was going in a palace or a temple, walking up the steps, the little boys would actually come up and lay right down in front of me or sit down in front of me and look right up my dress. Just literally look up it.

At first I was very offended by it, but then I realized they were just very curious, because they had never seen a woman running around with bare legs and were wondering what was underneath this short little dress. I was wearing little pants like shorts — short-shorts — like hot pants kind of thing, so it wasn't the underpants or something they were looking at, so they weren't really robbing me that much, but they were very blatant about it. They'd all but pull up my dress and take a look to see what was there."

Heather: Women were very fascinated by Liz and one woman was walking along with a load of laundry on her head, and she was so busy looking at Liz, that she walked right into a telephone pole and just knocked herself down. And the laundry came tumbling down and everything. She was just looking at Liz and not paying any attention to what she was doing.

That was kind of strange seeing all those people. Liz was with a guy and some other friends. Another girlfriend and her husband, who were Jewish, had black hair and darker skin. The guy Liz was with was a blue-eyed blonde with short hair, but it seemed wherever she went the people always singled her out physically. I think because of the way she dressed as a woman and because of her coloring. It was very unusual in those parts for someone with her coloring.

I had a girlfriend who was a nurse in Viet Nam, and she said that because she was blonde, the people acted very differently towards her, too.

Author: Liz, how did you feel when they were touching your hair or looking up your dress?

Liz: Well, the hair thing I thought was kind of interesting, seeing these adults acting like children who had just seen something for the first time, like a child who had never seen snow before. They kind of responded to me that way.

Of course, being a typical American, you're walking around; you don't really like people looking up your dress. You feel like you're in New York City with some weirdo. You just have to adjust your mind to the fact that these people are not perverted, they are just innocent little children; they're just plain old curious, and that's the way they are in countries like that. They are like children in a way, and they just wanted to find out, so that that was okay. That was no big problem. You get used to it, too. You really adjust.

Close Call at the Parker House

Pam Ross

B oston, Massachusetts, 1980. My other story happened in Boston. I had run the Honolulu Marathon and taken a flight to Boston. I think it was direct, but I cannot remember for sure.

I had a reservation at the then ultra-first-class, four-star Parker House Hotel (now the *Omni* Parker House) — the site of the famous Parker House rolls.

Anyway, I checked in about mid-afternoon. I was sore from the Marathon, so I ran a hot bath and later went out for a walk. I was meeting my friend Geoff H. there, and we were going to drive together to Vermont to meet his parents.

I probably went to bed around nine. Not sure when, but probably around 11 PM Geoff arrived. I had left a key in an envelope at the front desk for him, so he came up. It seemed to me he was not there very long, but I was exhausted from the Marathon, the long flight, stiff from sitting so long on the flight.

So, there we were there in the room together, when suddenly, we heard a key in the door lock and two men speaking. Geoff got up and by now these men were in the room. They were totally shocked to see Geoff and immediately began to make excuses.

"You ordered room service?"

But, of course, they had nothing with them. It was scary because it was clear they thought I was alone in the room. Not sure what they were up to or what they had in mind, but it was scary. Not sure what would have happened had Geoff not been there. Since then, I always put that lever lock on the door. That's it. We checked out the next morning and went to Vermont.

"Grizzly Man"

Barbara D.

Luxembourg, 1968. I just graduated from college and flew Icelandic Air, which was the cheap airline at the time, to Luxembourg. No sooner had I graduated I decided that I didn't want to be a teacher after all. I really didn't know what to do with myself, so I was going to Europe for the summer and would figure it all out later.

Of course, I was probably pretty uptight about the whole thing: did I do the right thing? I was doubting myself whether this was a good idea or not. The coup de grace was that I thought a friend was going to go to Europe with me, but she backed out at the last minute.

So, I'm pretty uptight. And I'm going to Luxembourg, which is not really that high on my list of places that I know anything about or really want to go to.

So, I flew, arrived, and somehow got to the train station downtown by taxi. My plan was to leave the next day for Amsterdam. I was looking for a cheap hotel, so I just wandered around looking, and someone pointed one out to me. For want of another term, it was a sleazy hotel. I went in and paid for the room. It was surprisingly cheap, but that should not be too surprising, being it was a sleazy hotel.

I went to my room, put my stuff down, then went out, got something to eat, and then came back. The lock on my door to my room didn't work. But, it was a pretty sleazy little hotel near the train station kind of thing, so what else is new?

I said something to the desk clerk about it, but the best he could do was mumble something to the effect, "Oh, yeah. That's okay; none of the locks work."

Was that satisfying to you, then? None of the locks worked in any of the rooms?

I guess I thought, *Oh, okay, well, this is, you know, probably pretty standard — not such a big deal, right.*

But you also didn't have a whole lot of experience either, right? So, what did you know?

True, and I just figured maybe, you know, poor hotels — it's probably par for the course.

So, I go to bed and I'm asleep. And then all of a sudden I wake up to this grizzly guy with his grizzly beard nuzzling my cheek!

So, he must have gotten into your room?

He just WALKED into the room — the UNLOCKED room!

What did you think? How did you feel about that?

I was appalled, frightened and totally freaked out.

What did you do?

Well, I got up and started yelling. I mean, I'm not a very passive person to begin with, so it was kind of like, "What the hell are you doing in my room? ... *Yadda yadda yadda!*"

You were yelling at the top your voice.

I was yelling as loud as I could.

I don't think he was the guy in the hotel; I don't think he was the front counter guy.

Then the front counter guy, himself, came up, entered the room, and then he hugged me. He *HUGGED* me!

He was kind of creepy, too? Both were in the room at the same time?

Yeah, of course, at some point, because I was yelling. And, I guess he came up to fix the situation or to address the situation, but he was creepy.

Finally, the guy with the grizzly face left, but in the end, he was stalking me, because in the morning he was standing right there just outside of the hotel, apparently waiting for me, because I guess he knew I was taking the train in the morning.

So, what did you do the rest of that night? Did anybody else do anything to you? You got them to stop whatever it was, huh? Did you put or push anything up against the door?

Yeah, I got them to stop and got rid of them.

I remember journal writing for quite a while because I was pretty hyped. But, eventually, I drifted off to sleep.

Did any other people come out of their rooms?

Winding up in the sleazy hotel in the first place was a big mistake. I didn't speak the Luxembourg language and no one spoke English, so I wound up by default in a very creepy area, and when I walked out in the morning to go to the train station there was Grizzly Man standing right there.

So, what did you think?

I was very frightened. I was even thinking at the time, *Maybe I should just get on the plane and go back to America* because I had an open return ticket and could return at any time. I was thinking that maybe this was a really bad mistake, and I should really just go back. I mean, I was only 21 and very inexperienced.

You know, I just hadn't much experience being a young girl from New Jersey.

What a beginning, huh?

Yeah, it was really a weird beginning.

What did you do?

I forced myself to get to the train and go to Amsterdam. I didn't start hitchhiking until I chilled in Amsterdam for a bit until I felt re-energized and safe enough to leave.

Did you have any other incidents during the rest of your trip?

Oh, yeah. I hitchhiked from then on. I was fine until I got to the Italian part of Switzerland, and later, in Italy itself where people got weird.

It seemed like just about everyone wanted to *"fare amore!"* (To make love).

How did you deal with these situations?

I had to constantly deal with these unexpected and unpleasant circumstances. Once, I even jumped out of a car. The guy had taken out his penis and was like playing with himself, and I jumped out of the car!

Was the car moving?

Yeah, but he had slowed down. He really didn't want to kill me, after all, so he did slow down, and I got out with my stuff. I was pretty rattled by it all.

And, if that wasn't bad enough, the next car, the guys were sort of like teasing me and not teasing me at the same time. Italian guys kind of have this idea of girls traveling alone being loose and fair game, I guess.

One driver decided that since I wasn't going to have sex with him, maybe I would give him one birth control pill for his wife — a birth control pill for one night of unrestrained sex with his wife!

What did you do?

I didn't have one to give him. But even if I did, it was some kind of naive innocence on his part; he didn't know that not only would it not work — I mean, one pill wasn't going to work — but, who knows; maybe there might even have been side effects with his wife.

Did they have some kind of attitude about American girls? What was and is that attitude?

I don't know what it's like now.

This was back in 1968.

If I was hitchhiking, to them, therefore, I must have been free and sexually active.

They had that attitude towards a lot of American girls, I'm sure.

Were you very discouraged seeing this all over where you were going?

Well, it was only mainly in Italy. I had been for a while in relatively safe countries where that never happened, but Italy did discourage me.

And I turned around. I did. After one week in Italy. I had had enough. I thought this was horrible and I was trying to train out, but for some reason, I couldn't get a train at the time, so I hitchhiked my way out of Italy safely. But it was all very scary.

The only other scary experience I had on that three-and-a-half months trip was while I was in Ireland. I'd been hitchhiking there for a month, and an American, of all people, picked me up and tried to seduce me.

So, how'd you get out of that?

I just remember it was really creepy. He was the only creepy ride I had the entire time in Ireland.

Was this a good idea to travel by yourself, after all is said and done?

I had to choose my countries, Europe at that point was still pretty much safe except for Italy. I didn't go into Spain. And in France, I was hitchhiking with somebody, so I don't know what it would have been like to do so alone.

Okay, remember back at that hotel in Luxembourg that we were talking about earlier?

In retrospect, you're older now, and you've done a lot more traveling. What would you have done differently back then?

I would have demanded a room with a lock. Or, if not, I wouldn't have stayed at that hotel. I would have persisted until I found a different hotel.

Also, I now trust my intuitions more. I'm feeling that there are creepy hotels, and if I get a bad vibe now, I wouldn't stay at such a place.

And under no circumstances — absolutely under *NO* circumstances, anywhere — would you stay in a hotel room that did not have a lock on it.

Right.

Maybe a bed and breakfast in New England, or something like that?

Yeah. Something that feels good.

The Blonde Gringa

Teddy and Karen Jacobsen

M y story is about my daughter who went to Mexico for three months by herself and then went on to Guatemala for an additional three months and was being sexually harassed.

And so, in order to stop the harassment, she decided to dye her hair black. She was tall, blonde, blue eyes, 6 feet tall and a nice-looking young woman (being, of course, prejudicial that I am).

And as soon as she got her hair black, the harassment reduced by at least 50 percent!

Mother, Teddy's Story

Was she being harassed a lot?

Quite. She was tall, and that's what the Mexicans liked, of course, the tall blondes.

And she could not even walk alone on the beach without being accosted. The beaches: that was the absolute worst part of the whole thing.

It was really funny. At first, I did not recognize her at the airport when she came back from her trip to Mexico and Guatemala for six months.

You were looking for her in the airport as a blonde, blue-eyed girl, right?

To hear about my daughter, Karen, tell you about her Mexico and Guatemala experiences, please continue on.

Daughter, Karen's Story

Mexico

1989-1990. Mexico. I had a backpack on and went to Mexico.

Had you been there before?

I was 25. And it was the first time I ever traveled by myself and with just a backpack on. No plans, no itinerary, I was going for six months just for the experience. I had been to Mexico previously with my parents and with other friends back down in Baja to very protective surroundings. I mean, you are going to very Americanized places. It wasn't quite the experience I wanted to get.

What did you want to do?

I wanted to go to really small villages. I wanted to try and pick up some Spanish and talk to people in Mexico. And just experience a culture, not from the outside but from the inside.

Did you have any apprehensions at all?

No. I started talking to my friends about my plans and then I started getting apprehensive because I was going to throw on a backpack and go to Mexico. Not a big deal.

Like what did they say?

They were talking, "Oh my God! White slavery!"

Just like worrying things — horrid things. That I was going to get robbed and I'm going to get raped, you know. I'm going to get kidnapped. The police are going to get a hold of me, and I'll be in jail for the rest of my life, and so on.

My intuitions were reacting to their thoughts with paranoia and what my friends were saying. It didn't worry me all that much, but at the same time, it affected me, until I was a little nervous, definitely.

But especially when I was on the flight, I really hit me like, *I am alone and it's the first time I've ever been alone.* It started off great. On the plane, the first thing I did was I ordered a Margarita. It was both a feeling of excitement and fear, but it was good. But it was scary. I can't really describe it in words.

It was a wonderful feeling.

I flew into Mazatlan, and then I was going to take the train to Copper Canyon and then go down to the middle of Mexico. It was fun. I had my dictionary and my book of Mexican phrases with me. And I was practicing them there with people.

No problema! I'd say phrases, but I didn't expect to get full sentences in response, which I did not understand. I could guess some of the meanings of what I had heard, but a lot of it was incomprehensible to me. And so, I began to see that there was a language barrier here.

I started thinking about where I could maybe learn Spanish in Mexico. I also started to notice that people were making comments to me a lot on the streets, but I just was not getting it. I often didn't understand what they were saying, and that was bothering me, too.

What were they doing? How were they reacting to you?

It was kind of sexual, you know, like "Come on baby, come over here," kind of thing.

I was in Mazatlan. I was just traveling for the day, and I ended up on a beach that was very deserted. I was just walking down the beach by myself, looking at the beautiful waves. It was gorgeous. And I was just walking. I was in this really great space.

And then a group of guys started hassling me. And I didn't realize how far away I was from anybody.

How were they acting towards you?

At first, I was sort of ignoring them and keeping my distance. And then two of the boys stopped and just continued to talk to me. I didn't respond. I didn't look at them. I tried to say in Spanish, "You know, you're bothering me." (It probably came off sounding more like, "I'm bothering myself," something silly like that.)

And, of course, they were laughing at my Spanish. They continued to talk to me for about fifteen minutes.

What was your feeling about this?

I was noticing that their friends were going farther away and they were staying there, hanging around, and I was getting nervous.

You know, I'm a big woman. I look like I can take care of myself. I don't normally run into problems like that around here at all (in the States). And, I didn't ever really think much about how I would deal with a situation like this. So, my adrenaline is going. And these two boys started getting angry and yelling. But finally, they just gave up and left.

I waited until they were out of sight and then went back to where I was staying. I realized then that, wow; I really needed to hook up with someone.

It was pretty much still daylight, but I was just not prepared to go out at night all by myself. And certain places I wouldn't be able to go to. Like I wanted to shoot pool.

It was just something that you never considered.

And I never really thought that walking down the beach by myself would be something that I'd have to think twice about.

So, I ended up hooking up with this one woman, and we stayed in this popular Mexican town called Guanajuato to learn Spanish. It was a pretty Americanized school. A lot of people go down there to learn Spanish. It was pleasant there, but it was really too Americanized for me. I wasn't in Mexico for that.

And as soon as I tried to get out of like the main 'Americanized' core of the city, where all the Americans were, I would start to get harassed.

Like people making comments. A friend of mine and I would take a walk up into the hills, and we would just get harassed. It was generally verbal, not usually face-to-face. I'd get past and something would be said.

It depended on the city. Like in Mexico City, it was a lot worse. People were more aggressive. On the Metro, I'd be yelling at someone, and no one would come to my defense. You know, like men touching my breasts, touching my ass. Very overt and no one really helping me at all.

What was your reaction? How did you deal with it?

I was serious, and I was yelling, and I was saying, "Get away!"

And no one was helping. It was all very surreal, because everybody was stone-faced, didn't smile, didn't get angry, even; everybody was pretending that nothing was happening.

You were losing it at times?

Oh, yeah!

I would say that by the time I left Mexico, I was seriously about ready to kill somebody. I was so at my wit's end, so angry, and feeling so powerless. No matter what I did, if I yelled, they loved it. If I said nothing, they loved it. If I pushed them, they loved it. Whatever I did, it didn't matter. It was as if they enjoyed provoking me into becoming verbal and out of control.

Were they ever doing this to Mexican women?

No.

In fact, I learned in my traveling, that if hooked up with a Mexican family, particularly a Mexican woman, an older Mexican woman, and I hung out with that type of person, I didn't get harassed nearly as much.

If I was hanging out with a Mexican man or with another woman who was American or another man who was European or American, it was not nearly as hassle-free. It was only safe if I was with women who were Mexican.

How often did you do that?

When I stayed in different towns, I made connections quite a bit. That was definitely really like the safest way for me. And I was really frustrated because that meant that most of my time was spent in the home or doing shopping, the sorts of things that women stereotypically do, and not doing the sorts of things that I as a free spirit normally liked to do.

It was interesting, but it was also frustrating at the same time, whenever I wanted to go out at night or see or do whatever or be freer to make a choice of what I could do, or what I could not do. I couldn't make that choice anymore.

Did you ever think of striking back?

I did. Yeah.

Did you ever actually hit somebody?

Yeah, I did.

Guatemala

This was in Guatemala. But, in Guatemala you never usually had problems.

It was the only time I've ever hit somebody, because of all this other stuff that happened before. All this pent-up aggression that I had.

What happened?

One time a friend and I were passing these two Latino men. Then one of the men touched my friend on the ass. They were drunk. I grabbed him by the shirt and I pushed him up against the fence, and I said, "Don't you ever fucking touch her (or me) again!"

In Spanish?

No, in English. I was too angry.

What was his reaction?

At first, shock. And when we walked away he started throwing rocks at me.

Did they hit you?

No. I didn't feel particularly threatened or anything, though.

What was your reaction to that?

Both good and bad. The good was the relief that I felt. The bad, however, was that like I knew better from my past experiences, that no matter what response I have, I'm not going to change anything — anyone's behavior or attitudes or images towards American women — who they are or what they do. That's the world we are living in.

This was not constructive.

Not at all. And I knew it right even then from the get-go.

But it was all this frustration pent up.

I was like totally acting without thinking.

What was your friend's reaction?

I think she was surprised because I'm usually a pretty calm person.

So, that wasn't a particularly good strategy, huh?

No, not at all. It wasn't a good strategy to yell back either because usually, the situation gets more volatile. And the geographic proximity was closer, too, and more threatening to me. I was usually with one other person, but when I was alone, whatever... I would grit my teeth and walk off.

Is that the best strategy?

No, the best strategy is to hook up with someone from the country.

What is strategy number two?

If you are alone, don't say anything; just ignore it; make no eye contact; close your ears, and walk past, and get to a place where you feel safe. Act like you know where you are going and look like you know what you are doing. Stand tall and strong and walk. And it works. People don't mess with you.

If you are looking around and wondering, *Where can I go?* If you do feel lost or out of control, just look and walk straight ahead!

If you find like a cafe that looks safe, or if you find, especially, a group of women that are sitting down or whatever, or are having dinner, or they are doing the laundry... And another place I'd often hang out is where the women did their laundry. And, I did my laundry right along with them. That's where I hung out!

So, anyway, I was getting really frustrated and surprised when other women I would be traveling with would say, "You know, this only happens when I'm with you."

Meaning that men would come up to us only when I was with them.

What were these women like?

They might have been shorter or they had darker hair. I just stood out because I towered over these people. I'm six feet tall, blonde shoulder-length hair, light eyes. I dressed really respectful of that community. I had dresses that were below my knees. I never wore short shorts.

What was it about you that got these reactions?

This was my theory: this only happened with Latino men; it never happened with the indigenous population there. The Indians had so much respect, a different demeanor, and a different way of approaching women.

The Latino men are just more socialized with television down there. I mean these programs like *Dallas* depict women in a bad way down there. A lot of the porn stars and negative characters were blonde women.

So, they treat you as if maybe they think of you as one of them, basically.

Who knows?

I don't think that they necessarily think of American women as porn stars, or me as one in particular, but they are conditioned to think of American women in this way. I look American; therefore, it is okay to harass, or whatever.

Were there any nice Mexican men who were friendly to you?

Oh, yeah. A lot. Of course. There were some men that I made a connection with who were Mexican, whom I met through introductions by Mexican women. I did not meet such men on the street, however.

A Change for the Better

So, it was when I was in Guanajuato that I decided to dye my hair black, to stop the harassment because I was at my wit's end.

What was your theory about that before you did this?

Well, several people told me that they thought it was because of my height and that I was blonde, and it only happened with me, and their other traveling partners were not blonde.

And this family that I had made a connection with helped me to dye my hair. They couldn't believe I was doing this.

They went, "Are you sure you want to do this?"

I don't think they really got how much I was being harassed. It didn't happen when I was with them. It only happened when I was alone. And also, I did it because I was leaving this community that I was in and that I was moving on. Thank God. And right away I got hassled less. Right away, the harassment cut in half! It was so apparent.

When I came back, some people liked the hair; some people didn't. My cousin said, "Oh God, I like it so much better in this color."

And, when I was a bartender, I got picked up on a lot more with blonde hair than I got with black hair. I don't think it was a good thing that I was hit on more; I just think it was interesting that this image of blondes is universal.

The Hotel from Hell

So, I left Guanajuato and I was back in Mexico City, which I told you about in the subway. I hooked up with different people. I was in safe places. Again, a little bit of harassment. And then I went to this small town that was outside Mexico City.

Every town has its patron saint's day, and it was their particular day this time — their big day, so, of course, it would be very busy there. I was going to check it out. I took a bus down there. I got into town. None of the hotels were open. Nothing was there.

I then went to this one travel agency, and they hooked me up with a hotel, but okay, a little bit out of town. I don't really want to be there, but at least it's walking distance. It looks like a very strategic place.

So, I get there. I pay. I get my bag. They put me in this room. And I go back down to have dinner. I meet the woman who runs this restaurant. It's dark out. So, I have to go. I start to walk back.

I'm inside. I just thought maybe I'm staying a little bit too late here at this restaurant, but I just had this great experience with this woman.

I get back to the hotel and go to my room. For some reason, there are now a lot of young men in this hotel. They are doing something with books. There are all these books in this hotel. I think that maybe they are doing some black market kind of thing. I don't know what they are doing. But they were definitely not there when I put my bags there in the beginning. And it is now abundantly clear that I am the ONLY woman at this hotel!

So, whatever. I lock my door, you know. I'm leaving in the morning. It's okay. I'll just spend the night here and deal with it tomorrow and go find another place.

And not 45 minutes pass, and someone is now knocking on my door. They want to enter. I say, "No."

And it doesn't end. They are knocking and knocking.

Did you say anything?

I didn't answer.

No, they keep on knocking and knocking.

I say, "What do you want?"

How were you feeling when they knocked on the door?

I was shocked. I thought that this isn't at all good. I'm pretty sensitive to things like that. Like I knew when I walked in what with all these guys there, that something was wrong.

This is what happened. I went to my room and I knew something was wrong, and I wanted to lock my door, but my lock didn't work. So, I went to the manager and told him, "My door doesn't lock."

And he goes, "Yes, it does. Yes, it does."

And I go, "No, it doesn't, and I want another room."

So, they put me in this other room. And the door did lock this time.

So, I locked my door. But still, I get the same knocking on my door. And then they want to come in and talk.

I say, "No, I'm going to sleep."

And then they finally left me alone. But it gets worse!

I go into the bathroom and there is this hole in a blacked out window. A HOLE! It is stuffed with toilet paper. It was there when I first came in. And then later, when I went in again, the toilet paper was NOT there. It had been taken away.

So, I put more toilet paper back in the hole.

And so, I'm in bed and just looking at my stuff. And I'm thinking, *I'm out of here in the morning, but I'm going to be here until the morning. Not much I can do about it for now.*

It must be 11 or 11:30 PM by now. And then, I go into my bathroom again and the toilet paper is OUT of the hole again! I'm going, *Oh damn, this is bad.*

And I'm thinking, *I'm out of here in the morning. I'll get some sleep, and I'm out of here in the morning.*

I'm in bed again, and then I realize there's another hole, this a small hole in the wall inside my hotel room. And now, I'm really freaking out. I take the toilet paper and I put it in the hole. And then, not five minutes later, the hole appears again, this time without the toilet paper. It means that someone is on the other side and they're looking in at me here.

I couldn't sleep all night. I was tense. I was in my bed. I heard like partying next door. It was the worst night probably in my life. I've never been as scared as I was that night. I never felt so alone. I felt very vulnerable for the first time in my life. I felt like I could disappear from the face of the earth. And it would take months for anyone to figure out that I was gone! It was like this for me the whole rest of the night.

As soon as I saw any light at all, I got up I took a shower. The toilet paper was still in the hole in the bathroom window. It must have been like 5:15 in the morning. Like way early. Like no one would ever be up that early. I'm taking a shower; the shower's on, and before you know it, the toilet paper's out of the window again, and someone's looking in. And I freaked out. I got my backpack together. I put all my clothes into the pack; I was soaking wet. And I leave my room into the hallway, and I yell at the top of my lungs, *"YOU MOTHERFUCKERS!!"*

I cannot think in Spanish, and I'm yelling in this ungodly hour early in the morning at the top of my lungs. I'm yelling at them, obviously waking everyone up, and all these guys are opening their doors and staring out of their doorways and probably going the equivalent, of "What the fuck."

There was apparently this door at the end of the hallway that led out of and up to my floor and down to the lobby. I grabbed the handle of the door to get out, and I'm totally freaking out. I can't get out. It won't open. It's tied up or something and it's locked, and not opening. So, I am pounding on this door that had evidently been tied shut, and I'm yelling, "Get me the fuck out of this place!"

I'm screaming at the top of my lungs. And I'm scared because I didn't think that this door was going to be locked.

And a guy comes creeping upstairs, who I guess is in charge of the desk. He opens the door for me... I don't think he even knows what was going on, and that he, himself, just woke up and that I was yelling.

And I just threw the keys at him, and I left and I ran right for the bus station.

I was on a bus for three days to get out of Mexico. Three days straight, I just beelined it to Guatemala. I took the bus at night. And I hung out in the cities during the days. I didn't think I was going to make it to the end of the whole trip. It was just the first three months. I could have just as easily given up at this point and just gone home.

So then, I gave it a couple more weeks. I'll see how Guatemala is. And if it isn't what I want, I'll just go home. No big deal.

And Guatemala was just wonderful. I love Guatemala. It was incredible. It was the exact opposite of Mexico. It was like 80 percent indigenous, twenty percent Latinos.

You weren't hassled in Guatemala?

No, it was just that one time that I told you about. And they were Latino men, not indigenous men.

The men there were so much different there. Even the Latino men were less bold. Maybe 'bold' is not the right adjective. They just weren't so bothersome there.

Maybe there wasn't as much television down there. And also, when I came back up in southern Mexico, the people were beautiful and the people were wonderful. Again, I think there were a lot more indigenous people in southern Mexico than where I was in the interior, in the middle of Mexico.

Guatemala was great. I then spent a week in Nicaragua. And then I came back up to Mazatlan.

Homebound

So, your hair was black, you were on the plane, and you were coming home. What was your expectation as to how you would be received when you got off the plane? Did you think about that and your appearance?

No. Not at all.

What happened when you got off the plane?

I don't really remember anyone being surprised. Oh, I remember walking out of the plane and looking for my parents, and seeing my parents looking down at me through the glass — I was down below — and not recognizing me.

I'm waving at them — and they're looking right at me — and they do not acknowledge me. I guess they forgot what their daughter looks like? I can't believe it! And, I was, of course, so used to my hair and my new look — I never looked much in a mirror when I was traveling. It's so funny. I'm like waving and waving and they're looking right at me, and I'm waving and waving at them, and they're not recognizing me!

It was great because my friends were also there.

Did they ask you why you dyed your hair?

Yeah. I think I had been so used to it by then, it wasn't such a big deal anymore.

In retrospect, should you have acted any differently in your hotel room that night?

I don't know. I think I did what I could.

But, if you had just kept quiet and silent and ignored them?

I don't know. I was as quiet as I could be.

When I left, all my yelling... If I could have controlled that better, I probably would have done that, but I was out of control.

I was thinking about leaving that night. But I just thought it would be safer to stay.

I think I stayed because I thought there's no other place available. I didn't know if I wanted to be at the bus station in the middle of the night, either. And I knew the door to my room was locked. So, I decided to stay until it got light.

So, how would you summarize overall the best strategy for dealing with harassment? Can you think of anything that sort of sums it up for you?

In sum, the best thing is to hook up with a Mexican family and live with them.

Sure.

You are in before dark. That's for sure. If you are going to a place where there's a festival and there will be crowds, make sure you make reservations beforehand at a place you know is safe. People talk when they travel, so ask around and find out the places that are good to stay in and the places that are bad. I wouldn't stay in a place by myself if I didn't first hear from some-one else that it is an okay place to stay.

What about what your friends were saying when you left? Did you ever think about what they were saying? Were they right?

In some respects, they were right. But at the same time, I had the worst time of my life and also had the best time of my life on that trip. I wouldn't go back and not do it! I would do it again; I would go back and do it again.

What would you say was the highlight of the whole trip?

The highlight was when I became very good friends with this poor family in Guanajuato, and when you make a connection down there you cannot attach a price to it. They were like a second family to me.

Did you keep in touch with them?

No, I didn't. I'm very bad at that, I know. (Laughs) But, when I returned from Guatemala, I went back into the city to say goodbye to them. And I was glad that I did that. They will always be a part of my life. I have great memories of them.

You know, it wasn't all bad. There were also experiences when I was traveling by myself and I wouldn't have met the people I met if I were traveling in any other way.

Whatever, like, there's good and there's bad.

Will you take another adventure after this to somewhere else?

Yeah. Oh, yeah! I have the travel bug. But, you know; I have to admit that if I travel again, I would travel with a male partner. And that although part of my Mexico experience was so unpleasant, that I would want to try that way of traveling, even though I know it has its negative points, too.

But, you know, that was the first time I ever traveled like that, so I don't know if I have enough experience, and maybe if I do more trips by myself, I'll find more strategies to deal with that, but no doubt, traveling solo for a woman alone can be very dangerous.

Travel Tip #1:
Do Not Be Distracted!

Michael Brein

I include some tips on travel safety and security for the solo woman traveler. The tips begin here and are interspersed throughout the pages of this book.

Distraction

Never allow yourself to be distracted. Always pay close attention to your possessions and your surroundings at all times.

Periodically scan the quadrants that surround you as if they were the 15-minute markers on a clock: i.e., 15, 30, 45 and 60 minutes on the hour.

Next time you see the Secret Service on TV, notice how they often appear to be scanning their surroundings in a similar manner.

The single most important way a pickpocket gets to rob you is to get your attention away from your possessions. The way he or she does this is to distract you. And there are a million clever ways to do this, such as dropping keys or other items right in front of you or by feigning to ask you a question, and so on.

Running from Shadows

Winkelle Godfrey

Tunisia, the desert, 1977. This is about a walk into the desert. This was in Tunisia, north of Gafsa.

Mid-Morning

I had just walked out of the desert after three hours of wandering northeast along an endless horizon of grey full of sand and scrubby dried bush. Here, on the edge of the gates of horror, I found complete silence except for the wind breathing over the sand stirring it occasionally.

It was surprisingly cold, a sky of pale gray. Occasionally a steely sun would strike metallically across from me, making a sudden companion in a shadow. You could walk and walk to nothing. Merely a slight change in the desert structure in nature of a rise or mound, hopefully, to view a continuation.

It was a wonderful sensation. Fearful a little, because the desert for me is an unknown. I'm not acquainted with its ways or inhabitants; therefore, they are not friends. I'm essentially an outsider.

I was passing close to wild camels un- hobbled or -guarded that would raise suddenly their heads, lumber slightly sideways to stare. I didn't know if they were simply curious with their heavily lidded eyes or not; they would watch me from under their lids.

Some of them graze; some walk aside, yet one larger one continues to follow my progress. I couldn't help but feel a little nervous. Nowhere to hide and camels come on fast and kick with those great padded feet.

I sometimes noticed a huge ant pop into a perfectly round hole bearing a pellet. They would both disappear cleanly.

Then I would hear the clear and lovely sound of a desert bird and see it fly from bush to bush, landing to stand still and straight.

You did feel slight fear about the camels? Why?

Because there was nowhere to hide if they'd run at me, and I don't know how camels react when they see strange people. I know deer run away, and I know if you shout at a cow it runs away, but maybe a camel is different.

But when I was coming back, I had no fear of them at all. I walked straight past one.

What about... You said you saw a small one?

It was a young one. It was drinking from the mother.

Yeah? Milk? Then what happened?

It was a very good feeling. Milk, yes.

And what happened? You got close to it and then what?

I didn't get close to any of them. I just left them alone. You leave them alone; they leave you alone. But they were grazing very close to the trucks of the... a Land Rover, whatever it was that was going across the desert.

The thing I was following, because I thought it was best to follow something like that. If I had followed my footprints back, there might have been a bit of a wind and they'd be all covered up.

Well, I was hoping I wouldn't meet anybody I didn't know. In fact, when I passed all the camels I wondered whether they might have somebody with them. I looked. But it's difficult to see the people in the desert because they are camouflaged so well, the clothes they wear.

I stand out because my coat's bright blue and they can see you, so I felt a slight anxiety and I thought, no, I'm going to walk on. I thought, *Well, if they're aversive or dangerous, what can I do out here? I can't run indefinitely through the sand, so what I would do is I would just have to walk past them. Just turn some friendly gesture and just hope they'll be friendly back. They might well be.*

Then I remember thinking, *I'd much rather meet some Nomad in charge of camels or goats or some children or even a group of men in charge of animals, rather than a whole bunch of dogs, such as we meet at every crossroad, because I'm damn sure I'd get a far worse time from them than I would from any person herding animals.*

So, I thought, *Well, they probably will ignore you.*

What is this fear that you have of the people in Tunisia?

Because I don't know what kind of people... I don't know how they feel, and I don't know what they think. For instance, I feel a great deal when I am walking through the desert, but I just wonder whether they just take it for granted now because they've been born here. I don't know how people in this part of the world feel and think, and their attitudes towards me. Because I don't know, I'm afraid.

What is your feeling of the attitude of the Tunisians towards women as you walked into towns? What's happened to you?

I'm sure their attitudes towards their own women is different from me. They see you as some kind of target, I think. I don't know whether it's our fault or whether it is just inbred in them to see Western women as some sort of symbol of sexual freedom; something they can touch and get away with or look at and get away with it.

Well, what's happened to you, for example?

Nothing really. I suppose you just... when you walk around the streets you just can't avoid being noticed. You feel vulnerable and naked. They watch you and comment, sometimes in French, sometimes in Arabic. They might say something to you, might say something in German because they probably think you are a German tourist.

And once or twice I might have gone through a group of boys and they touch you.

Where?

Touch your ass, or let's say I'm buying something from a market. A guy reaches out for money and brushes my tit just ever so slightly. It's all very clever and cunning, and it's made to seem that it hasn't been done, but maybe it is an accident, but I don't know. I feel unnerved slightly. Not flattered or anything like that. Slightly unnerved when I walk in the streets, but they do have a sort of smooth charm about them. They're different from the Italians.

How are the Italians and what's happened to you there?

Well, they're more blatant. They just cruise about and annoy you. They just generally won't leave you alone. They're very unpeaceful.

This is when you're walking on the road?

Exactly, yes. Every car that... Every Italian sticks his head out and stares. I don't know why they do it; it's just habit. It's almost habit. It's almost as if they think they should do it. They're expected to behave like that. I feel when I'm walking in Italy I don't — I can't — relax. Probably nothing would happen to me, but there is always that fear something might, and what the hell could I do about it, especially if there were a lot of them.

It irritates me because it inhibits my freedom because I'm used to being able to walk where I want. Every time I see somebody on the road here I think there's a man walking and I want to run away or hide. I don't want to be seen walking alone because for some reason I'm more afraid of them than I am of the Italians, but simply because I think of the Italians as another... as Europeans.

But Tunisians aren't Europeans, and their life is completely different here. Their lifestyle is so different. Therefore, they must be different. They must think in a completely different way. Until I could understand that, I'd always be afraid.

Early Afternoon

This afternoon I decided to take another walk, this time up into the mountains just off the main road. I think that was the nearest town. I saw some mountains and I thought they look pretty isolated, and I couldn't see anybody, so I concluded that that might be a good place to walk.

There was a sandy and rocky hill in the shape of a mountain. So, I set off and I climbed, not to the summit, but to one of the peaks. I had to cross, traverse the ridge, and I suddenly noticed a group of goats. I first thought they were unattended, and then I looked closely and I noticed a man was with them.

A fraction of a second later he noticed me, and he stopped to stare, and I stared at him. We looked at each other for a little while. Maybe we were only about 500 meters apart. Then I noticed he was moving toward me, so I immediately panicked.

I didn't know what the reaction would be. I thought, *I'm alone up here, so I'd best get off the mountain.*

So, I hurried over to where I thought would be my best way out. But it was quite difficult because it was very rough and there were a lot of loose stones, but I didn't lose my balance — I just kept going down.

Then I looked up once or twice and noticed that he had reached the edge and was looking over and watching me and in fact walking along the ridge. I thought, *Oh, my God, he knows a quick way down; he'll cut me off.*

And he was shouting at me I thought. I also noticed below me there were other shepherds that suddenly came from nowhere. I didn't know whether they were children or a man or woman, but they were shouting, too, and there was a lot of hurrying about as if a commotion.

The dogs were even barking, and I thought, *Perhaps he's told them to cut me off. Maybe he thinks that I was going to steal his goats.* I could see the van (Author Michael's VW bus) in the distance by now, and I think, well, I must make it to the van.

So, I hurried on as quickly as possible and eventually got out of there, but by that time, in fact before I could see the van, I remember a real fear had gripped me. I was panting with fear. In fact, I felt just how a hunted animal must feel. It's not a pleasant feeling. I could have waited. I could have stood my ground. I could have let him come right up to me, but when you are alone like that, and you don't know the people, and you don't understand how they feel, eventually, if you're me, you don't want to wait and find out.

Eventually, I got down onto a sort of track and slowed right down. I thought, *Don't hurry now. Don't make a fool of yourself. Just calmly make it back; you're okay now.*

Got back to the van and, of course, everything was fine, but I didn't know what would have happened if I'd waited and confronted that man alone up there.

Earlier

And that reminded me of an instance that happened earlier in the day. First thing, I'd been for a short walk out into the desert. I'd come back and I'd been entirely alone. Hadn't even seen a car, but then later I thought I'd just go for a run, too, because it was a lovely morning, and I felt I'd like the exercise and the fresh air. So, I ran down the road, a kilometer, and decided to run back again to the van.

As I was running, a car passed me. In fact, it came upon me very suddenly, which surprised me, because in the desert you can see and hear cars for miles. They passed me pretty close and they'd just gone past and they must have reacted rather slowly; then they pulled up.

Brake lights went on and I thought, *Oh-oh.*

So, I veered over to the left onto a sort of sand track. Kept on running, but faster, back to the van.

They backed their car down and swung it over towards me. The doors opened and they started to get out. By this time, the van was in view and they could see me looking very possibly at something. They glanced over too, saw the van, immediately got back into their car, shut the door and drove off.

I remember thinking, *Oh God, oh the Arabs, I hate them!*

That was my sudden reaction at the time because I'd been afraid, and I remember thinking, *What if I'd been alone or anything?*

I'm not saying anything would have happened, but just supposing they'd leaped out and chased me, caught me, dragged me back to that car. Anything could have happened. So, it seems to me when I'm in this country, I'm always running. Running in the morning. Running from people. Running again in the afternoon.

The Same Evening

In fact, I had another run that early evening, and I saw a car approaching, and I thought, *My God, I must run again!*

So, I ran off the road into a muddy field, far enough away. I hoped for the car lights not to spot me. But the car drove past me and I thought, *Oh, they haven't seen me,* and ran back onto the road behind them.

But to my amazement, their brake lights went on. Now, they couldn't possibly have seen me, but I saw those brake lights, and the first thing I did was turn right around and run like hell back to the van.

I thought, *My God, they couldn't beat me,* so I ran on past the van, looking all the time for lights. Ran down faster and faster and then turned around and ran back again.

But it's amazing; I've done so much running since I've been in Tunisia, I'm going to be very fit by the time I leave the country. It was a coincidence. I think that their brake lights went on, but it was significant to me, and, of course, my first reaction was to stop, turn and run away again.

What do you think it's all about really?

I think it's a lot to do with my imagination, and I am probably conjuring up a lot of these incidents, but I have this fear. It's become almost an obsession now, that if someone does meet up with me, that something is going to happen to me, so I don't allow these things to occur. So, I get out of there before there can actually be a confrontation, but I still think it's rather unusual for a Western girl to be seen running along all the time, that maybe I'm asking for trouble.

"We Don't Live by Your Rules"

Jennifer Utter

The biggest thing I learned, despite the fact that I really loved my trip — it doesn't sound like I did — was that it was beautiful. I learned that being a young, single female traveling alone just really isn't an option sometimes — not a real good option; it's not always a safe option.

So, I was in a position often where, whether I liked it or not, I had to be with my male travel companion. He was my security; he had traveled before; he was smarter, and; he was much bigger; and he was a man, and it was essential.

I'm not saying that all women need to travel with men, but I think as young women, we do not always understand what we're getting ourselves into and probably how to protect ourselves.

It's kind of interesting, you know; we live in a society where we talk about the equality of the sexes, and yet, you know, when you're traveling in some places, you're getting down to a sort of a primeval, more primitive level almost, when you're a single female traveling by yourself.

And, it really is a dangerous world out there, I mean, especially if you do not have a whole lot of experience traveling in some of those areas, that it's definitely different. It's much more basic, you know, than it is here in America, where we live such sheltered lives.

And, you almost feel there's almost a natural order going back to where the males were the protectors of the females, you know, in a very basic environment of, say, Italian men, who do not respect foreign women much at all.

And yet, I'm sure that they have their own way of respecting their sisters and their mothers and their aunts and their grandmothers, and so on.

Exactly, yeah.

But culturally, these men see women in a completely different light than we do here in the United States. And, it seems to me that we live in our own little bubble. And it's a very sugar-coated little bubble at that.

And you get out of that, and you understand that every single culture is different, and they are not going to operate by your rules. They won't.

For a moment, let's revisit this groping situation in Italy.

What could you do now? How could you avoid that?

I'm not sure how to avoid it. I found it very unpleasant, and, you know, I guess the best way I dealt with it is to get out of Italy, at least the southern part of Italy, and that's that!

Did you ever think of trying to fight back?

No. I thought I might get arrested. I was not. You realize very early on, you're not in the United States anymore; you don't have constitutional rights.

Do you want me to talk a little bit more about the Italian incidents?

I didn't learn much more about that except that Italian men were schleps!

Which is why I wanted to get out of there.

The 'I Hate Italian Men Club' #1:
In the Church!

Barbara Bridges

———◉———

Italy, small town, the late 1980s. I'm Barbara Bridges (an assumed name). I was with a girlfriend and on the bridge where we were sitting. I took my shoes off. A tall man approached and started asking us all these questions in broken English:

"Where are you going? What are you doing? Where do you come from, and so on?"

All these persistent questions. He wouldn't leave us alone. And he could not be discouraged. We didn't answer him, but he still followed us holding my arm, and then he followed us all night. We couldn't get rid of him.

We just sort of tried to ignore him.

Finally, we dipped into a church. Well, they were working on the church, and I lit a candle. I'm just standing around in the church when I'm lighting a candle, and he's now pinching my buttocks. I cannot simply believe it. I turn around in disgust and I yell at him, and I walk away. I just push him away in this church.

"Come with me to make me your lover," he says.

"Go away, you," I shout as loud as I can, and I walk out of the church, out the door, and just as I walk out he comes and he pinches me again, but this time really hard. I wheel around and then punch him in the face.

And then I just stand there with my fists clenched. I am so furious by this time. I'd just had it. People have probably never seen this sort of thing happen there, before, and I just wheel around and simply punch him. I really mean it.

So, everybody in the church heard it, huh?

Yes, it was in the church, and everybody turned around. He was so embarrassed. He stood for a minute and looked at me. and then being macho masculine, being right in the church, and what with the noise, this idiot ran back somewhere deep inside the church, and then I walked outside.

"Don't you do that again," I shouted in English. Everyone, including him, got the message. I'll never do it again, punch a guy in Italy. I mean I've been pinched in the buns in France, and in Italy, I was really pissed off being pinched in the buttocks.

A girlfriend of mine was really puzzled when I told her about it. The Italians, they pinch you on the bottom. She went to Italy. But in her group, nobody got pinched on the bottom. She was almost disappointed!

She told the Italian waiter when she was leaving Italy that she hadn't been pinched by men.

"Something wrong with you?" was his reply!

There must be.

Can't imagine what. He was a Southern Italian probably.

Anyway, I'm awfully tempted to form the '*I hate Italian Men Club*' and be the first member!

Travel Tip #2:
Do Not 'Run on Automatic'!

Michael Brein

———◦◉◦———

Do not run on 'automatic.' Pay attention! This is just a simple, all-important catchphrase that's well worth becoming something of the 'new mantra' for overseas travelers and adventurers.

I think the 'ordinary' tourist (one who's not so particularly steeply immersed into the travel experience versus the 'traveler,' who is more travel savvy as a result of a more in-depth travel-life history), may all too easily just pay lip-service to the notion that one ought to be running on all cylinders overseas rather than just 'running *(blindly)* on automatic' as we tend to do when we travel, just as we typically do when at home, when we need not be particularly 'conscious' or aware of what is just at the perimeter of our envelopes, bubbles, what have you — our personal psychological and physical space.

The above is not meant so much as a warning that "the sky is falling; the sky is falling," as it is a bid that we all need to be more conscious and aware than we tend to be in our overseas travels. The world is 'a changing', so please pay (more) attention!

The Elevator Guy #1:
The Night Crawler

Debra Denton

Rome, Italy, the 1990s. I'm Debra Denton (an assumed name). When I was a junior in college I traveled to Europe with a German girlfriend. Her mother had come over after World War II, so she was an American citizen but she spoke fluent German.

So, we were going back to Europe to visit some of her relatives in Germany and travel around. She had met this one guy who was traveling with a study group, and so we were on our way to Rome, and we were going to meet up with them in Rome. They were staying at a very fancy hotel, but, of course, we didn't have any money. So, we couldn't really afford to stay at this hotel, but we were able to find a tiny little room at the top of the hotel, which they rented to us for not too much money.

So, one evening my friend went out with one of her friends, and I decided to stay in. I was reading Ernest Hemingway's "A Movable Feast," or something like that.

Earlier that day, I was coming up the elevator, and it was one of these old-fashioned elevators, you know, an old wrought iron one that you could see through. And I'd got in. As I was going out, the elevator guy was just smiling at me and talking to me. I don't know what the hell he was saying. And just as I was exiting the elevator, he *PINCHED* me!

Where?

On the derriere. Oh, my God. That night I was by myself in the room, so I was very nervous being there by myself.

What did you do when he pinched you?

Well, I didn't quite know what to do. I was just really shocked. I mean, I was really surprised, I thought, *Oh my God.*

I was getting really upset because we had had an incident earlier that day walking down the street, where we were just practically attacked by these Italian guys. There must have been like six or seven guys that were just following us and pinching us and pushing us. It was really very scary.

And we saw a couple American guys up ahead. We ran up to them and said, "Please, please, can we walk with you? Could you take us back to our hotel?"

And then those Italian guys finally they let us alone. I guess they didn't want to get into a big fight, you know. It was really upsetting to be treated like this way. So, I wasn't very happy about being pinched.

So, my friend that evening went out with her friend, and I stayed in the hotel and was reading. And pretty soon — there was a door connecting the room connecting to another room, which was locked — I heard a lot of moving and rustling around in the next room.

So, I was reading, and I then heard this noise at the window, and I saw this arm and a leg, and here it was this elevator guy from earlier in the morning trying to crawl through my window. The ELEVATOR guy! Unbelievable!

I was just petrified. I didn't know what to do; so I started yelling at him. I then called down to the front desk and was trying to tell this desk clerk guy that there was somebody trying to crawl in through my window. Someone — a male — crawling into my window!

I mean, they were so fucking casual about it. He was going, "Yeah, yeah lady." It was like they spoke only broken English, and they didn't really understand what I was saying or they were pretending that they didn't understand. They wouldn't do anything about it.

I was petrified; I was so scared, and; I was yelling and screaming. Finally, I called one of the guys who was on our tour, and he went and found the girl I was traveling with and her boyfriend, and they came up and rescued me.

So, what did they do? What happened?

Well, the guy apparently got scared when I started getting on the phone and when I was yelling at him, and then, I guess they went and knocked on the door of the adjoining room to see if there was anybody in there, and they never got any response.

He disappeared?

Yeah.

You ever see him again?

I never saw him again.

What about the elevator?

Oh, he wasn't there the next day. You know, he mysteriously disappeared. But it was real; I was so scared.

What did you think about it?

Oh, I thought he was going to climb in and rape me. I was really scared to death. I still don't like Italian men now. I mean, I was very happy to get out of that country.

And we got hassled and leered at and everything even on the train out of the country. I don't know whether other American girls have had that experience.

Tell me a little more about that. What you thought and what you were feeling just walking down the street.

Well, it was very frightening and very degrading.

In what sense? Tell me what happened.

Well, it was just having people come up and pinch you and whistle at you. They were actually pinching our bottoms and making clicking sounds with their mouths, you know, that sort of thing.

Oh God, it just felt like being a piece of meat. It was awful. In all my years of experience in traveling, I've never had the experiences like I had in Rome.

You know, even like when I was in Malaysia, sometimes I'd get people when I was riding my bicycle, the guys would yell out at me or whistle or something, but I never got the treatment as I did in Rome. I suppose maybe if I went to a Middle Eastern country maybe it wouldn't be so different. But, God, was that scary.

Is there maybe some sort of an *I hate Italian Men Club* that I can join?

The Elevator Guy #2:
Operator Assault

Eleanor Ellis

Kabul, Afghanistan, the 1960s. I'm Eleanor Ellis (an assumed name). This one chick, she's in an elevator and she's in Afghanistan, and she's going up the elevator. And this guy that's running the elevator stops it right in the middle of the floor and says, "I'm going to fuck you."

The chick just looks at him thinking like, *Well, it looks like I'm going to get fucked.*

But what does she do? She then grabbed him right by his cock.

The fucking guy, as soon as she touched his cock, he came all over the place.

Otherwise, she could have been killed.

She looked him right square in the eyes

What happened then?

The guy was really distraught. He said, "I'm sorry. You know my problem, that's all I wanted to do was just have an orgasm, I was all excited, and excuse me."

And you know, he opened up the doors and away they went. She went one way; he went the other, but she could have easily been killed. She did the right thing. That's what she did, though. The right thing. She did. She grabbed him in the groin to help his frustration, his situation. She just grabbed him right by his cock. She wanted him to come. And as far as she was concerned, that would be the end of it. He didn't have to do anything.

All she did was touch him. He was so fucked up, the guy; that's all she had to do to him, she said. Just reach down and grab him and the guy was just fucking eggs spread all over the elevator.

Would he, in fact, have hurt her, really?

Yeah. She thinks that guy probably would have killed her if she hadn't done that. It was a better option than getting raped and maybe murdered in the elevator.

The Elevator Guy #3:
The Ditchbed Hotel

Judy Lee Rosenzweig

Cairo, Egypt, 1996. Unfortunately, I have definitely had my share of negative experiences. Definitely. Purely as a female living abroad. Not at first, though. But, in an odd sort of way, I almost thought of myself as being sort of immune to it. Imagine that!

Yeah.

These sorts of experiences can actually be quite negative, but one occasion, it was kind of funny, too.

The "Ditchbed"

My friend and I were staying in Egypt for six weeks. We went over to work on an independent documentary project. We were staying in this really grungy hotel from hell called the "Ismailayya Hotel." It was only five bucks a night at the time, and that even included breakfast in the price! It was all about shared bathrooms, and you were lucky if there was any running water. That sort of thing.

What's your definition of 'grungy'?

Actually, we had the nicest room in the whole hotel, believe it or not, because they liked us. But the floors and the carpets were dirty. The mattresses were yucky and foam. One side of my bed had like a ditch that ran through it. So, I called it the "ditch bed," ergo my pseudonym name for the hotel, "The Ditchbed Hotel!"

But the one thing this hotel had going for it was that it was central and very convenient to everything, right in the middle of downtown Cairo, of course, a huge city of nearly 16 million people who were very, very tightly packed in together like sardines.

We're right in the center of the downtown, and right below us, there was this makeshift mosque, where they used public loudspeakers to call

76

people to prayer. It had, like most mosques, what they call, a *'muezzin,'* that
is, its own guy who calls the people to prayer. Only, this particular muezzin
seemed to have a penchant to be rather mean, loud, and in an angry-sound-
ing disposition. He was the one in charge of doing the first call of the day
at 4:40 AM, and who, somehow, seemed to us particularly intent to do his
God-given duty very righteously and always right on time. So, we were duly
awakened every morning by that.

But, at any rate, given our hotel's good, central location, our staying
there provided us with no lack of really interesting people that came
through there.

Down to the Casbah!

For instance, we met one night, a group of particularly interesting girls
that were all traveling alone, but who seemingly 'teamed up' together in
Cairo, somehow. And so, we happened to meet these various girls and all
decided to go to view the famous-for-Cairo Sufi dancing event together.
But before we went to see the Sufi dancers, we decided that we would all go
and have something to eat together.

This was particularly interesting, because the Sufi dancers were in this
area in one of Cairo's biggest outdoor markets, one of the largest in the
world, as a matter of fact. It is the *Khan Ai-Khalili Market,* simply a fabulous and famous Cairo landmark and tourist attraction.

It was an absolutely fantastic place to watch people and to sort of take
the pulse of Cairo. And so, all of us girls were getting to know one another
better, and after a time, as often happens among a group of travelers, we began sharing some of our greatest travel stories with one another.

Two of these girls were particularly interesting. One of them, for instance, was from America and one of them was from Sweden. I don't remember much about the other girls, but I was really intrigued with these
two, in particular, because the American girl had been traveling in Africa
for six months all by herself, and the Swedish girl was actually a flight attendant before, quit her job, and now spent a year-and-a-half in Africa traveling alone, on her own, as well.

She would go from one country to another and find these piddly little
jobs, you know, like, for instance, working in a youth hostel to working in
this one interesting little restaurant, and so on.

And so, we began to share these travel stories, and one thing led to another. So, it's not surprising in the least, that especially among a group of traveling girls, that at some point, we would get onto the subject of women travelers being sexually harassed.

And, as they were going on and on with their stories, actually, these girls were saying that some of the worst sexual harassment they'd ever experienced was in none other than Egypt! It was as if the floodgates suddenly opened!

Of course, sexual harassment of Western women has always been known to be rampant all over North Africa, but, apparently, it turns out to be particularly the case in Egypt.

And my friend, who I still work with, and who was also with me on that night, started telling us her own stories about being hassled that included, for instance, guys coming on to her all the time, and guys even exposing themselves to her. You know, just continuous hassles and lots and lots of problems.

And I find I am saying to these girls, "Well, I guess I'm lucky, or something, but this really hasn't ever happened to me. I mean, I guess that I just must look like a bitch or something, because I have never really been hassled. And, it doesn't mean that I look down at people... Everybody just leaves me alone. I won't engage myself with people. I can kind of feel it, you know. You can feel people looking at you or trying to get your attention, and I just won't even respond to them. Even if somebody is looking at me or talking to me, a lot of times I simply won't answer them. I know that's really weird in our culture. But, I guess, just out of self-preservation, you have to learn how to deal with things overseas, and it seems to work for me. Well, at least, most of the time.

That is, before I got to Cairo and to the "Ditchbed Hotel!"

Did it work?

It worked mostly well for me as a general rule.

Why did the others seem to have all these hassles?

Well, take, for instance, especially this one friend of mine whom I'm now traveling with to Cairo. Most of her experiences that were negative were due to her walking alone at night. Well, du-uh, this is a big 'no no' for me; this simply is not smart! You observe the same kind of caution any-where that you would observe at home, and maybe even more so abroad.

You know, this doesn't mean you need to be paranoid, but you just don't go out walking alone at night by yourself. That's just ignorant, isn't it? It just makes good common sense not to do that.

And also, a lot of the other problems that she had had were things like getting into the front seat of a taxi with the driver. No, no; you don't ever do that, you know; that's just not smart.

What happens in the front seats of cabs?

They just love to feel you up, the taxi drivers! That shouldn't be a sur-prise to anyone! I've even had a taxi cab driver try to do that to me once, thinking that I was going to do a trade with him — *A TRADE!* Can you believe that?

I crossed my legs once. I accidentally lifted up my skirt a bit too high so that I could cross my legs. It was rather awkward and unintentional, but when I did that, I guess he instantly took that to telegraph a message to him that I did not at all intend: He instantly gets excited and gets this idea in his mind that I'm actually going to "trade' with him, somehow, that he can cop a feel in exchange for the taxi fare as some sort of a perverted notion of exchange of favors. I had to tell him, "No, no, no ... you misunderstood me! Don't go there, you know."

It worked?

Yeah, yeah.

How about the other two girls?

Just mainly verbal harassment. For instance, they tended to have a lot of the experiences of the sort which would be that a lot of men will say such things to you like, "You are very, very beautiful: I want to marry you," to the really nasty things that are unpleasant, but that don't really hurt you. Thus, a lot of the problems that the girls tended to have were more of a verbal and non-physical nature.

And at times, on rarer occasions, some girls say they had been grabbed — a lot of grabs — both tops and bottoms... everything. Anything is fair game to some people.

What do women do in reaction to these things?

A lot of women will simply say or do nothing at all. And when I say "nothing," it's because it's really so shocking to have somebody do that to you — absolutely so shocking — that you're just so dumbfounded by it, and by the time you even realize what has just happened to you, generally it's over... and done with... and the person's gone!

My friend got grabbed about two months ago. We were in a very crowded shopping area and some guy grabbed her front. He full on grabbed her. That was a big mistake! She had been studying karate for like ten years.

She slugged him as hard as she could in his lower back causing him to reel. And although I was right next to her, I hadn't actually seen what he did and her reaction to what was all going on. She told him — she actually speaks some Arabic — that what he did was very, very bad and that he was a bad man, and of course, everyone will come to your rescue at that point.

He just acted like he didn't do it; he would not even acknowledge her, and so be it. And yeah, he knew he had been caught.

Did he grab her breast?

No, no. He just started to put his hand under her skirt.

So, on this one night, when we went down to watch the Sufi dancers in Cairo, we kind of got into this sort of conversation.

I was REITERATING about myself, maybe somewhat cockily, that nothing like this has *EVER* happened to ME! But was I immune to such things? And why? Or, why not?

Obviously, I've heard people tell these sorts of things to me, but so far, no one's ever grabbed me, and nobody's ever exposed himself to me. I attribute this, maybe to the fact that I probably look very unfriendly, and therefore, am unapproachable to them. Maybe it's just that I have been very careful.

And so, my friends who have been victimized by these sorts of things, had been harassed and were naturally upset by them, but it was just not quite the same for me.

Until that very same night in Cairo, *THAT IS!*

Maybe you just had some good rules!

But, I was sure soon to learn a <u>new</u> rule on that night!

Back to the Ismailayya

We went back to the hotel. It was very crowded downtown. We then walked through a dark hallway. And my girlfriend and I were together.

And their elevators over there are quite something else again; like when you stand in an elevator there they're really very fancy, left over from the British occupation. They're really cool, too. As you go up floors you can reach out and touch the walls actually; you can even jump out if you want to. There are no operators, as we've been used to in those days in America in some places. And, especially in this five-dollar-a-night hotel, there was no operator at all, in "The Ditchbed Hotel," the Ismailayya Hotel in downtown Cairo. (Laughs)

This building was a really busy building.

So, we went through this long, narrow hallway there and got in the elevator. And, as we step on, there is a guy that's on there, too, this young guy — a young Egyptian guy who was maybe 18 or so. And so, it's one of him and two of us. He is definitely smaller than both of us. And you can only fit three people in this elevator. This is a really small elevator. And so, it's a tight fit. We get on the elevator and close the door and it starts going up.

This young man now looks at me and says very politely to me, "Fornication?"

Okay, now I hear him saying this and I'm doing a double take of sorts. I'm thinking, *No, this isn't a word. There's no way that he is saying this to me. No way.*

So, I now look at my friend, and I say, "What did he just say?"

She just starts laughing in complete disbelief as if trying to just shrug it off. She shakes her head and goes, "I don't know!" It is either something that she just doesn't want to have to deal with and like it's my problem and not hers, "So deal with it!"

Keep in mind, that in Cairo, as in a lot of other places, lots of people, of course, speak some English, and it is very, very possible a lot of times, what with accents and such, that people get confused, and, indeed, say the wrong things at the wrong times that can give the wrong message. This is true with any language. *Is this what is happening, maybe,* I'm thinking?

So, trying to get some clarification, I look back at him and I say, "What do you mean? Tell me again."

Well, he says, "Fornication," as he now brazenly reaches out and grabs my breast! HE grabs my *BREAST!* And I am going like, "*Ahhh? HEY-LO-OH?*"

Hey, this is now after I've just been a wise ass earlier that evening, bragging and now just outsmarted, like nobody has *EVER* done anything like that to little old me!

I am so pissed. I get in his face and I am just like, "*YOU* do *NOT* do that!"

And I am so intimidating that I imagine I am even dangerous. And I am telling him that what he just did "is very bad" and "that you should not treat women like that," and that, "You are very bad, and you are very ugly."

And we're doing this bantering back and forth.

Did he let go?

He did.

At first, I thought I had something on my shirt, but it was his hand, you know. His one hand. He just reached around and grabbed me with his right hand. It was weird; it was like a full motion distraction. I mean it was as if we were frozen in time, the two of us, locked in this strange interaction.

He just reaches out and grabs me while we are standing there. It's like I cannot leave and neither can he. So, what to do? I am so totally in his face. And, normally, I generally would be a non-confrontational kind of person, especially in a situation like that, but I mean I am really pissed.

I was not done with him at all. By the time we got to our floor, the sixth floor, I just held the door open, because the door has to be shut in order to go up and down, even though you can still jump out, so I held the elevator door open.

And the guy at the desk, who is this guy we had just been so frustrated with earlier during our stay because he had such a bad attitude. He was always pissed off about one thing or another, like his life, maybe, which, of course, must have been pissing this guy off.

It is no wonder that this desk guy was always really grouchy. He was super big, burly and way strong. However, over the six-week period we were there, he had gotten somewhat protective of us, so yeah, we could expect him to be on our side.

So, I hold the elevator door open, and I next holler for him. And I am like, "Can you come over here?"

I am meanwhile going back and forth with this guy in the elevator, and my friend who was riding up with me starts telling the guy from the desk the whole story.

The desk guy says, "What's the problem?"

She then says that the guy in the elevator just "grabbed her" (me), and so on.

She's trying to be polite about it. But the man from the desk is all about business and goes right into the elevator, makes the guy get off, and asks him for his ID. He has him empty his pockets.

He then asks the guy what happened, and they're going back and forth on this. And I'm thinking, *This guy's lying to him.*

So, then the man from the desk turns back around again to him and he says, "What's the big deal? What happened?"

The guy now apparently tells him that he had grabbed my breast as if to say, "So what? What's the big deal?"

The guy from the desk next reels right around and slugs this guy full on. He then picks him right up and throws him back into the elevator. He then tells him that if he EVER even as much as comes into the building again, that he is going to kill him!

And then the desk guy turns back to us and asks, "Do you guys want me to call the police?"

And, of course, I want to reply, "Yes!"

But I felt better about it; I mean, I am a fighter, but it wouldn't have done any good; it wouldn't have made much of a difference, really, for all the effort.

What was the guy in the elevator's attitude towards all of this?

When the guy from the desk was talking to him, and when I was talking to him, he was just acting at first like he didn't know what we were talking about, like "what's the big deal?" or, " I didn't do anything."

I mean, he was acting like he hadn't done anything, because, of course, all along he knew exactly that what he was doing was wrong.

There is such a great misperception of our Western females, as you know. That they are loose and they just will do it with anyone, and that all Western women are just whores and such. That's all they are good for.

And, no doubt, due to the great influence of television and movies, these kinds of attitudes are not surprising. I'm really embarrassed living in a Middle Eastern country that is likely the most progressive probably of all of them; if I see foreign people dressed in ways that is so disrespectful to their culture, it just shocks me.

For example?

Mainly, like I have on slacks and a sweatshirt. I'm practically okay. This is perfect; this is fine. But, I see in Cairo foreign women with shorts on and tank tops, halter-tops, bathing suit tops, and miniskirts which are just so totally inappropriate. It is their Muslim culture; they have norms that they expect people to live by as visitors, so I think that it's really important for us to respect that.

Now, here is an important question? What was the new rule that you learned that night?

We should not have been on the elevator with that guy. I would say if I was in the States, if I was getting on an elevator, I wouldn't normally have gotten on an elevator with him alone.

And that even with both of us, the two of us, I still wouldn't have done it, gone onto the elevator with this man.

Elevators are places where things like this happen. I don't suppose that this is that unusual a circumstance, as women here, particularly in Egypt or North Africa or elsewhere in the Middle East. But, I think that a lot of foreign women here, when you get on an elevator, if you're not with a large group of people, you shouldn't ride up alone with a man. I'd think twice before doing so. I really would.

That's a good rule. You have to exercise good common sense. You don't put yourself in situations that would not be good, that would not be good even here in America.

The Rock

Lainie Liberti

———————◦———————

Cusco, Peru, 2013. The day I picked up a rock to defend myself was on June 10, 2013.

Why?

Never in my life have I experienced a physical threat. I did not know what that feels like to have aggression directed at me. I have never been confronted physically by another person. Nor do I live in fear.

I consider myself lucky.

I also feel on many levels this sort of violence doesn't come into my life, since it's not something that really enters my consciousness. I know it is out there, but I do believe wholeheartedly that that which you give your attention to becomes your reality.

I tend to take the high road on most occasions. I don't like confrontation, nor do I like aggressive behavior. So, choosing to live a peaceful life is my conscious choice.

Overall, I consider myself a gentle person.

Two weeks ago, I had to let all that go and pick up a rock to defend myself.

This was big for me.

During the afternoon, I was walking down our street, just returning from the bakery. A man was walking towards me. He was Peruvian, somewhere in his early 30s. He was looking at me, and as he walked past me, his hand reached out and grabbed my crotch!

What the fuck just happened? I thought.

I flung my body around to face this man, who had already passed and said in the deepest, most powerful voice I could muster, "ASSHOLE!"

He stopped, looked at me and laughed in my attempts to be powerful.

I felt humiliated, small and powerless.

I kept on walking, breathing through my teeth.

I could feel his energy, his thoughts. He had anger and aggression towards me, a *gringa* with blonde hair, walking down his local streets. He had so much anger towards what I represented to him in that moment and there was a heavy story playing in his head and I could feel it. I felt like a non-human in his presence, and his Latino machismo was so big, there wasn't room for me, the person, on that road.

I walked further, still about 5 minutes from my house.

It started to rain, so I ducked into the little *tienda* just a few feet in front of me. As I stood in the doorway, I noticed the man had turned around and had been following me, and I hadn't even noticed. I was caught up in my thoughts, not aware of what was happening around me. The man walked past the *tienda*, slowed at the entrance where I was standing, looked in, and smiled at me.

His look was menacing, and I felt my blood pressure rise. For the first time in my life, I experienced rage ignite within my body; I understood the expression "my blood was starting to boil."

In that moment, I realized I was not afraid of this man.

I was angry.

I was angry that he was fucking with me and approached me with the attitude that he had power over me.

I stood in the door of the *tienda* and gave him enough time for him to pass. Then put my scarf over my hair in an attempt to stay dry from the rain and set out.

He was standing there waiting for me. I looked at him, gave him a scowl, made my eyes smaller and meaner pressed with anger, and bent down and picked up a rock.

I showed him that there was a rock in my hand and took all the physical power in my body, and channeled it all through my hand, into this palm-sized rock. My arm was rigid and I was holding his glare.

He laughed at me, turned and walked down the road, the same direction I was walking, but in front of me about 50 paces.

Halfway between the *tienda* and my house, he stopped on the side of the road. I could either pass him, letting him walk behind me or I could, too, stop.

I stopped, held the rock in my hand and faced him with my face scrunched up but holding dynamic power in my body that was able to snap in any moment.

Again, he laughed.

Just beyond him, but before my door, was the gate to a hotel. There were people standing out front of the entrance to the hotel. I walked past my predator, gave him a look of death, and stopped where the other people were in front of the hotel. I stood with them while watching this man pass me. I figured he should think I was staying there and not know where I was going, nor know where I lived.

He laughed at me while he passed. I could read his energy, a game of cat and mouse with him, he believing he had the upper hand.

He reached the end of the road, just past the entrance to my house. He stood there, at the end of the road, while I remained at the entrance to the hotel, just a hundred feet behind him. He turned around, spread his legs and grabbed his own crotch and made an obscene gesture at me. Then he broke into laughter once again and exited down the steps and was out of sight.

I waited another moment to make sure he wasn't popping his head back around the road. Maybe he was waiting for me beyond the stairs, maybe he wasn't. I crossed the road, put my key in the door, and turned around once more. He was nowhere to be seen, so I dropped the rock.

Safe inside my house, I felt angry. I felt angry that another human being was so aggressive to me for absolutely no reason. I felt angry that it was necessary to embody such rage. I felt angry that this was the interaction I just encountered.

Then I felt empowered that I found my own strength.

But I equally felt pissed off that this man had flung his aggression upon me.

I've seen this man two or three times since. I walked past him with my son, Miro, as he was tending his newspaper stand on the street. Yes, I know where he works, and he didn't see me that time. The second time was with a group of friends in the market. It had just started to rain so we were standing at the entrance waiting for it to stop. Then he walked through the entrance and was standing face to face with me. My heart raced, but I stood with my feet solidly on the ground. I think he realized that I was standing with a large group of people and many men.

He looked frightened. He looked small. He even looked remorseful. He scampered by me very quickly and got lost in the crowded market.

Guess what? I felt sorry for him. I can't even imagine what was going through his head to make him act so aggressively towards me. But the dance we dance with one another is just that, a dance. He didn't hurt me, and in my heart, in my soul, I don't believe this man is a bad person.

The 'I Hate Italian Men Club' #2:
Meet the Parents #1

Unknown

———————◦———————

Florence, Italy, 1970. I came to Europe in the summer of 1970 with a friend of mine, and he went to Italy. I refused to go. I went to Denmark instead, because I said I had absolutely no interest in Italy.

He went down to Italy and had a great time. He met all these wonderful people and he told me all about it. So, when I came to Germany this year I froze, first off. California girl coming to freeze in Germany, and I had a two-week ship/rail pass that my parents had sent me for Christmas, and so, I thought, I'll go south before I have to come back and start school.

Of course, that warm country was Italy, no less.

I had heard nothing but good stories, so thought I'd go. Plus, I'd been to Venice already. Somewhere along the line, I'd been to Venice for a day. I thought it wasn't all that bad.

There wasn't anybody else who had a rail pass at that time, and there wasn't anyone who really wanted to leave Germany, so I wound up going by myself. All I wanted to do was to find a beach somewhere and someplace to stay for a few days and warm my body before I had to return to my studies back in the States.

I first went down to Austria, which I knew really well, and then from there into northern Italy, which is almost like Austria. I got to Venice, which was just packed with tourists. Nice and warm and beautiful, though, but it was way too crowded, and I didn't have that much desire to remain there. I couldn't find the camping ground, either, and there wasn't a youth hostel, so I decided to get on the train and go someplace farther south on the line — Florence.

Comparing notes with everybody, Italy gets 'worse' the farther south you go. In Florence, you start noticing that people start looking at you — guys — saying, "Hey baby," and that sort of thing.

As a friend of mine would say, these guys start making all these comments to you. I don't speak a word of Italian, and I was there for four days, but by the end of my stay there I came out learning how to say in Italian such things as:

"Are you married?"

"You've got beautiful hair."

"Are you alone?"

"I love you."

"We'll go someplace."

I also learned, on the other hand:

"Leave me alone."

"Where's the train station?"

"I'm going."

"The police will arrest you."

And that was just about the extent of my Italian for very good reasons.

The first thing that happened was actually on the way to Florence. I get on this train; I leave Venice at about 10 PM at night, and I suppose we got into Florence about 1 AM. I got the kind of impression that there were some pretty raunchy Italians running around there late at night.

I'd been living in Germany, and I had really gotten into the culture if you know what I mean. Going and not just seeing and looking at the famous buildings and museums, but really talking with people and getting to know the people and their customs and what they think about.

I did want to go down to Italy, but I felt bad about not speaking Italian. I wanted to get to know some people, and there just are no single Italian girls traveling around, or even Italian girls traveling in pairs.

I never saw any of them, and if you did, they were either married with kids and husbands and grandmothers, or else they wouldn't talk to you. Whatever. They just wouldn't talk to you.

So, the train got into Florence. I'm thinking, *I'm going to get into Florence in the middle of the night. There's no place to stay, so what am I going to do?*

This really nice soldier — dumb that I was — came over and sat down with me and started talking. We were having this really great time trying to understand each other, what with my broken French and English and German, and the Italian that I knew at that point was just nil, and his broken French and English and Italian that he knew... But it was just perfect.

We were sitting there, and he said, "Well, where are you going to stay when you get to Florence?"

This, of course, is all in terribly unclear. I said, "I don't know."

He then said, "My parents live in Florence, and I'm coming home from leave. I'm stationed down in Sicily. I'm coming home from leave and my parents would be glad to put you up. My brother is meeting me at the train station, and we'll give you a ride to my parents' house."

I said, "Okay."

Mistake Number One

Saying okay. We get out at the train station, and there's this one guy and these two other guys waiting for him. They take one look at me and they start jabbering away in Italian. I kind of figured that this might not work out. And there might not be any parents waiting for the guy.

Why?

Well, just because they started jabbering together and were all kind of looking at me at the same time going *umm-umm-umm*. You could kind of tell that they were complimenting him on the fact that I was either good looking or that he had caught someone, or just the fact that it seemed to me that neither of them looked like his 'brother.'

I just didn't have the impression of a brother meeting his older brother at the train station to take him back to the family house. It just didn't look like it. I don't know why.

I'd just gotten uneasy because there were three of them and there was just one of me, plus the fact the other guys started helping me with my suitcases and putting his arm on my arm, and getting kind of friendly.

We get in the car, and we start driving out of Florence. I'm thinking, *I better remember the way just in case. If anything happens, I'm going to have to walk back to the train station.*

I was just being cautious because I had heard bad stories about Florence; I'd heard bad stories about Italy, and that's why I didn't want to go the first time I was here.

I kind of kept my eyes open and I asked, "How far is it to the house?"

They said, "Oh, oh, it's not far. It's not far."

I said, "How far, exactly?"

They said, "26 kilometers."

Mistake Number Two

I shouldn't have gotten in the car! I should never have gotten in the car with these people. We drove out, and I don't know if it was 26 kilometers or not, but it was way outside the city in this tiny, little village.

What village? There were about six houses on this road that was about four kilometers long. No lights, no pavement, nothing. It was desolate.

We get to a house and stop. I don't think there had been a woman in that house for at least six years. There were dirty dishes piled up to the ceiling. There was what I think what used to be a little fireplace that had been blocked up and full of garbage. It had this tablecloth that I swear hadn't been cleaned in the last 100 years, and the chairs didn't look like they had been cleaned in the last 1,000 years. And they had this refrigerator that was growing its own mold in it. The mold had a good healthy growth on it.

It was just a disgustingly dirty place, and I thought that this is certainly nobody's parents' house. Can you realize, 26 kilometers out of Florence in the middle of nowhere and I don't speak Italian?

I thought at first that they were just being very nice and respectful of me. They were all kind of giving me these looks about "gosh, isn't she a nice young lady" kind of look, but still, they were respectful, and so, I thought, *Well, maybe we'll pull this off.*

They gave me a pear. Cut up this pear, gave me this pear to eat, and they all ran u and were doing all these strange things upstairs. And I heard all this noise upstairs, and I'm thinking, *What's going on up there?*

Wait a minute. By this time I am not cautious. I am downright armed to the teeth, ready for anything. Ready for them to attack me in the next minute. These three guys and me in this house in the middle of nowhere.

You say you are *armed*?

I'm armed mentally. I was ready. I was ready for them to attack me and I was ready to flee. I had my hand on my suitcase. I had my eyes watching them every second, listening to every sound, to make sure that I caught any kind of nuance that something was going to happen.

I go upstairs and there are three rooms upstairs. The bathroom, a big empty room, and a bedroom. The bedroom had three beds in it, and they had moved a bed out of the bedroom into this empty room for me.

I'm thinking, *Well, this is okay. Putting the bed in the empty room for me...*

However, the problem was that this empty room kind of served as a hall, because the stairs went up, but then you had to go through that room to get into the bedroom, and you had to go back to that room to get in the bathroom.

Now, the bathroom had a toilet in it and a sink, and it had running water out of the sink. And a bucket was under the sink because there was no plumbing connecting the sink to anything else. After you went to the bathroom, you took the bucket from under the sink that had caught the running water and poured it down the toilet, because the toilet didn't have any running water in it.

For some reason, I guess, they didn't keep real close track of the toilet.

They had water all over the bathroom floor; it was filthy. The place was just filthy.

They all said goodnight. We turned out the light, and I laid down in my bed, took my shoes off, period, and just laid down.

I had just started to fall asleep, and sure enough, I'm half asleep, and all of a sudden, I feel this person sit down on my bed. I wake up and I said something like, "What are you doing here?" or "Who is that?" or something in my broken Italian.

He started saying my name and saying something, and I said, "Get out of here" or some such other.

It took him aback the first time he heard, "Leave me alone."

He got a little upset and said, "I just want to talk to you."

You could just tell by the tone of his voice that he was kind of whining. "I just want to talk to you."

"Let me lay down by you for a second. I won't do anything. I just want to talk to you."

"Get out of here."

He'd kind of stood up, and then he'd just sit there and he'd say, *"Oh Susan."* (He called me 'Susan,' because they couldn't pronounce my name, so they called me 'Susan' at times, instead, which was my middle name.)

He'd go, "Oh Suzanne," and you could just tell that he was just ripped. So, he'd sit down again, and I'd say, "Leave. Get out. Get out!"

And he wouldn't.

So finally, he laid down and I jumped out of bed, and I pushed him off the bed and started putting my shoes on.

Of course, the place was pitch black. He gets up and he turns on the light. He sees that I'm putting on my shoes, and he says, "What are you doing?"

"If you don't leave this room, I'm going to leave."

He said, "Oh, don't do that. Don't put that on. I didn't mean to be rude. I didn't mean to..."

He started to go back to the door. Turned off the light. I kind of sat there, and five seconds later it was, "Oh, Suzanne" again and he came back.

I put on my shoes, grabbed my backpack, and ran out the door. Got out in the street. Pitch black. Not a street light for a thousand miles.

There's only one country road luckily, and I was so furious at myself for going out there with them in the first place, and I was furious with the guys for letting me go. I was furious with this one guy for coming in here and bugging me in the middle of the night when he knew perfectly well it wasn't what I wanted.

I was also furious with the entire world for having Italy. Just seething mad, that I walked the entire road in pitch dark without a second thought except for the fact that I was angry.

I got about 3/4 of the way down the road and I heard a dog. All of a sudden I realized that I was in the middle of nowhere in Italy, and I didn't know where I was going or what I was going to do.

I started thinking about that.

Twenty-six kilometers is an awfully long way, and the only way I knew to get back to Florence was on the highway. I get to the highway. What happens is there's this long country road and then it hits a kind of... It's still a country road, but it's a busy country road that kind of connects the three or four little villages around.

It's got trees, and it's got light. I get to that street and every other car practically — and there weren't that many — because by this time it's 2 or 3 in the morning, and they pull past me and stop. I walk past them. They'd wait until I got a few feet in front of them. They'd start up the car, drive past me again and stop. I have to walk past them again, and all this time they'd be giving me the eye, trying to check out what kind of person I am.

You had to get this horrible look on your face, just very upset; your lips firm together; keeping your eye on the road, meaning business; you didn't dare look at all happy or pleased or even semi-normal. You had to have this really rough look on your face or they'd start calling out to you, "Where you going baby?" or whatever.

I couldn't understand it. I didn't pay any attention. I figured this is not the absolute ideal situation to be in. You go down this road and then there was the highway, and before the highway, there's this about 20-foot high sign saying in every language possible "Hitchhiking Illegal."

And I knew perfectly well what it meant and what it said, and at the same point, I didn't know how to get home except to go on the highway. It also said walking on the highway is prohibited, I think. Anyway, it was pretty well restricted: you couldn't walk on the highway and you weren't allowed to take rides with strangers. Damned if you do and damned if you don't!

I kind of went, *Well, there's nothing else I can do. I am not going to sleep out here in the country, because I just had a little sleeping bag, and I would die from the cold.*

It was November or December. It was cold at night.

I went on the overpass and a car stopped. These two guys were in it.

They said in their Italian, "*Ponati! Ponati!*" — (they'll arrest you!). And they kept on going, clicking their wrists together, gesturing that I'd get thrown in jail, and they would say this sentence over and over that, "They'll arrest you; they'll take you to jail."

I kept saying, "I have to go to Florence. I have to go to Florence. The train station in Florence."

And they kept saying, "The police. They are going to arrest you."

And I kept saying in my pitiful voice, "*A Firenze Stazione!*" (To the Florence train station.)

So finally, the one guy looks at me, decides I'm a hopeless case and they go, "Get in the car."

So, I get in the car, curl up into an absolute nothing in the back seat, holding my pack in front of me to protect me, ready for anything. I'm expecting these guys are going to give me the same bad time as the guys at the house.

Not that the guys at the house were really bad, it was just...

So, the guy turned around and asked, "What are you doing?"

And I just kept saying, "*A Firenze, Stazione Firenze!*"

And they kept saying "*Politi*" (police).

It got across that they were going to Florence. They were going to a town outside of Florence.

Then he finally said, "Do you want to kiss me?"

Any time he asked me any question I would say, "*No, grazie.*" (No, thank you.)

He'd say something about like, "You want to come to this town with us?"

And then I'd say "*No, grazie.*"

He'd say, "You can come stay with us."

"*No, grazie.*"

"You want to kiss me?"

"No thank you."

He'd kind of look at me and they'd laugh. Here's this petrified girl sitting in the back of the seat, and no matter what... they could have said, "Do you want to sleep with me," I would say the same thing: "No, thank you."

It must have been how it sounded to them, but finally, they decided that I was pretty shaken up so they left me alone.

They showed me, "We're going here," and they drove past.

I'm going "hmm."

It turns out there are tollgates on the Italian highway that policemen sit in. They drove me past the tollgate, got out and stressed the fact that those were the police and I wasn't allowed to let them see me. Then they turned around, went back and went off at the exit they were going to, which was really nice.

To make a long story short, I got beyond the police station, hitched at this point. I hadn't hitched with them. I was just walking and they stopped to tell me about the police. Stuck out my thumb and this drunken Sicilian stopped. I knew he was Sicilian because he was playing Sicilian music and he was telling me, "*Bella, bella,*" (good, good).

And I'm going, "Oh, yes, it's really nice, really nice." He took me all the way to the train station, walked me into the train station, offered to buy me coffee, and I said, "No thank you, no thank you."

The thing was that they were very respectful in their lecherous attitudes. It was a very strange predicament. I was so upset at the whole situation that I then went to Trieste, and I was just so resentful of the fact that I couldn't even be halfway myself for fear that one of these people would take me wrong and start to hassle me again. The worst thing is going up to Trieste. Another night train.

Mistake Number Three

Trust no one, well, almost no one. This conductor comes through and he says, "Let me see your ticket."

I show him my ticket and he says, "I'm going to come back in a minute."

I figured there was something wrong with the pass.

He comes back in about 5-10 minutes, sits down next to me. I sit up in my sleeping bag, trying to look semi-normal and intelligent. He starts stroking my hair telling me how beautiful I am and how he is madly in love with me.

I almost died.

The *CONDUCTOR* of the train!

If the conductor of the train isn't going to protect you from perverts — and if he is a pervert himself — what are you supposed to do?

He starts telling me he's madly in love with me, and so, I say, "I'll bet you tell this to all the girls."

And he says, "Oh no!"

He got very upset when I said that.

He said, "Oh no. I'm only in love with YOU!"

I just go, "Give me a break!"

Really.

"Give me a break."

He sat there for 20 minutes, petting me, trying to kiss me on the ear, in the hair and telling me that he loved my hair and that he was madly in love with me.

Finally, his end station came and he had to get off the train.

At that point, I was ready to go back to Germany, where all the men are very cold, formal, and sane.

Just get me away from that crazy country!

I mean, the train *conductor!*

I heard a story about one girl where the train conductor came in and said that he wanted to sleep with her.

Big kind of chesty bosomy blonde girl.

She said, "Uh-uh, uh-uh," but he kept insisting, and she kept saying "Uh-uh, uh-uh." Finally, he picked up her pack and threw her out into the hall and said, "Get off the train." And I can believe it because this guy — I didn't do anything rude — I just kind of sat there going, "What in the hell is happening?" I just couldn't believe that this conductor was stroking and kissing me on the ear. I guess that was really all that he wanted to do was just sit there and stroke and kiss somebody on the ear, because he didn't really give me any further qualms, but I was so disgusted with the entire mentality of the Italian men.

They can't even discuss anything civil with a woman. I couldn't even understand, "I'm in love with you," or "You've got beautiful hair," and stuff like that, but they couldn't touch my mind or person at all.

They were really turned on to the body and to your outside appearances, and I got so sick of a country filled with men who thought nothing more of females except for the fact that they were bodies, that I'll never go to Italy again.

It's just, the whole idea of that kind of mentality — and that's my impression of the Italian mentality — just turns me off so much that I wouldn't spend another lira.

A friend of mine and I have formed an '*I Hate Italian Men Club*'; although for some other girls they just love it, because they (the Italians) do have a sort of respect while they are trying to rape you. It's not a violent rape, but they don't know the word "no." You can tell them no a thousand times and it just doesn't sink in.

Oh, the Italians!

What's the best way to go?

Go down with a boyfriend and a ring on your finger and pretend that you are either married or engaged.

One girl told me that she told some guy she was a virgin and he left her alone, but she'd had a good experience in Italy.

Mainly I think, don't go by yourself if you are a good looking or even semi-presentable female.

Don't go by yourself, but if you do have to go by yourself, don't wear backless shirts or skirts. Dress fairly decently. Go to a town and find a "*pensione*" or hotel or something, with a protective landlady, or some kind of place that is sympathetic, you know.

Not one that's full of drunks or dirty old men or where the proprietor himself lechers at you.

Go to someplace where there are older ladies and get on their good side or something so you can go safely back to your room and close yourself in your room without fear.

My main problem was the fact that I'd never stayed overnight in any town.

I got there, and I then got so disgusted with just walking around trying to find someplace to stay that I left.

I just didn't know the city well enough, so I was lost and I didn't know the language well enough to really ask directions, so I was kind of vulnerable to any kind of crank or pervert who wanted to come up and try to help me.

I really didn't know where I was going or what I was doing.

People who have gone to Rome or Florence and found a nice hotel — and maybe the first one you go to is a real dump — well then, you spend your whole day looking for someplace nice. But try to find a nice hotel where the lady who runs it is sympathetic to single German girls. They are around someplace.

The other thing to keep in mind is if you are traveling on trains, don't sit in a compartment with only guys in it. Take a compartment that has a family in it or that has a sister traveling with her grandmother or daughter traveling.

Pick a compartment that has a few other Italian females in it, or pick a compartment that's entirely foreigners.

Don't get in a compartment alone with men. It's the biggest mistake that you can make.

If you are going to be traveling for a long time, I'd say find someone who wants to travel in Italy for a long time and travel together.

You probably would find lots of people who have really good experiences in Italy, because people really are terrific and nice if you hit them right, from what I've heard.

People have had just great times in Italy, but I just got so sick of having to screw my face up into a scowl and look terribly unnatural and rude or something, or else they wouldn't leave me alone.

I just found myself going back to Vienna. I was never so glad to be in a city in my entire life as I was to be in Vienna. Vienna's got a lot of scummy areas to it and really scummy workers, but nothing happens to you there.

Geez, I'm ready to start that '*I Hate Italian Men Club!*

Travel Tip #3:
Vary Your Daily Patterns!

Michael Brein

———◆———

Always vary your patterns. The shortest distance between two points is usually the straightest line between the points.

It is all too easy to become predictable in our comings and goings. All kinds of people are looking to victimize people who exhibit regular patterns, i.e., who predictably, reliably, and dependably — and like clockwork — always do the same things, go the same ways, exhibit the same unchanging patterns — can be regularly depended upon to be at the same places at the same time and exhibit the same patterns repeatedly, day after day.

The more your behavior can be predicted, the easier it is to 'plan' for you to become a victim.

By varying your comings and goings, you are less likely to 'stand out' or be noticed.

The 'I Hate Italian Men Club' #3: Bella Italia!

Flora Fielder

———◦———

Florence, Italy, the 1990s. I'm Flora Fielder (an assumed name). It was my 50th birthday that was coming up so I wanted to do something that was over the top. So, I thought to myself, *What could I possibly do that would be absolutely over-the-top.*

I thought, *Well, I need at least to go on a journey at some point in my life.*

So, I thought, *You know what? I'm going to Europe for three months, and that would definitely be over the top.*

That would be what I want to do!

What was your definition of over-the-top?

If somebody says behind my back, "Who does she think she is anyway?"

Then, that's over the top.

I started out in Paris.

Did you know any French at all? Were people nice to you?

Absolutely. If you smile at someone first and have a warm energy coming out, you're going to get that warm energy back. There were no more rude people than in my hometown.

Any highlights of Paris?

I definitely love the culture. I would have a two-hour lunch every day and would sit in the cafés. And eat and drink. It took me two weeks to get the courage to sit by myself in a café, and then I'd see maybe after getting to know the lay of the land, so to speak — I would see who I might like to talk to and go and sit by them. If a conversation happens, it just happens.

Did you feel self-conscious, yourself, a woman traveling alone?

Like the first or second day, but after that, I didn't care.

Did people talk to you?

With my freestyle traveling, I didn't have everything planned out. I typically would find things that are of interest to me. I stayed in a hotel, and I saw two American women look down their noses at me because I didn't have things planned. I was living a lifestyle that I liked and was really getting to know people and talking to people.

Nearby my hotel there was a bar at the corner, and I just went in there one night and the locals all embraced me, and the bar was just filled up with people. By night's end, every single person without exception came up and spoke with me — embraced me. They are all buying me drinks! I stumbled back to my hotel. This is in Paris. And it was an incredibly beautiful thing. These are people from different walks of life than I was used to.

Be specific.

They were totally lovely people; they didn't have a whole lot of money, but they had a lot of heart.

And so, I felt really honored that they were buying me drinks and being so nice to me.

So, what about the stereotype that Parisians don't like Americans?

The one thing I noticed about Parisians is that they are really nice amongst themselves. But what I definitely relate to is that they always *kiss kiss* whenever they were meeting with each other, And it's also especially nice when they do this with Americans occasionally.

And so, they just kind of came up to you? What was it about you that they all took you under their wing? I mean, this is interesting. Was it so unusual that an American girl, an American woman like you would walk into a bar by herself?

Well, it's one of those tiny little bars that are like the size of a typical living room, and so, when you open up the door, I mean just everybody turns around and looks at you.

[Like the TV series "Cheers!" — where everyone knows your name!]

Exactly, I mean I'm like "hello! I'm here!" you know.

And you broadcast that friendly vibe.

And you do this! And they just gravitated towards you?

Entrainment. That's what it is, huh? What I mean by that... entrainment is casting a kind of a mental framework or vibe about/of, which you are in, and which encompasses other people. To some extent, affecting, bringing others to the thought form that you are projecting. Is that a possibility?

A metronome effect. It all got started in the 16th century. If you put a bunch of metronomes together that are initially out of sync, pretty soon all the metronomes are together in sync. And that's how entrainment is.

Whatever vibe or energy you bring into a situation, and you get other people in motion with it... In life, it's about getting entrainment back to the positive... Because we have so much negativity and dark nastiness in the world.

It's an interesting theory, huh?

So you entrain other people with your presence of mind and relate to them that well? I mean, to have everybody in that bar treat you the way you described is a gift; not everybody can do this. But, I don't think it always works as you may think because I know you are about to tell me something of an incident where this beautiful sort of thing might not quite apply.

Okay, so let's move onto that.

That was in Italy.

So, how would you summarize or sum up Italy for me?

Simply this: I'll never go back to Italy as a single woman or with another woman, that I will only go back when I am being accompanied by a man.

So, you were a woman traveling by yourself; you are an attractive lady, although it doesn't always matter to Italian men. What happened?

So, by this time, I had been traveling into my second month, and I hadn't cried even once, but when I landed in Florence, I cried the first day that I was there, because men were following me. And they wouldn't leave me alone, and it made me feel very uneasy.

How did you deal with it? That's the important thing.

How I dealt with it was I moved from staying at a hotel and I went to a hostel. And that's with gals, and then that's when I started going on tours, being involved with them and going more as a group than by myself.

Did that harassment then kind of stop by that point?

It wasn't nearly as bad.

Was there any particular worst experience of the whole thing? Did they follow you into places? Did you have to literally get rid of somebody?

There were two particular guys that were following me all over town and wouldn't leave me alone, but finally, I was able to ditch them.

How did you ditch them?

There's a lot of people in crowds, but the thing that made me the most upset, though, is that most of these guys were married or had girlfriends. That was even the more upsetting thing.

How did you know that?

Because I asked them. And their answers were pretty much always the same that, you know, "It's the culture. It's what we do here. She (girlfriend or wife) knows that this is what I do" (but she really doesn't!). (Laughs)

They tried to make it sound like "this is what we do... Okay, so what's your problem?" (As if to give it some semblance of credibility, legitimacy, and acceptability.)

So, that was my experience.

Was anybody particularly aggressive? Two guys that were very aggressive?

Not really. I mean it was just a bunch of guys coming at me but not necessarily someone who was going to rip my clothes off or anything like that.

How close did any of them get to you?

About as close as you are! (Laughs)

You were talking to them. Did you argue with them? Did they speak English? Were you angry at them? You were talking to them. You were trying to reason with them. Like, "Don't you have a wife or a girlfriend?"

I would just turn around and walk away. You know, there's no sense in trying to have a conversation, really, once you figure out what their motives are.

Was pointless, right?

At that point, you had to like disappear into the crowd and ditch them?

The MO is that they always ask you if they can buy you a coffee — which is interesting — in that at least you get dinner. (Laughs)

You don't dare do that!

You get a coffee out of it! (Continues to laugh)

I've had women tell me that they've literally had to run from these guys. And different things they did to escape. Going into somebody's house! Or attaching themselves to some other people just to be safe.

I didn't do that; I walk with a lot of confidence and I carry myself with confidence, and I don't put myself into dangerous situations. I was always back into my hotel or wherever I was staying by dark. I didn't drink more than so many drinks alone unless I was super close to my hotel.

You never left a drink unguarded?

Exactly.

I was wondering if this technique of entrainment discussed above might work with people who harass you. I guess you haven't brought it to that degree of mastery, huh?

It will give me something to think about. (Laughs)

Say, do you know of an '*I Hate Italian Men Club*' that I can join?

All According to Plan

Julie Wiley

Portugal, 1987. We were hitchhiking in Portugal. We were going to go up into the mountains to see Fatima. And before that, we were in Oviedo, Portugal.

We had had a few close calls with hitchhiking and just some kind of weird energy with rides, and I was getting to the point where I didn't really want to hitchhike as much. I just didn't want to have to deal with the hassles of it.

Can you tell me a little bit about that?

Well, the fact that being light-haired was not the most opportune thing for two women to be hitchhiking.

Andrea is darker and taller than I. She could, therefore, pass easier than I could for being local from the country, whereas I could not. So, I would be the likely target for harassment, or so the theory went.

And so, we developed a strategy of sorts. What we learned to do was to have her get in first and have her sit next to the driver, and have me sit in the back seat. It seemed to make good sense at least in theory.

Nonetheless, we were still a little bit leery, in general. So, we had been sitting outside of this town waiting for a ride for a while. We even had a big sign. We were waiting and waiting.

Finally, this one guy pulls up in a pickup truck with a flatbed on the back. And so, we say, "Where are you going?" And he counters with *"blah blah blah,"* and so, we hop in, and of course, according to plan, she gets in first, sits next to the driver and I get in the back.

But the first thing we see is that he's got like this skull hanging from his rearview mirror, and then he's also got like this plastic fornicating couple hanging there. So we're looking at each other, going, "Oh, great!"

Our packs are in the back of the truck.

A little late for regrets, we drive on and are thinking, *Okay, well, let's just hope for the best.*

As we go on, he starts putting his hand on Andrea's leg, and we go, "Oh, No, No."

And Andrea moves his hand away.

And we're going up through the mountains and he keeps on just kind of pursuing that. Then he indicates that he wants to stop and points to the woods inferring that she and him would go into the woods.

And we're emphatic like, "NO, uh-uh, NO WAY, NOO WAY."

And it goes on for quite some miles, and we're kind of like still in the middle of nowhere.

So, what are your options?

Not a lot. Not a lot of options.

So, we just finally just shout, "STOP!"

"You need to stop this car and we were going to get out."

Another strategy is we always kept our passports and our money on ourselves. For instance, I had a pair of pants where the pockets were on the top part of my thigh, so I always had my stuff on my person, and so did Andrea.

And so, we jumped out of the car and he took off with our packs. Our packs are in the back.

Oh no! What's you're feeling about this?

We're going "Oh, my God."

He takes off, and we're just like, "Oh, my god, I can't believe this just happened! What are we going to do? What are we going to do?"

And we're just kind of like in shock and talking to each other and trying to reassure one another with, "Well, at least we've got our money; it'll be okay."

And then we hear a truck approaching in the distance. We hide in the bushes and we see that it's him approaching, and we kind of just come outside of the bushes just as he's passing by, and he sees us. He then comes to a screeching stop just long enough for us to grab our packs out of the back, and then he takes off down the road. We're now kind of stranded in the middle of nowhere.

But you feel relieved.

And, yeah, we're quite relieved and we're really grateful. I think that there were several times during our trip that we felt like we had guardian angels watching over us because there were just some situations that could have been really freaky. But they weren't.

So, he wasn't out to steal your backpacks, but look how easy it could have been for him to do so.

He was looking for some action; that's what he was looking for.

And so, we put our packs on, and we could see way down in the valley there was a little town. So, we just started walking and we walked and we walked and finally got down to the main part of the town. It wasn't very big at all, but there just happened to be a train station, and we waited around until the next train came.

Was there a better way to have dealt with the situation, do you think?

Oh, you know, the only thing, retrospectively — when we got in the truck and saw those weird things hanging — those then should have been our cues. We should have just said, *"No, gracias"* (no thank you).

But it's hard; I mean, you don't want to assume the worst about people. But that's the only thing I can think of.

Hitchhiking

Winkelle Godfrey

Australia, in the desert outback, the 1970s. This story is about a New Zealand gal friend of mine who used to spend a lot of time in Australia. She was hitching once in a desert area and she got a ride with a guy.

My Friend's Hitchhiking Experience

Everything is perfectly normal, but he drives her up a very quiet road. No one around for miles, and decides he wants to rape her. She tries everything, pleading with him. Everything. Screaming, shouting, trying to be calm, reasoning with him. But nothing seems to work.

The only way around it, in the end, was to masturbate him. So she gets away with it — meaning probably saving her own life — by doing that. He doesn't actually have intercourse with her, but she had to beat him off, so that's how you escape, which is preferable to being raped or murdered or both.

What did she say about that?

When she told me about it, she said, "I'm afraid I had to..." I don't know what term she used, but she was afraid she had to 'wank' him in order to satisfy him. She sounded almost apologetic about it. Obviously, she was very, very scared at the time, but I think she still hitchhikes alone, actually.

She and I were talking about hitchhiking alone and how safe it was, and we were both agreeing that it was relatively safe in Scotland and parts of northern Europe, but to do it alone in other parts of the world would be too risky. She agreed, because of the bad experience she had.

I've never been raped or had to do what she did.

My Own Hitchhiking Experiences

I, myself, got a ride once in Sweden with a truck driver. Everything was fine. He was telling me about his family and where he'd been. He men-

110

tioned that he'd been on a long trip to Europe somewhere and had had a good time since he was alone without his wife.

"Oh, it's good to get away once in a while."

I thought, *Yeah,* sort of half-hinting that he had a good time both *WHILE* and *BECAUSE* he was away from his wife.

He had some magazines. We were together for quite a few hours. So, he slaps the magazines with his hand and suggests that I take a look at them. They looked harmless enough, but upon opening them I saw that they were some sort of sexy soft-porn magazines with dirty, crude embraces, and so on.

He asked me whether I liked them.

I said, "I can't read Swedish, but I'm not really interested in that kind of thing," so he pushed them aside.

What do you think about that now?

I thought, *Oh-oh, I wonder what this is leading to?* They obviously didn't interest me in any way. They weren't classy magazines, but they weren't out-and-out hard porn, either. They had other articles in them as well, but I had glanced at them a bit more, and eventually, he stopped the truck and he offered me a Coca-Cola and that sort of thing. He was pretty friendly.

He then stopped the truck and jumped out and had a piss. I don't know why, but it suddenly crossed my mind that I associated having a piss with intercourse — before intercourse — because quite often guys prefer to piss before they make love. It's more comfortable for them. It just crossed my mind that something like that might happen.

He got back in the truck, and then he just looked at me and as calm as he could be and said, "Shall we try the bed now?" As if it was quite understood that that's what I wanted to do.

I just looked at him and I said, "No."

That, fortunately, was all I needed to say. Whew!

He said, "Okay," and drove on, but the time was on his side. Who knows what he was capable of?

The mood was cooler now, and I felt distinctly angry for various reasons. I just left someone I was extremely fond of, and it upset me more than a little bit that he dared to ask me as an infringement of my personal freedom and an invasion of my privacy.

So, I felt angry and a bit disturbed. I couldn't relax after that, but, luckily, I was getting out in about a half an hour, anyway.

He seemed a little shorter with me after that. But he didn't try to touch me, thank God.

So, I got out and we were amicable. I didn't start screaming or anything, because the lift, after all, was useful. I got down. Walked away and that was the end of it.

On numerous other occasions I have had lifts, even in Scotland, and quite often the driver has brought the subject of sex up quite calmly and casually without a qualm. Almost as if it was understood between us that there might be something like that, like some sexual contact or intercourse or whatever. I don't know, but they seemed to think it was their right to ask in a way. Not ask, suggest.

Often, if you decline, they don't push it... I've never been forced. Never actually been touched. Of course, it makes you feel uncomfortable.

It spoils the relationship. Just an ordinary friendly relationship you can build up between the people you are having a lift with. It destroys that. Puts you on your guard and ruins everything. It makes you want to get out.

I just think it's more than a little unfair if a girl takes a lift, and if she doesn't lead the man on at all, and she's just sitting there talking about normal things, and they start bringing up the subject of sex and marriage and boyfriends. Private things like that. It's just a pity. It's a shame that men have to look upon women in this way.

But, of course, if a woman leads a man on and is suggestive and behaves as a kind of cock teaser, then she asks to be raped in a way. But if she doesn't, and if she's just friendly like a man will be friendly to another man or a woman to another woman, then I just think it's a shame, unfair.

It ruins good lifts and possibly a good friendship.

Travel Tip #4:
Have an Exit Strategy!

Michael Brein

Always have an exit strategy — a way out! Avoid getting yourself into a situation in the first place that you cannot get out of if you have to. Not always easy to do. Probably the single most frequent cause of people getting into trouble is where and when your options are reduced to the point where 'there is nothing you can do,' i.e., your options or choices go to zero! You may become a victim when you allow yourself to have too few escape options.

The best example of this is people hitchhiking: getting into a stranger's car or truck at night by yourself or into a third-world taxicab where your escape options are too few or non-existent.

Maintain some degrees of freedom. Hold in reserve some kind of an escape valve.

Sadly, a good deal of dangerous situations discussed in this book were for women travelers who wound up having NO or few degrees of freedom, that is, they got 'boxed in' into inescapable situations in vehicles or with strangers and with few, if any, ways out.

The Conductor!

Unknown

S omewhere in France, 1973. I was traveling on a train in France. Never had been to Europe or anything. I had a second-class ticket and I knew I had to be in a second-class coach, but I didn't know what else was involved in it. I sat down in a seat in a really crowded compartment.

The Conductor comes along and he looks at my ticket. He then looks at me and says, "You're in the wrong place." In broken English. I looked at my ticket and I thought, *Okay.*

Then he says, "You must come with me."

I looked at everybody else and nobody else knew English, so they didn't help me any. He says, "Come on, you're in the wrong place, you must not ride here."

So, I gesture meekly to the others, "Okay, I gotta go."

We keep going down and down through the train, seemingly forever, through all these people, and I'm thinking that this is pretty strange, *Surely, he knows where I'm supposed to be.*

Finally, we come to this one compartment, like almost at the end of the train. He opens it up, and nobody's in there.

He says, "Here, it's for you. You can come in."

I think this is interesting; *Now, I've got a whole compartment to myself.*

He goes out and then comes back in a minute. He locks the door, pulls down the shades, and I think, *Oh my God, what have I got myself into?*

I say to him, "What in the world?"

He says, "I just want to come in here. Now you can have a place to sit."

He then starts sitting closer and closer to me, and I'm thinking, *Oh God, I've got to get out.*

I say to him, "I just want to get out of here!"

He doesn't know very much English, and I say, "Look, you go!"

He says, "Why?" and he tries some more to get fresh with me.

Then I say, "Look, I'm not interested in you. Goodbye."

Finally, he gets the message in his head. He seems very sad that I don't care! In the end, I talked with him a little bit and I got a few free tickets for the Metro out of him.

And then he said, "Okay, go, find your own place."

And then I left.

And I thought to myself, *Even the conductors are crazy!*.

Travel Tip #5:
Trust Your Intuitions!

Michael Brein

Always trust your 'instincts.' If it doesn't 'feel' right, the chances are very good that it probably isn't. Better to over-rely upon or over trust your intuitions sometimes and your so-called 'sixth-sense.'

We are always trying to talk ourselves into 'rational disbelief' of unusual or unlikely situations and are prone to feeling and wanting to convince ourselves that 'this cannot be happening,' or 'it cannot happen to me' — i.e., it CANNOT be happening, so, therefore, it is NOT happening; 'This is too unbelievable,' therefore, I DON'T believe it, and so on.

It is much easier to talk oneself into being complacent than it is to believe or rationalize or convince yourself that something bad or horrible or unlikely is either about to happen or is actually happening.

Rationalizing, judging or 'reasoning away' a bad or difficult situation often robs you of invaluable 'escape' time, so that it can become too difficult, too late to deal with a bad event in a safe and effective manner.

Often paying attention to one's inner self or gut level opens you up to attending to inner cues that you might tend to just too easily dismiss or rationalize away before it is too late.

It is better to be safe than sorry. If escaping a bad situation because you err a little on the side of paranoia or caution, just observe how good you feel when you finally manage to extricate yourself from a potentially troublesome situation.

Double Exposure:
Beach Encounter in Mexico

Linda Taylor

Teacapan, Mexico, 1993. A woman friend of mine and I were walking down the beach and we went round the point. We were coming back, and I found a piece of driftwood on the beach. I was dragging this piece of driftwood along with me, and we were walking therefore quite slowly. Suddenly, I heard this whistling. Nearby, there was a big chunk of coconut husks at this point piled up on the beach. I turned to look, and there was this man exposing himself.

The first thing that ran through my mind was, *if this guy only knew how old we were!* (Laughs) I guess from the distance he couldn't tell that we were in our 50's! He wouldn't be wasting his time with us. (Laughs)

So, what was that instant like for you to see something like this?

I thought to myself, *Gee, I wonder, if I'll feel comfortable walking by myself on the beach anymore?*

And, you know, I don't at all. I have never gone down to the beach by myself after that. And we had moved specifically to this area so I could utilize the beach more, and I don't do it.

Do you need to work on that?

I think so.

What was your reaction when he did that? What did you do next?

I felt fear, and then it struck me as funny. But the fear has stayed with me. I didn't even say anything to my friend. I didn't even point it out to her.

You saw it but she didn't?

She didn't turn around. We just kept on walking.

Of course, this happens anywhere, right?

Yeah.

Did you feel that there was any potential harm that was going to happen?

No, I didn't feel that there was any harm. But I just never felt quite the same way again about that particular beach.

It's a shame.

What is your philosophy about bad things or good things? How do you feel about that? I mean, this has affected you, because you say that every time you walk that beach, you think about that.

Right.

Have you ever seen that guy again out there?

No, well, I wouldn't recognize him! (Laughs)

You didn't really see his face, huh?

Yeah.

Well, that is funny in a way.

Yeah.

So, how should a woman deal with a situation like that?

I think you should probably tell somebody about it right away, and maybe talk about it a little bit so that it doesn't fester and become such a big thing. I think maybe that would be the thing that I would do. I mean, I'm sure it's the same about rapes, anything that involves feeling a loss of power over your own destiny, even if it's just momentary. I think that my suggestion to anyone in any situation like this would be to please talk about it.

The Roman Baths

Aileen Agricola

Rome, Italy. This is my story about sexual harassment. I'm actually the crazy tourist sightseeing in the pouring rain, and I'm entering the Roman Baths in downtown Rome. At first, I think I'm the only one there — at least I *think* I'm the only one there. And the Baths are pretty much open. You pay in advance, and then you enter the ruins and go room to room.

As I was moving from room to room, I noticed that there was a gentleman on the outside with a raincoat and an umbrella seemingly following me along from room to room on the outside. I thought that was odd. Why would he be pacing me from room to room?

By the third room, however, I realized that he was looking at the ruins, too, but strangely, the same ruins as I was looking at, at the same time?

Of course, by the fifth 'Bath' room, it all became very evident: I noticed that he had his raincoat open and he was masturbating, using me as his target! And, I'm now going out loud, "Oh, my God! Where is his hand? Oh, my God!"

Did you begin to be worried at all at that point?

Well, not worried, per se — more like infuriated — because I knew what he was doing. I was astonished. It was pissing rain and I am like the only one in here. And I'm like running away from him now.

I'm going, "Oh, my God!"

And, I'm trying to find a security guard or someone to make him stop. By that time, I bump into this English couple also visiting the Baths, and they're viewing my obvious discomfort and are going, "Oh, just don't worry about it; he's not bothering you! Just ignore it!"

"What do you mean, he's not bothering me?"

"He's on the outside."

"I don't care if he's on the outside. He's upsetting me."

It was almost as if, by my very presence, that I affected *HIM*, somehow, and not the other way around, and made him do whatever he had to do. It was all crazy and absurd.

It wasn't seen by them as a dangerous situation. In fact, I just felt that it was more like I was seen as the one who was responsible for provoking his behavior in some way. I felt totally violated and disgusted with the whole thing. And I just left.

So, what other ways are there for dealing with something like this? You got upset, and that was probably part of the motivation of that guy that was doing it. To have this effect on you.

Yeah. I guess it's just the accepting that, "Okay, there is really nothing much I can do to make him stop."

I guess, I just had to let it pass, you know, just walk away and not let it affect me.

But you say that now. But, I have a feeling that you would probably react the same way if it happened to you again.

But, the funny thing is, now that I've been talking to my friends about this, if it were a reverse situation; if, for instance, it was a woman doing this, fondling herself, a man would not even get angry at seeing her do this. In fact, a man would probably, instead, just laugh and enjoy it. He probably wouldn't even think twice about it. He wouldn't likely even get angry or upset with it.

Like, what's wrong with this picture? Why does a man enjoy a woman in this situation, and why does a woman get upset with a man doing this?

Does it have something to do with their upbringing perhaps?

Probably. Well, I think maybe that's just how the world works. It's a man's world, you know! So, I'm thinking like, personally, I don't think I could laugh at a man doing that; I don't think I could ever enjoy it.

And, when I'm traveling around the world, I always get these little reminders from people, like, "Oh, you are a single woman traveling around. Aren't you just afraid?"

Or, the other thing is, "Oh you're here in our country. You're going to marry a local man, aren't you?"

It's that reminder of who I am as a woman.

It's a reality check — a reminder of who you are.

West Bank Assault

Jackie Matthews

Palestine, West Bank, the 1970s. This was in Israel (or Palestine) on the West Bank. I'd gone for a walk, because I was fed up spending three weeks solidly with hundreds of people around me, so I just stormed across the fields where I was picking vegetables and just went for a walk. I could see a lot of old buildings on top of a hill that I wanted to explore.

Suddenly, on the other side of this wall was this Palestinian youth; he was probably about 15, it appeared. He said hello, so I said hello back, and he seemed to be fairly friendly and chatty, so I chatted back. Why not?

He asked me where I was from, and I said I was staying in the nearby Palestinian village. I said "No, I'm English; I'm not from Israel," and I turned to go away, because I was feeling a little bit nervous by this time.

I think it was just something. I can't quite think of the word, and I can't put my finger on it. Something was not quite right. Threatening, I suppose, in the way he was just standing there. So, I started to walk away, and he started yelling.

I turned around, and he'd undone his fly. There was this great big circumcised erect penis right in front of me. I thought, *Well, this is it. I'm miles away from — well, I wasn't really miles away — but I was certainly nowhere where I could run.*

All through this, my sandal is broken, so I really couldn't run, because it's full of little rocks and thorns and things. I thought, *Christ, what am I going to do now?*

He started to grab hold of me, to push me. I managed to get away, and I picked up a stone. I thought, *Well, I'm going to throw the stone at him.*

So, what did he do? He picked up a stone as well.

I thought, *Oh boy.*

And he got hold of me again. I was yelling at this time. I was so angry more than anything else at this stupid situation I got myself into.

What was worse than anything else, I had walked out on my friends, because I was fed up with being with them, and had had this sort of childish fantasy to strike out on my own after being there for three weeks.

It was the day before I was going home, and I asked once to be on my own for a bit, but, for some reason, I couldn't be on my own — they were not allowing me to — and I was so angry.

I was now shouting at the top of my voice, not really thinking about what was going to happen next. Perhaps just resign myself to the fact that I might be raped. I don't know.

He was stronger than me. I couldn't get away.

Fortunately, I heard another yell coming from over the nearby ridge of the hill like the fifth cavalry. It was the younger brother of my friends whose house I was staying in. He came galloping up, and the chap who was pushing me around, of course, heard him, let me go and then started to walk off.

He came up. He said, "What's wrong? Why were you shouting?"

I said, "It's all right. This guy was bothering me!"

But I just couldn't bring myself to explain to him exactly what was involved, because it might have had terrible repercussions. I could imagine some kind of a blood feud starting over that, because I was like a 'sister' of theirs.

So, that was really the end of the story, because I went back to the house, feeling thankful that he'd bothered to follow me up the mountain and not leave me alone on my own.

He kept at a distance, and he hadn't quite let me go on my own like I had wanted to. I was very rude to him. I just walked out of the field, because it felt somewhat oppressive; I just wanted to be on my own a bit, and I didn't even bother to tell them where I was going. Fortunately for me, this guy had followed me back a ways.

He said, "What was wrong? Why were you shouting?"

I said, "Well, that guy was annoying me."

I just couldn't it explain to him. I don't know why. Perhaps I was shy. I don't know.

I would have embarrassed him probably, and I would have been embarrassed as well to tell him what had happened. And he would have probably done something very terrible to the guy, like maybe beat him up.

I think the reason why the guy attacked me was that he probably thought I was an Israeli prostitute because there were quite a few of them at that time that used to go over to the West Bank. And so, if you are a girl and you're traveling around, what else are you? You're a prostitute and therefore you can be raped. That's it pure and simple.

Did you ever see him again, the one that bothered you? Could you have recognized him?

No. I don't think I even knew what he looked like. It wasn't the most obvious thing about him! It was such a shock. I just turned around and there he was waving his thing about. It was strange.

Accosted in Jerusalem

Lyn Dee

Israel, Palestine, East Jerusalem, 1984. The reason I'm telling you this story is because I want to help women who aren't thinking straight.

I am Lyn Dee (an assumed name). I was living in Jerusalem and was walking in the part of the city known as the "Old City," mostly Arab East Jerusalem. I would typically walk up onto the rampart walls of the Old City and just walk around. I had never really had any trouble before. And on this one beautiful sunny summer Sunday afternoon, around 4 o'clock, I'm walking along the ramparts of the wall as I always do, passing a few people here and there.

I come down to a corner and I turn, and there's a young Palestinian teenager, maybe 15 or 16 years of age, probably 15 pounds lighter than me, and possibly an inch or two shorter than me. I just kind of nod a friendly "hello" and keep on going.

Well, I don't realize is that he is trolling for tourists. And, I don't know where my instincts were on that particular day, so I suppose that this was meant to happen.

I walk down some steps into a small area that's about 10 feet long by about 6 feet wide, and it leads into a room where they used to keep ammunition to shoot from the walls years ago. Then you have to go up another set of steps on the other side, like 15 steps or so, to get up and out of this enclosed area.

You did not know that yet.

No, I did not.

Yes, hindsight's 20-20!

Anyway, as I am walking down the steps, he sneaks up behind me, unbeknownst to me, and simply grabs my head and smashes it against the stone wall.

What is in your mind at that point?

I'm going like, *What the fuck?*

And I'm like, *I can't believe this!* This hasn't all quite registered yet. And then I realize that he is, indeed, attacking me. And I've NEVER, ever been attacked before in my life! So, okay, I now have all kinds of thoughts in the back of my mind — all of my book learning, you know. I even had studied Tae Kwan Do, martial arts, and all that crap. But, because it does not come naturally — most karate classes they teach these days they simply pencil people through and give them their belts so that they can keep getting more money! It does not come naturally to you, unless, of course, you're somebody like a Bruce Lee or a Chuck Norris that uses it every day of your life.

It was surreal, and I did not react at first, which is to say, I couldn't believe it was actually happening to me. I simply could not believe it. Then he spins me around, and I'm going like, "Why are you doing this to me?"

And he is laughing all the while. Obviously, he wants to rape me. He then tries to drag me into the little ammo room, where he presumably plans to rape me.

He knew the layout?

Oh yeah. He absolutely knew the layout. And he's like trying to drag me into this room. I then stick my feet down, trying to prevent myself from going in. I'm slapping at him; I'm trying some karate kicks and stuff, but all to no avail. He just kind of merely turns sideways, deflecting all my efforts, and then just totally laughs at me.

I am totally ineffectual. It's like a living nightmare! So next, I try even poking my fingers into his eyes. And, in response, he tries to do the same thing to me. I think, *Hmm, okay, better that I don't do that!*

And, all the while, if you can believe it, I'm still sort of in denial! I'm being attacked! I do not scream, however. I will explain to you later why I didn't scream because it would have only made matters worse.

I'm continuing trying to fight him off in this small area, and at one point he even gets me in a headlock. Now, I'm trying to punch him in the groin, but nothing I am doing is working.

None of the crap, and shit and stuff, that they tell you to do, works, I'm sorry.

And, all the while, I'm still sort of in denial; not believing that this is really happening to me. I'm just not at all reacting very well to this.

So, next, he is saying to me in Arabic, the equivalent of: "A teeny kiss, a teeny kiss."

I've also been harassed in the streets by Jewish men, too, by the way. So they're all from the Middle East, and we all know they all think we're bait and fair game. It doesn't matter: Arabs, Israelis — it's all the same. It's Middle Eastern culture. They're all products of their culture. I don't blame them. I love the people over there. They were very hospitable and kind to me, but this was a teenager, and he was an opportunist.

So, I finally acquiesce and say "Okay" to the kiss.

He comes forward and I let him kiss me, which is so absolutely unbelievably abhorrent to me. I just pull him against me, put my hands behind his head, and give him a nice kiss!

Oh, but I had a plan, an ulterior motive! So, when "French's" me (French kisses me), which I KNEW he would do, I simply clamp down on his tongue about an inch back — I bite down on his tongue as hard as I can. I mean, you can't really bite a tongue off, because it's cartilage.

But, I'm going to tell you something: I was truly prepared to bite *something else* off if it came down to that. And, you know what I'm talking about, right? (Use your imagination!) But, I certainly wasn't going to ever let it get that far if I could help it.

So, I'm hanging onto him, and I even tilt his head toward mine, to increase the pain. I mean, can you even imagine how much it hurts?

He starts screaming and gagging. Now the tables have definitely turned! Now, he's trying desperately to get away from me, but I'm just hanging on to him like a pit bull. Just hanging on. I probably held on to his tongue for a good 10 to 15 seconds, and that's a hell of a long time.

Then I shove him away from me. The blood was pouring from his mouth. You wouldn't think that a tongue would have that much blood in it!

My mom said to me years later, when I told her about it, "You know, he could have bled to death." And, indeed, he could have.

Anyway, he's screaming, and he's trying to run up the steps, and I'm trying to jerk him back down again. *You want a piece of me, buddy?* is all I could think of.

You know, my next thought was to even follow him up the wall and push him off of it. But then I thought, *No, if he grabs hold of my clothes, I'll go with him,* and this, of course, I did NOT want to do.

So, I just let him go, and he is all the while screaming. I always wondered afterword, how he could scream that much, especially with a chunk of his tongue almost bitten off. Geez, I'll bet he has a speech impediment to this day.

So, you did some real damage to his tongue, huh?

Oh, I'm sure I did.

So next, I ran down the other way and ran out. I was crying and upset. And some other guys saw me. They were shouting, "What's wrong? What happened?"

I then got down and ran into a coffee shop, where my husband and one of his friends were waiting for me. My husband goes, "What's wrong? What's happened?"

And I told him.

He starts talking and gets all these people there to go out and find this kid. If they ever found him they would have killed him, probably. They went looking for him, but they never did find him. They even checked with all the doctors they knew in the area; they checked with everybody. I guess I'm just lucky they didn't ever catch him. Who knows what might have happened.

I didn't go to the police. And in talking to other young women from different countries in the youth hostels, and so on, I heard that it was not uncommon to be attacked this way up on the walls — not just by young Palestinians, but even by Jewish Israelis as well.

So, the reason that I did not yell for help... Okay, I had been up on the wall before hanging out by the Damascus Gate, looking at the nice view there. I would go there and I would see Israeli soldiers at times. They never patrolled with less than like three or four of them together.

Once, I saw an Israeli soldier, and there'd be like a tourist girl there. He'd be standing with her in a corner with his rifle blocking her, kind of preventing her from getting out from underneath.

Right, okay, so something clicked in my head, and I went like, *Okay, you need to be careful here!*

If I had screamed while I was in a remote corner of the wall where the soldiers did their patrol, maybe there'd have been three or four very well-built, strong-armed Israeli soldiers in their 20s or 30s there.

If they would have come, they might have dispatched that kid, maybe even killed him — I don't know what they would have done to him, but then there would have been me — I'd have been left to their mercy, the three of them.

And did you know for a fact that Israeli soldiers actually did this to girls?

I don't know.

I'm only telling you what I saw, that there was one of them who had this rifle blocking this one girl. I was just not going to take a chance of having to fight off three well-built armed guys, two of which could have held me down at their pleasure.

What was he doing to the girl?

He wasn't really doing anything to her. He just had the gun so, such that it was up against her throat. He just kind of had her blocked, and he was talking to her. Nonetheless, she didn't appear to be in any obvious distress, so I don't really know.

My guess is that the soldiers wouldn't have likely done anything to you. It would be people who weren't soldiers, probably.

Remember how we were talking about eyes earlier? About cold eyes and cold blue eyes? Have you ever seen anybody with cold brown eyes?

Probably Turks. Some of the bad Turks I've met. Well, some of these Israeli soldiers had cold brown eyes, too.

I know that sounds odd. And some of them were very sweet, very nice people. But, let's face it: soldiers are soldiers; they are predatory by nature. I probably would have trusted them more than I would have, say, Egyptian soldiers, though. Yeah, yeah, but I don't know. I just don't know.

But, it's a good point: a young woman shouldn't just trust anybody.

This is true.

Trust no one.

Now, in retrospect, I want you to go back and revisit your experience on the wall. What might you have done differently?

Number one: I wouldn't walk alone up on the wall again. But, I've always been the type of person who realizes that if I didn't do things by myself, I probably was never going to do them, because if you wait for somebody to do things with you, you'll just never do 'em. Say, I want to go to Europe. I want to go here and there'll be, "oh yeah, I'll go with you," but the minute it comes down to buying tickets or getting a passport, they'll suddenly back off. And then, where are you?

Number two: Although some of the best traveling experiences I had when I was alone, going alone can be kind of hard. I'm going to say, however, go alone if you have to. But follow your instincts and try to let somebody know where you are if you can.

But, in that specific situation on the wall?

I don't know where my instincts were on that day. So somehow, it was obviously meant to happen, because, generally, I do get an odd feeling or a prickle in the back of my neck or something — a warning — like "don't go down that way" or something like that. And that did not happen to me at all on that day. But, after all is said and done, I did come out on top of things on that day, because I prevailed and sent this attacker off packing.

Maybe, you're not invulnerable. None of us are.

Well, no I'm not, but now, you know, I learned an important lesson, because I wouldn't do that again. I wouldn't go somewhere without company, without someone else with me, either male or female, because when I've heard the stories of all these other girls who had been accosted, you know...

Nobody did that 'bite the tongue trick' of yours like you did.

Well, I talked to some girls that, yeah. They got in their kicks, too, because none of them were actually raped — at least that's what they said. But, as you know, yeah, they did stuff alone; they did their thing. At least they went to all different places.

I've certainly heard my share of rape stories of women traveling alone, you know.

I'm sure.

You know, there was one guy who groped me from behind one time in a busy marketplace, somewhere in North Africa. I don't recall exactly where it was. But I swung around and I caught him with my elbow right in the solar plexus and totally knocked the wind right out of him. And he went down like a ton of bricks.

Did people turn around and look?

Nah, they just stepped over him and kept on going.

They've seen it before, huh?

Very likely.

I toyed with the idea of kicking him while he was down. Kind of like I had the similar thought to push the guy who attacked me in Jerusalem over the wall. But, in this market situation, as well as on the wall, I thought better of it, *Let it go. Let it go.*

"Maureen's Place"

Maureen Malin

―――――⊙―――――

Wasilla, Alaska, 1999. I am Maureen Malin (an assumed name).

So, you have been a student of the martial arts, correct? For how long?

Twenty-five years.

Have you reached any level of attainment?

As far as belts are concerned, I do traditional martial arts that use belts only that hold up your pants! (Laughs)

No belts, really?

Just the ones that hold up your pants! (Laughs)

But, do you feel that your skills now are at the level of, let's say, other more traditional martial arts, that might be at the level of a black belt?

Oh, easily, I'm sure. (Laughs)

This is not a time to be shy.

You went to China to train?

I went to study Shaolin martial arts for three months in Dungfeng, China.

What was a highlight or two of that experience?

The food was awesome. And the people are wonderful. They are just open, and gentle, and loving, and they thought I was hilarious because I had huge feet.

So, you're a fairly tall lady, right? Did you tower over most of the people?

Always, and a lot of people have never seen an American or talked to an American before then. It was in a little village of 60,000 people.

Are you the first American woman that they've ever seen?

Female, yeah.

And, were you the only female taking martial arts there at this point?

131

Oh, yes. Mostly guys. And children. There were a couple of girl children there as well.

But as far as adult women, yes, a few.

Were there any other foreigners besides you?

There were four young men from Europe.

So, this is kind of amazing that you went over there to do that.

Did anybody ever want to challenge you there?

When I was in China? No. But, of course, we'd play around and practice and spar, but definitely no challenges there, per se.

All right, you're now in Alaska and you had been studying martial arts for years prior to your trip to Alaska?

Correct.

Tell me the story of something pretty profound that happened to you there.

In 1999, the girls (friends) and I went out drinking and dancing, just me and three other women, us girls. A girls night out sort of thing.

We left everybody at home.

And, I'm usually the designated driver because I don't usually drink a lot. But on that particular night one of the other women said she would drive, so I decided to have a couple drinks and dance and just have a great time and not worry about it.

We went to a nightclub and just danced and had a lot of fun. It was Wasilla, Alaska, the home of Sarah Palin, of all people! We don't need to talk about her right now, though! (Laughs)

We went dancing, had our fun, and then decided that it was time to go home. And, on the way home, two of the girls wanted to stop at the biker bar.

I did not want to, however, because we had been drinking, and I had had enough by that time.

And so, one of the other women and I were like going, "We're not stopping."

But the other two begged us with, "Please, please!"

So, finally, we gave in and said, "Sure, for one beer! And, that's that, and then we're out of there!"

All right, now describe this step by step.

So, we go into some non-descript biker bar. I can't even remember its name at the moment.

So, what was that like going through the door?

You know, bikers drinking beer, being loud, leather. It was winter in Alaska, but I mean they're still wearing jeans, Carhartt leather jackets, scruffy hair, and big beards.

It's fairly wild and rugged in there, and they look like a lot of typical Alaskans, you know, males and females, and lots of hair.

So, we went towards the bar and sat down at a table. We were rather near, however, one of the younger women who was very short, maybe five feet tall or so, and her mouth just never stopped. And she was very drunk to boot. She's one of these people that always thinks that she can say just about anything she wants. Anything. Her father was supposedly in the mafia, and she could get away with just about anything because he would take care of it. Again, supposedly. Who knows? So, she had a mouth on her and she was using it.

Next, she moves up to the bar in between these two guys and she just starts talking away, and I couldn't hear what she was saying, but it was escalating.

You knew that it was. What did you see?

Just her standing there in between two guys.

But, they were louder and louder and becoming obnoxious, turning one to the other and getting louder by the minute. Enough! And so, my girlfriend, Angie, decides she was going to go over and take care of it.

She said, "I am going to take care of it."

I said, "No, this is my turn."

She goes, "Really?"

Because I usually actually just watch people.

So, I go up to the bar and stand next to this obnoxious young woman, between her and one of the guys.

Are you taller than the guys?

Yeah, I'm pretty much taller than that girl and taller than just everybody else in the bar. You'd say I stood out, all right!

So, I am standing there, and I start talking to this young woman. Jenny was her name. I say, "Jenny, let's go sit down and have a beer."

She goes, "Oh, I'm not causing any trouble."

"Yes, you are. Let's go sit down and have a beer."

Well, the fella next to me decided that my butt was a place to put his hand evidently — and distinctly without my permission!

He just reaches over and sticks his hand right on my cheek!

I'm thinking, *This is MY butt! You don't have my permission. It doesn't work for me.*

So, I go, "You! You do NOT have my permission to do that. You know, it doesn't work for me."

You know, you have these pressure points in your hand. So, naturally, I just reach behind me and grab these pressure points in his hand and just twisted his hand and hit these pressure points. And he literally buckles to the floor screaming, "Oh my God; she's killing me. My hand! My hand!"

I look at him and I say, "Apologize and mean it!"

He said, "I'm sorry."

I say further, "Tell me you'll never touch a woman again without her permission, especially if it's me!"

He goes, "I'll never touch a woman without her permission."

So, now I look over at Angie, and I say, "Girls, let's go home — *NOW!*"

And we're outta there in a flash!

So, that's it. Yeah, that's the only altercation I've ever had.

So, we left the bar and went straight home.

That's beautiful. How did you feel about it?

It felt great. I was like. "Oh, my God, it worked!"

All the training?

Yeah, all the training. And I still train, you know. I train two to three times a week now, and I love it because now it's just a matter of your body knowing what to do. Muscle memory is a phenomenal thing, and with enough training, physical muscle memory works.

Did you feel that it was a good idea to get out of there?

You bet. I thought it was a great idea to get out of there.

Were people beginning to notice what was happening by that point? What with the guy screaming and such?

Oh, yeah, they were looking all right. I was half drunk, myself, at that point, and I certainly didn't want to deal with anything else that night. I just wanted to go home.

You destroyed that biker's life! You know. I mean, you know, machoism is king, right?

Yeah, it is. Right. And this is one woman (me) who brought this man buckling down to his knees!

How could he have any more respect from the other bikers from then on?

I thought it was great, and I'll never even remember his face. But I will certainly remember that day.

And they will certainly all remember you! But you know, you are now a legend in that bar, and they will probably rename it for you to, say, "Maureen's," or "Maureen's Place," or something like that, don't you think?

Nah, it's not like that. It's more like they're probably going, "Make sure she never comes back in here!"

Do you feel like you never want to go into a biker bar again like that?

It wouldn't bother me. I used to live with bikers when I was a teenager, and bikers don't scare me. It's the drunken fools that are idiots. They don't scare me, either.

"Wander Woman": Fighting Them off #1

Barbara Swanson

———◦———

P aris, France. 1977. Okay, now, that wasn't the first time or the last time for you to be wandering around almost penniless. Tell me what happened to you in Paris.

I had very little money, and I was staying above the famous Moulin Rouge, which was in a very rough district of Paris, in the red light district, especially in the 1970s. It was where the whores were. It was in an area referred to as the *'Pigalle.'*

Above there, are the popular tourist areas of the *Place du Tertre* and the cathedral, the *Basilica de Montmartre,* which is often also referred to as the 'Artists' quarter.' And down below was the infamous whores' quarter or the red light district.

It was there that I actually learned to not look at anybody and just to look straight ahead and keep on walking because I was dragged into doorways by pimps. It was really, really very rough back then.

So, you looked at somebody once?

If I looked at anybody.

It was mainly because I was white and because I was obviously young and naive that I was dragged into several doorways, where people would try to drag me up flights of stairs.

Why?

To have sex with them! (Laughs)

So, how did you deal with this?

I learned to look down at the ground and never make eye contact with anybody because to make eye contact was considered an 'invitation.' And, I learned to never respond to any remarks, because to respond was also considered an 'invitation.'

And I didn't actually realize I had done it until I got back to the United States and my friends were asking me why I wouldn't look at anybody (including them) in the eyes. I had learned to do this without even realizing it.

I was there for about three weeks by myself. It was rough.

You say you were wandering around the streets in the Moulin Rouge district. What time of the morning?

Well, this was at any time, but actually, the day before I left I was so disoriented that I woke up at what I thought was at five in the morning to catch a train to get to the airport. But, it was actually one in the morning, and so, there I was wandering around the red light district for about two hours trying to find a train that ran, because, in reality, they didn't run that time of night back then.

Luckily, nobody approached me, and nobody hurt me, and I actually sat down near some strangers and wasn't even approached in any way. They just left me alone. And I was safe.

So, you say, at times people were trying to drag you into doorways, did you actually have to fight anybody off?

Yes, I did. More than once.

So, how did you do that?

I kicked them in their privates. I did! (Laughs)

I did that about three times!

And that was mainly during the daytime, but for some reason, at night when I really probably should have been hurt, I was not. I was totally safe.

Did they fight back at you when you did such a thing?

This was when they were trying to drag me into the doorways. But, no, I wasn't actually hit or anything. I was never hurt that way.

I mean, did you actually send some of these people reeling onto the sidewalk, holding their privates?

Yes, I did. A couple of them! (Laughs)

And you're fairly petite. You're not really tall. I think we should rename you, "Wonder Woman," or maybe even better, "W*a*nder Woman."

She laughs.

Fighting Them Off #2

Unknown

What can you say about the French and Paris?

Paris can be terrible. I was only recently in Paris. I was in Toulouse for a while a couple of years ago. I don't think it was so much the Parisians per se, but rather, the Algerians who are appalling.

You can walk down the main Boulevard St. Michelle, for example, which is usually fairly well lit at 8 o'clock at night, and you can get picked up, literally, right up off the street. They'll just sort of pick you up and walk off with you. Just physically pick you up around the waist. And sometimes they'll pick you up at the back of the legs, drape you over their shoulder, and just take off with you and disappear to another part of town with you.

They picked me up once one night, and the only thing that put them off was that my sister spoke French. I didn't speak very much French at all and was just sort of yelling, "Help, help, girls! *HELP!*"

My sister ran immediately to my rescue and spewed a mouthful of vulgarities at them. And they dropped me, literally, like a sack of potatoes right onto the pavement and simply walked off.

They'll stand very close to you in the Metro, too. And they'll rub up against you, given a chance. We used to carry scissors around with us and keep them open and very visible. That would keep them at a distance.

They'll grab you anywhere if given the chance. They are disgusting. And, they are much worse at pawing than the Spanish are. But, at least, they are, thankfully, relatively easy to put off. You sort of turn on the heat with them, and they'll usually back off.

Aggressive Men in India

Roniq Bartanen

N ew Delhi, India, 2006. I went to India and it was very exotic. However, it's a most difficult country to travel in. The infrastructure in India is very backwards. They're not a very progressive country, you know. For instance, when I was there, the train schedules weren't computerized yet. For instance, you'd get to the train station, and you'd stand in line for an hour waiting to buy a ticket. And after waiting such a long time, you'd get to the window and they'd simply say, "Come back tomorrow."

I mean everything kind of runs on Indian time.

It's also a very male-dominated country. Being a woman traveling in India, we got cut in front of many times in line. Men would just step right in front of you, and it's just part of their culture. It's the way they are. It's like women are kind of slightly invisible there.

One day I went to the post office to buy stamps. As the ONLY woman in the post office, there were 20 guys there, and every single one of them was staring at me. I suppose it's just that they're not used to seeing Western women there so much.

It's a huge country of a billion people in India. And it's a very rough existence there. There are a lot of people living on the streets there. But, you know, they're also very progressive in some ways with technology, for instance. But then, you are struck with such scenes like we saw these people working, and they'd be piling rocks into these baskets and putting them on their heads and carrying and dumping them. There's no machinery, so you have this.

And yet, people are coming out of India that are engineers and doctors and highly educated. But then, you have this really old way of life. It's what makes India so fascinating, I guess. And even though it was a very difficult trip, I would still go back in a heartbeat.

Did you feel safe in India?

Not always. Sometimes, I felt a little unsafe, only because men would stare at you so much. And they'd often travel around in packs, and so, that's just a little daunting. So, we would just make sure to keep ourselves in areas that were well lit and with plenty of people around.

And you know, physical safety, too, is often an issue in India. For instance, what with the power and lights quite frequently going out, and the streets aren't lit all that well, you could encounter, for instance, a sidewalk that will suddenly disappear into a three-foot hole in the ground!

And so, anybody traveling to India would do very well to bring a flashlight with them. I would say that's number one on the list of things to bring because we used it there every day.

Have you ever had to deal with aggressive men in your travels in India?

Not especially, other than I would say that the men could be slightly more aggressive in India. They'll come on to you, for instance, with, "Come out with me and let me take you..." Or, "I want your name..."

But, as soon as you assert yourself and just say, "I've got to go. Leave me alone," they'll usually back off.

Stalked at Gandhi House

Katharine Clark

A hmedabad, India, 1990. I was traveling in India, and I was very excited to go to Gandhi's home, the one in Ahmedabad on the river, the one that's in the movie, *Gandhi*. When I got there, while I was walking around enjoying the grounds, I noticed there was a young man, and he was trailing me only a few feet behind.

What was your thought about that at first?

Well, at first it didn't bother me, but after a while, it became obvious that he was indeed following ME!

What was that feeling like to discover that moment?

I just felt violated and not safe. So, I said *"Chalo Jalili,"* which means "Go quickly," and I waved my arm at him, but he didn't.

And, I sat down and I noticed that he was looking at my breasts.

And, I could see my husband, the man I was traveling with, over in the field taking some photographs, but I couldn't go directly to him; I had to go a roundabout way, and sure enough, this man was just about nearly on my heels.

And, if I hadn't been where lots of other people were, I would have been terrified, but I was getting pretty scared.

When I got over to my husband, he was quite annoyed to be disturbed, so he had a couple of words to say to me that weren't that pleasant. And then I said to him, "This young man has been harassing me and following me, and I came over here for your protection and your help!"

And then he said, "Oh well, I didn't know that; I was taking a picture."

So, we were both a little bummed out, and we decided to just go home for the day.

What happened to the kid at that point?

Well, the boy was nowhere to be found at this point. He disappeared when I got to my husband. Because we were having words for a few minutes, we both had our mouths turned down and were frowning, and not feeling very good. And as we were walking out of the grounds a man dressed in white robes suddenly jumps right out in front of us and says, "Oh hey, how are you guys? How are you doing? How did you like this place?"

I say, "Well, it's very nice."

He continues, "But why are you leaving?"

I say, "Well, you know, I just had this bad experience."

He says, "That boy; we have beaten him!"

I'm thinking, *Beaten him? We're in the Gandhi Ashram for God's sake!*

He says, "We've tried to throw him in jail!"

He says to my husband. "Come with me. We have to find him now. You have to beat him!"

So, I have to sit down. I'm thinking, *This is adding insult to injury! My goodness, we're in the Gandhi home of nonviolence and peaceful protest, and here's this man who wants my husband to go and beat this boy."*

So, they came back. They couldn't find the young man, but the Indian guy knew who he was.

He says, "Well, I'm the curator here. I manage this whole museum, and I'm so sorry you've had this experience. I don't want you to leave like this. I have the keys. Come with me.

The keys to all the rooms that you could only peer into through the doors and windows. And he next opens up Gandhi's personal room. He insists that I come in, which really meant a lot to me.

And I sat on Gandhi's mat, played with Gandhi's spinning wheel and then even sat behind Gandhi's desk where the famed "*hear no evil, speak no evil, see no evil*" monkeys are.

And he says to my husband, "Take her picture! Take her picture!"

And so, what really was an upsetting experience turned into quite a peak experience for us. I got to be in Gandhi's personal space!

So, you were harassed by a boy that's been known to do that there — they've had problems with him before, apparently.

Yes, he harasses the tourist women, and honestly, some of the ways the girls dress there, which is perfectly fine in your home country, is completely inappropriate there, in India. And that would be quite provocative to a young Indian boy.

I wasn't dressed showing a lot of skin myself, but to his credit, there may have been circumstances and experiences that got him into the habit of following foreign girls.

That's on the face of it. I wonder, aside from that, in an ironic sort of way, could there be a higher purpose for you?

It's quite possible, maybe to see how I would handle it, to see how my husband would handle it, and then the incredible reward when we were open to talking to the man and got the 'keys to the kingdom,' so-to-speak.

Did you ever hear any more about that boy again or anything further on this?

No, just that he had jumped over the fence and was gone for the day.

Did this experience change you or your husband in any way as a result of this incident?

Well, he felt very remorseful that he had been so snappy with me when he found that I actually needed his protection and help, and so, he wanted to treat me to a nice meal that night to make it up to me.

Travel Tip #6:
Know the No-Go Areas!

Michael Brein

Always consider where you should or should not go! No stranger knows better than the locals which places are to be avoided for safety's sake. There are bad and worse neighborhoods to avoid during both days and nights. If you 'feel' that an area is too remote, too quiet, too still, too dark, too many 'questionable' types hanging about, then maybe re-routing yourself is not such a bad idea.

Travel Tip #7:
Do Not Be Over-Confident!

Michael Brein

———◉———

B e careful of over-confidence in both yourself and others! 'Quantum,' unpredictable, or chance events do pop up or occur from time to time that even experts may find difficult to deal with. It's too easy to become over-confident that 'I can deal with this' or 'I can handle this' (or anything) that comes my way or crosses my path, or 'I'm not afraid of anything!'

All too often, unforeseen dangers pop up and happen to people who become ever-so-slightly less observant or prepared to deal with, simply because they become too complacent or careless due to over-confidence.

Introduction to White Slavery

Unknown

Well, basically what happens is a lot of women want to trip around the country, and so they get onto the desert. When you get onto the desert, a lot of people would hitchhike in trucks, because the only thing going down through the desert is trucks, going down to Mali and Mauritania, etc.

So, they are just really naive. Women, female travelers from all over the world, think that they can just cruise down with these local truckers.

That's not the way Muslim men are. If you are a woman, and you are by yourself with them in a desolate place, of course, they are going to take you. There's no question about that, but I don't really know anybody that lived in white slavery to tell about it. A lot of women that went down there never came back. They just went down into the desert like that and they were never seen again.

A lot of them?

Yeah.

What supposedly is happening?

Well, I don't know. I guess they get into some kind of trouble. I suppose they're passed around to different men like that. I don't really know. It's never really heard. You never really hear about specific people.

It's just that there were people that went traveling down there that just get lost in the desert and they never come back, and that something called 'white slavery' exists.

I heard of another woman who traveled a lot in East Africa, just more or less being used by different people — just being passed on from one guy to the next like that, but I don't know if you'd actually call that *white slavery*,* per se.

A typical white slavery picture also used to happen in this country, too, In Chicago, for instance, and different places. I guess it's a lot associated with Chinatown opium places. Just people that are like in a harem or something, part of a harem and just owned by men who use them and have other men use them. I don't know. I really never heard anything definite about a place where women were kept.

Women also disappeared from the cities?

Oh, yeah. Yes, I suppose. Mostly what I heard about was the desert, but yeah, there's some pretty seedy-looking places in the souks and the *medinas* and places like that in the different North African cities.

They're like mazes. You cannot easily find your way out unless you really have a guide. I heard mostly of people that got drugged out and just hung out in those *medinas*. Like a lot of Western people, like hippie type people that maybe went over there in the 1960s, and that lived back in the deep parts of the *medinas* like in Fez or in other Moroccan cities and just do hash all the time and burned out. Just totally burned out, basically.

2

Well, I had a friend that had problems in Istanbul, and I had been told to be careful in Africa, too, that there is a lot of white slavery, or whatever you want to call it. A lot of kidnapping and stealing of white women.

Had you heard anything in particular?

No, but everybody said the same thing, "Never be alone. Always stay with groups. Go with men. Don't ever go alone — just a couple of women, with at least a few, two or three women."

Always have men around, too. As many men as you can, and when you are in bazaars and crowded streets and places like that, even hold hands and stay close to each other.

Don't get separated, because, apparently, that's the way they work it; they find ways to get you confused and try to come between you and your group and isolate you and then just take you away in the crowd.

Whatever they are doing with white women over there that they were stealing and selling, I just don't know. I don't know if you are aware that it's considered a prize to have a white slave or what.

What the deal is over there about that, I really don't know what happens. I just know that everyone said that — travel agents, guides — anybody you talked to, anybody that lived there — would all tell you the same thing, namely, to be careful, because it does happen. It does exist. They know it exists.

And nobody really seems to do anything about it, either. There is not too much they can actually do about it. Once you disappear, the chances of finding you aren't too great, either.

I had a lot of concerns about that, but I was pretty crazy and didn't pay much attention to those kinds of things. I'm careful enough so that I wasn't really careless at all, but if I wanted to go, I'd go anyway and just assume it wasn't going to happen to me. So, nothing happened to me, nor were any attempts made towards me or anything.

I know a girlfriend of mine who had been dragged away by some people in Istanbul (from whom she managed to escape), but I don't know of anyone who's actually disappeared. But, I do know that it did exist and that it did happen.

There were just too many people talking about it and too many warnings for it not to be true.

Disappearance #1:
A Close Call

Unknown

———◦———

N orth Africa, Morocco. A friend of mine was with her husband and some other people, and a fellow was talking to her trying to sell her something. Another guy came by and was telling her that he knew where she could get it at even a cheaper price and a better deal than the shop she was in. He had a friend that had this place, and he would take her right to there.

Was she interested?

Everybody barters over there, and that goes on all the time, all the trade and stuff. She was asking him how much was it at his friend's place or something like that, and he says, "Come on, I'll show you."

He just kind of held her in a way where she couldn't actually break away from him, and he took her several blocks. Quite a way away, actually.

By herself?

Yeah, just by herself. I don't know how she got away or what happened, but she just kept pushing him about "Where is your friend? How far is it? Where are we going?" and so on.

He just kept kind of smiling and shaking his head and wasn't actually talking to her anymore. He was just kind of smiling. It was weird. That scared her, and I think she did something physical and then managed to wring herself free and run away from him.

Fortunately, the others who had been with her now had begun to look for her, so they were moving in the same direction that she was coming back and intersected her, and that was that.

But, it certainly seems that he wasn't just taking her to show her a better price, because of his attitude and the way he had just stopped talking and had this weird smile and had singled her out and had literally taken hold of her.

And, to boot, she's a blue-eyed blonde, and it just seems to be that fair-skinned, light-haired people are what they seem to try to steal over there.

Now, in the North African bazaars, are there any rumors that you've heard as to where these white women actually go?

No. I kind of remember hearing something. I might have, but to tell you the truth, I don't remember what I heard. I'm sure I heard stories at the time; I just don't remember what they were exactly. I don't really know now. I just know there is such a market, and I know it happens. I just don't know where they go and what they do with them. It's a murky area.

But there is a slave market?

Yeah, well, I don't know if it's a slave market, per se; I just know that white women, particularly fair-skinned, fair-haired women are stolen in these countries or kidnapped, abducted — whatever word you want to use — and that there's a price for it, and that they are valuable.

Who buys them, what they do with them, I don't really know. I have no idea. I don't know even if it's slavery, per se. I have no idea really what it is, but it happens, and it's the blondes and the light-colored women, and it's Europeans. It still happens now. I'm sure it still does.

Travel Tip #8:
Attend to Drinks!

Michael Brein

———◆———

Never, ever, ever walk away from your drink! Also, do not drink (or shower in) the water!

Rule #1 Never Leave Your Drink Unguarded!

Never, ever, _EVER_ leave a drink unguarded, even for a moment! Who among us has not witnessed a girl (or woman) getting up from her table or barstool to go to the restroom, glibly abandoning her drink to anyone and everyone to be potentially tempted to do the dastardly deed as 'slipping her a mickey' (dropping something untoward in her drink), i.e., something as evil as like a date rape drug or God only knows what other incapacitating substance!

Has it ever really happened? You betcha! Such goings on have often been reported to have happened to travelers to Mexico, for instance. And it's certainly not limited to there; it happens at home; it happens everywhere.

Rule #2 Don't Drink the Water!

When in doubt, don't drink the water. Bottled Water: A corollary to this is that you get what you drink! Just never simply take a chance and drink that bottled water UNTIL YOU CHECK THAT THE CAP IS SEALED!

Bottled water is touted as the be all, end all for drinking water overseas.

They say that bottled water is as pure as a newborn baby. Maybe so. But they also say, "Hey, that's nothing more than tap water!" Can you be sure you can trust third-world bottled water? Hell, you never know if it is just tap water, but the chances are these days that you can pretty much count on it being purified, with this one caveat, however.

All too often people simply will drink the bottled water without first checking that the bottle is COMPLETELY SEALED! Make absolutely certain that the cap is firmly sealed, to begin with!

Rule #3 Be Careful of Shower Water!

Be careful of the shower! Be aware that shower water in third-world countries CAN do you in! And, finally, here's another thought about drinking the water. Well, I don't suppose you think of shower water as something that you strictly drink, do you? But here's something I'll bet very few people really think very much about.

When you take a shower, water enters you just about everywhere — *EVERY* orifice: your eyes, your nose, your ears, your mouth, your skin. It can be tantamount to taking a drink. And, let's face it: it only takes but ONE vermin to give you *"Delhi belly,"* doesn't it?

Disappearance #2:
Another Close Call

Unknown

North Africa, Morocco. I do remember one particular story involving a group of Yugoslav architects, including one of my friends and his girlfriend. She was a very sexy, very good-looking, blonde-haired, blue-eyed woman.

They were walking in a medina full of small shops, talking and looking around. There were four of them, two men and two women. The two men and one of the women were just talking about architecture, and the other woman, the architect's girlfriend, apparently just moved off a few steps away. She was looking at some jewelry in one of the shop windows — there were some jewelry shops in the immediate area.

Suddenly, his girlfriend disappeared. They turned around and looked, and, suddenly, she was not there anymore. She was absolutely not there.

Again, there were a few shops just a few steps away — very close by, only a matter of a few meters' distance — and suddenly, and oddly, she was just not there anymore.

They began to go from shop to shop looking for her, and it turns out she happened to be in one of those shops fairly close by just behind them.

She had been looking at something in one of the windows when the shopkeeper said to her, "Well, why don't you come into my shop and I'll show you..."or something to that effect. "I have something really good to show you."

She was hesitant, but suddenly he kind of grabbed her and took her right in and brought her to the back of the store. She was just sitting there, wondering what was going to happen next.

Again, meanwhile, the others were going from shop to shop looking for her. Turns out they found her sitting and talking to this man in the back of one of the shops. She just simply disappeared out of nowhere after she just kind of separated herself, somehow, from the rest of the group.

She had been looking in the window, and suddenly she simply disappeared. The store guy literally took her in and then apparently locked the door, and that was it.

All these shopkeepers are connected. They won't talk. They all know what goes on, but they won't tell. They are connected. Nobody would say anything.

Were they going to keep her?

They probably would have kept her, I don't know. I don't know what they would do, and the man telling me this story said, "Well, the shopkeeper resisted at first; he was a very strong man. The three of us came up there, and we asked what is going on. And we were very insistent; we asked for her to come out. And so, of course, he had to let her go. He had no other choice at that point. But it was all pretty brazen!

Because, of course, it's prohibited and illegal, but she just disappeared. My friend told me, "I couldn't believe she was not there anymore."

She could have really disappeared for good. It really is dangerous there.

Yes, she could have really disappeared, because the problem is that they are all connected. The people at the airport, the policemen, taxi drivers, all the shopkeepers, they are all connected. They won't tell anybody. You just don't know whom to trust.

There is just nobody who can give you any protection, any security. I don't think I'd ever go again by myself. I think the best way to see those countries is just to go in a group because it is well organized.

Although it's not the best way to go — after all, you don't get to meet the people, and you don't really see the life there — but it's the best and safest way. A small group. Yeah, small group and maybe a few men, at least one man, so not only women. Even two women is a lot better than one, but it also can be quite dangerous; it really can be.

Disappearance #3:
Shopping in the Arab Sector

Michael Brein

Marseilles, France, the 1960s. I had heard the story about a young French couple from northern France traveling and sightseeing in the southern French Mediterranean city of Marseilles.

Of course, being along the Med, and under the partial cultural influence of Arab culture, given its proximity to North Africa, Marseilles was full of interesting places to go as well as having an Arab sector full of an untold number of shops.

The wife wanted to peek into one of the shops, but the husband was a little tired of it all by then, so he simply told her, "You go ahead. I'll wait for you right here. Just come right back out when you're done."

After a seemingly inordinate amount of time, the husband began to become a bit uneasy and more than a little concerned, as there was no sign of his wife, and the longer he waited, the more anxious he became.

After a bit, he went to the shop that he saw his wife go in and asked the shopkeeper, "Where's my wife? She said she would come into your shop to look around and then return to me. And she hasn't."

The shopkeeper responded somewhat cheekily and tersely, "Oh, she left — she went out the other door quite a while ago. She is not here."

You can imagine how perturbed the husband must have been after the shopkeeper's response. "You are lying! She said she would come right back out the same door she came in. What have you done with her?"

The shopkeeper simply repeated what he had said earlier. "Your wife is gone; she left out the other door. She is not here."

The husband then ran out the door, frightened to no end and sought out the first *gendarme* (policeman) he could find and explained the whole thing.

The policeman, with the assistance of one or two other fellow policemen, promptly returned to the shop in question, pushed the shopkeeper aside and began a thorough search throughout the whole store.

After a few minutes, they entered a room, discovered a closet, opened it, and what to their surprise, they found right there and then, not only this man's missing wife but several other women as well. All were bound with duct tape and unconscious, apparently given something like chloroform to knock them out.

The man was arrested, the women freed, and that was the end of that. Apparently, the intention was to take these kidnapped women out at night and deliver them to their next destination, which had, no doubt, something to do with white slavery.

This actually did happen, and it most certainly was neither the first time nor the last, either. Apparently, it is quite common in Arabic areas, especially in North Africa. What was surprising, though, was that this was in France!

Disappearance #4: The Real Deal?

Unknown

Tangier, Morocco, the 1970s.We met a tour guide there, a German man, who was in Morocco in Tangiers at the same time I was. He said that he'd had a young wife. He was about 30. They went looking for things to buy. So, one day they went into the medina to shop and look around and wandered the spider web of interwoven tiny nooks and crannies of the souk.

It was very crowded, and so, his wife said, "Oh, look here at that nice carpet, and the leather wear," and so on. But the man was a little bit tired by then and simply said to her, "Well, go in and have a look. I'll wait for you here."

So, that's what the woman did. She went in, and after a little while, well, about after 10 minutes or so, he wanted her to come out. So, he looked in and did not see his wife at all. He asked the owner, "Have you seen my wife here?"

"No."

He looked around, but his wife was nowhere to be seen. Then he called the police. They made a thorough search all throughout the whole bazaar, but still, they could not find any sign of his wife.

And, by the time we met him, he had lost her for about three days. She didn't reappear. She'd just gone away.

He never saw her again?

No.

He didn't know where she was. He tried to do everything possible to find her. And even after five weeks, there was still no sign of her.

She just went into a shop?

Yeah. It's weird. It seems she was that kind of woman that the people there like because she had blonde hair and a good build.

What do you think happened?

They must have simply loaded her into a carpet and just took her away. That's all.

What's the moral of that story? Not to go alone into a shop. I don't think something like that happens very often, though.

Apparently, he did nothing more as far as you know?

No. I don't know what happened to her because we parted.

But for at least for five weeks he had no idea where she was?

He must have been very worried. This is in Tangier. Maybe she got sold into slavery — white slavery.

I don't know. I don't think this could happen, nowadays.

When was this? When did this happen?

About five years ago [from the time of the interview].

It's very frightening and disturbing.

Very few people have told me about good experiences in Morocco.

Abducted in Morocco?

Eleni Papadakis

———————————

Tangier, Morocco. 2005. I got abducted in Morocco, I think.

What were the circumstances?

When you asked about the people who I travel with, this one is about a woman who's never traveled without an itinerary. She's always been, "I know where I'm going to go, where I'm going to be, where and when, and how I'm going to get there, and everything,"

How about you?

No, I don't do that. She was supposed to be going to India, but her trip fell apart at the same time that I was going off to Spain with no itinerary. I just really wanted to rent a car and drive around Spain.

And so, she said, "Oh, I can't go to India, so can I come with you?"

We've traveled in small bits together in the past, and we did some work together, so I said, "Sure."

We're driving along, and we get to the Costa del Sol, in the southern part of Spain. From there, they had ferry trips going to Morocco.

So, I convince her that she wants to go to Morocco, too.

Did you have any other knowledge or opinions about Morocco before you decided to go?

I just love Moroccan food. But it's also an exotic kind of atmosphere. And then, of course, there's famous Casablanca. Of course, we start talking about Casablanca and the Casbah, and I thought it'd just be an intriguing place to go, so we talked ourselves into going — it's just a day trip, after all.

Did you have any fear or trepidations?

No, no.

So, we signed up for a day trip tour. I am thinking, *What's there to fear? I'd never do tours, ordinarily. But what the heck, I'm just going to give myself over to the tour.*

We just basically stayed in Tangier in the main medina there.

It turns out, however, that there's much more to the story. Our tour guide in Tangier, it turns out, was in collusion with some criminal elements, apparently.

The tour guide meets us at the ferry. You come off the ferry, and they ask you which group are you with, and so on. And it's all very easy and well organized. You've got your little card that assigns you to a tour. And, it's all good.

But there's this other little weasel of a guy who's the tour guide's assistant and he said that he would be bringing up the rear.

"We want to make sure that you're all sticking together, because when we get into the medina, the marketplace, it gets a little maze-like; we just want to make sure you're all together."

And so, we're now in the shops, and I'm looking at rugs. I decide I'm going to buy a rug. Well, the rest of the group now gets shoved out of the rug store into the next store, and I'm left behind all by myself. I'm a little concerned.

I keep saying to the rear-end tail guy tour guide weasel, "Is everyone still here?"

"Oh yeah, yeah. They're out in the other part of the store."

I'm thinking, *Oh, they must all be looking at rugs too, just in different parts of the store.*

And then I finish paying for the rug, which they're going to ship to me. I now go to the other part of the store to find the others, and, of course, there's no one there!

I go, "Where is everyone?"

The weasel then goes, "Oh, they just left; they're just at the next store."

How did you feel then?

Oh, I'm thinking like, *Uh oh!*

It's like, there's something going on here. It was an immediate instinct that I was being targeted in some way.

How does that feel?

It feels like crap. I don't like being the target of *anything*.

I like to blend in.

And all the other folks on the tour were couples, except for this one woman and I, so we were seen as a likely vulnerable pair to split up in some way.

I was targeted for some reason, so they apparently separated me from the rest of the group.

And the other thing that usually happens to me when I'm in these fear-inducing situations is that I get this amazing sense of calm that comes over me. It's the weirdest thing; I just get really calm and focused. So, I decide that I'm going to go with this guy. I'm just going to do whatever he does and play really stupid and see what happens.

And so, he's taking me around to these shops, and he's instructing me to buy these spices.

And I say, "Yeah, you know what? I just don't have the money for these right now."

Actually, I do want *SOME* of the spices, but not *ALL* of the spices. And I want to use my Visa card, but the shopkeeper says, "Oh, we don't take VISA."

But I say, "But, you have a sign on the door that says you take Visa! The people who were here before me used Visa cards."

And he says, "Yeah, but the machines are down right now; we can't take it; we can only take cash. But why don't you use your Visa in the ATM just right outside the shop."

I say, "No, I don't really want to do that. I'll just leave then."

"No, no, no," the little tour guide weasel says, "No, you need to do this. I'll help you with the ATM."

I say, "I don't really need help, but okay."

And it's interesting; I knew exactly what was going to happen. I knew exactly that as soon as I put my card in and the cash comes out, a hand will come from out of nowhere and take that cash! And it won't be mine any longer.

And lo and behold, sure enough: I press the button; the cash comes out, and; a hand comes, as if on cue and grabs the cash. I swing around just in time to see my little tour guide weasel wink at the guy running off with my cash!

Oooh, now the pill takes effect! I call it my "Give me the asshole pill" routine. When I'm in these potentially stressful, scary and dangerous situations, I'm often quite calmly in control. But, I can get really bold, you know, and I can be trouble. I call it *giving me the asshole pill,* and once someone gives me the pill, it's like, "Okay, you really don't want to mess with me!"

Yeah, nonetheless, I'm at the ATM machine, and I am, oddly enough, still and calm.

You knew this was going to happen, but yet you continued to do it. Why?

Because I honestly thought that they'd kill me, otherwise. I really did. I thought that there was a real chance that I might not come out of this alive.

Really? What gave you that feeling?

I don't know. I just had this sense that there was something bigger than me with the tour guide going on here.

First, it was the feeling that they were just trying to get you to buy stuff. Then they steer you to the ATM.

Although they did want your cash in the shop.

Yeah, right, so that wasn't connected with the shopkeeper?

Oh, yes. I know it was.

It was?

It was because he was taking the Visa card from everybody else, right?

I wanted some of these spices, and the tour guide knew that, because in the beginning when they started the tour, they said, "What are you looking for?"

And I'd said, "I want some of the Moroccan spices."

So, they were more interested in your money, more than merely buying something, figuring you had money.

Yeah.

You saw him wink, then what?

I didn't mention it at first. I just say, "Well, I guess I need more money to buy the spices don't I?"

He says, "Yeah, you know, you have to buy the spices because now you've promised my friend, the shop owner, that you're going to buy them."

How much money was stolen from you at that ATM?

At that point, it was like a hundred dollars, maybe a little more.

So, I take out another hundred dollars.

Were you watching for hands at that point?

No, because I knew that was what was going to happen, and then that this was going to be about keeping me going and seeing what else he could get from me.

And so, I'm not getting upset. And he knows that I know now.

And he doesn't think you're as stupid as he thinks tourists can be?

It's hard to know, but I think he knew because I turned around. Like I said, he saw me turn around, so he knew that I had a sense of something.

And so, he says, "Where else do you want to shop?"

I say, "I'm through shopping now. I simply don't have any more money."

He says, "But, you need to spend the money that you have."

And, I say, "Where would you like me to spend my money?" (Like the sheep leading itself to slaughter with the wolf!)

Yeah.

He takes me into this other shop, and I say, "Well, there's nothing in here that I really want."

So, finally, things kind of move on, and I do buy something — a little elephant curio in a shop. He then says, "That's not enough."

And I say, "Look. What are you doing? I want to go with the rest of the tour group. You tell me that the tour group is right nearby. Either you are going to take me to the tour group or you're not. What's going on?"

And he coyly says, "What?"

And I say, "Come on! You know, that charade with the ATM! Why are you doing this, and why did you pick me?

Good for you! This is interesting.

He pauses for a moment and then says, "Do you know what it's like living here and watching these tourists come off the boat with all their money?"

And I say, "Well, but this is your living! You're living off of these people."

He says, "Do you know how little we get? How little these shopkeepers get? Do you know what living is like here?"

And I say, "I thought there was all this great wealth in Tangiers."

He said, "Yeah. See up on that hill? That's where the wealth is. Do you think any of it comes down here?"

And I say, "Well, I imagine that must be just really hurtful and frustrating. Do you have any option of getting ahead and getting past this?"

"There's nothing here for us. We're good people, and we work hard."

And then he says, "Do you want to see how we live?"

I say, "Yeah, I would."

So, he takes me to his family's home, which was like a one-room apartment with three sets of families living in there.

This is incredible.

I say, "Well, I get it, and it is unfair. It's not right that you should be living like this!"

So, I go back to the ATM; I get some more money and I give it to him. And he says to me, "The money that the guy took from you at the ATM is going to his sister, who is going to have a baby, and she can't get the care she needs at the medical clinic."

So, that's when he says, "You know, I can show you I'm not making this up!"

And she is there, indeed. And the sister clearly needs medical care, so I give them a couple hundred bucks more even!

That's a twist of irony, isn't it?

Yeah.

Did he ever apologize for their stealing from you?

Yes, he did. And he says, "You know, we don't want to live like this, and we don't want to do this, and I'm sorry if we scared you."

And I say, "You'll make it all up if you get me to the ferry before it leaves."

And so, he calls ahead to the tour guide, which is how I knew that they were all in collusion, and he asks, "Where are you and where's the ferry?

The guy says, "You'd better get down there. The ferry's about ready to pull out."

So, I say, "We'd better run."

And he says, "No, don't run."

He does this whistle thing, and this cab comes right up and we jump right in and we get down there. I go to pay the cab driver, and he said, "No, don't bother doing that. You need to get up the ramp now; they're pulling up the ramp."

And I run right onto the ferry.

My friend is standing there in tears. I mean, she's been yelling at all the authorities, "You can't leave! You can't leave! They've taken my friend!"

All the other people on our tour are coming up to me and hugging me now.

"We thought you were dead. What happened? "

You were abducted in Tangier.

Yeah. I was, well, sort of!

When we got off the ferry, I went to the tour company where we bought the ticket for this thing, and I tell them this story.

And they said, "You're lucky you got back alive!"

It just confirmed that apparently there were a couple of tourists who never made it back.

I said, "Do you think you might want to tell people that before you put them on this boat? At least tell them to 'stick together and be aware.' "

How could you do this to people?

You know, people do tours all the time to dangerous places; they're on their own. The tour company never gave me an apology. Nothing. But it confirmed my suspicion that there was a chance that if I had made any kind of a big deal out of this right in Morocco or tried to fight back, I might not have made it out of there alive.

So, this sort of thing is real, and what you say is an explanation, but in a strange way, of how you related to these people. These guys liked you after all, didn't they?

Yes, in fact, they even offered to give me one of their nephews as a husband.

I said, "Thanks. I really appreciate, but... *(Thanks but no thanks!)*"

He went, "Moroccan men make very nice husbands; he'll take care of you!"

He then came up and was hugging me."

And I'm like really going, "Thank you! Thank you!"

Do you think that this group may have been involved in the disappearance of people in Tangier?

I don't think this family, in particular, was, but I think they're connected to the network nonetheless. I think it's all one network, including even the gendarme who waits by the ferry and takes your passport and stamps it, or whatever they do. Because he was called by the cab driver and told to hold the ferry.

Very sophisticated, yeah?

Oh, yes. It's an intricate network.

And, you know, after all is said and done, you really have to applaud their ingenuity for getting this all together.

Indeed!

Caught with Your Pants Down

Ellis Ender

Mumbai (formerly Bombay) India, the 1960s. I'm Ellis Ender (an assumed name). My girlfriend and I were hitchhiking on trucks throughout northern India. It was really a better way to travel. You're riding on the top of the truck, not crammed into a bus with a lot of people, and you see the countryside. We were riding along on the tops of trucks that were really beautifully painted.

We were on top of this one truck and had just stopped for curry, which was real hot.

My mouth was burning so that tears were rolling from my eyes. I was just burning, and I was so thirsty that finally, someone handed up a dirty glass of grimy water. It was so dirty and so grimy I would have never dreamed of drinking it. But I was so thirsty; my mouth was so on fire that I just guzzled it down without even allowing any room for thought.

As a result of drinking that water, I got really sick. For the next few days I was so sick that at every stop I was running to the nearest tree — there are no toilets in India, so you go wherever you can.

On one beautiful moonlit night, very late, towards morning, the drivers made a tea stop. I ran to the nearest tree and was standing there with my pants down. The drivers walked by me. They saw me, of course, and I figured, "Well, I got a minute. They saw me here, that'll give me a minute."

But as soon as they went by me, they took off running, jumped in the truck, and took off at full speed. My little Chinese wife-to-be, Lily, was in the back still sleeping up on the top of the truck.

I was already a little bit worried, because they had changed drivers from the original ones that had picked us up, and these guys were a little bit weird. For example, one of the boys climbed on top of the truck and was sleeping there. But he kept moving over towards us. I'd push him away from us. It was getting really weird.

My first thought when they started up the truck was, *Oh well, I'll be able to catch them.*

I pulled up my pants and started running, and really didn't have any worries about catching them, because I'm a fast runner and I'm in shape. But they took off at full speed. They were trying to get away, and Lily was up on top.

I just started running at full speed, and then I started to get afraid because I wasn't catching up to them. I was running as fast as I could, and I was just running and running, and they were still just right in front of me. I was running maybe about 80 to 100 yards at full speed like you would run the 100-yard dash.

As I was running, the most frightening thoughts were going through my head. I was just thinking, *God, if I can't catch them, if they get away, what will they do to my lovely little Chinese girl?*

I was running at full speed, and that's when I'm sure I started to pray that I would catch up to them because I was getting really close, but I was also getting tired. They seemed to be picking up speed. I thought, *One last effort, one last burst, maybe a 20-yard burst of speed.*

They were still about six feet in front of me.

On these really decorated trucks, they have a bar in the back for climbing up. I dove and caught the bar. Thank God! I was holding on for dear life, flapping in the breeze like a flag. I was just holding on, but I was so happy that I at least had a hold. I knew that once I had got a hold, I could make my way up.

I slowly inched my way up the side of the truck to the cab. As soon as I got to the cab I started screaming. I reached in and grabbed the passenger, one of the drivers, by the throat. I started yelling at him. Of course, they went "Oh-oh-oh? We didn't know. What?"

They played ignorant. But that's the typical thing they do there. I was so mad. I just wanted to kill them, beat them to death. But I let go of the guy and climbed up top right above the cab where Lily was sleeping under the canvas.

It was so darn close to being a horrible situation. Lily wakes up and says, "What? What's going on here?"

I can hardly tell her, "You almost got kidnapped."

She goes, "What? What?"

I go, "Aw, just go back to sleep."

I was just totally stoned from the adrenalin and just looked up at all the stars. It was cold desert air. I couldn't go to sleep; my heart was still beating so hard. I just laid down and thanked God that He had allowed me to catch the truck.

About two hours later, they stopped the truck in the outskirts of Bombay.

"You have to get out now. You have to get out."

I was still real mad at these guys. I was ready to punch them out.

One of the guys said, "Just give me 60 rupees for the ride."

I said, "You can go the fuck away from me."

I was so mad at them.

They didn't understand the language, but they sure felt the vibes. They knew I was totally mad. I was distracted, however, from any revenge on these guys, because a dysentery attack came on again, which forced me to forget them and run behind a close-by building.

Another attack of dysentery came on, and I ran behind the nearest building. Just as I was bending over, with the rats scurrying around me, a guy came out of the back of a restaurant and tried to shoo me away.

I yelled at him, "Get out." I just yelled at him and he ran back into the restaurant. I sprayed my dysentery onto the pavement and ran off.

Meet the Parents #2:
The Family Man

Unknown

Fez, Morocco, the late 1960s. I met one American girl in Fez who was raped by a Moroccan.

She got to know this Moroccan in a street cafe. A suit, white shirt, tie, everything, drinking his coffee.

She said, "Sir, do you mind if I sit here?"

"Sure, sure." A little attaché case. Businessman.

"Ah yes, you are very nice. You are from America? Very good."

He spoke English. He said, "May I invite you for coffee at my family's house?"

"Your family, oh yes. Sure."

After 2 PM, and two hours later, she was really loosening up. They walked around the bazaar. They went around here, went around there, and he said, "This is where my family lives."

So, they went up the stairs. He opened the door. They went into a room. She said she heard some voices out of the next room.

He says, "You go in here first. I have to tell my family first that I have somebody. It's a very old Moroccan family. I have to prepare them first and then we will come and say "hello," and then the coffee will be served next door. So, you sit down here for five minutes."

He goes for five minutes and she waits; then he comes in and locks the door. He's already half naked and grabs her and fucks her and rants, "White woman, white woman, white woman, white woman," while he is doing this.

Then, he's about to kick her out. Dresses. Slaps her. She wants to scream; he slaps her again. She doesn't scream again because she fears for her life.

In the meantime, it was getting dark a little bit. He took her outside the house and was running around crisscrossing through the bazaar in order to confuse her, and then gave her a push and he was gone.

She went to the police, but she couldn't find the place again afterwards. She said the only thing she noticed were two guys working together and one lending the other one his apartment. So, when they finally found what they thought was the apartment where she had been, another guy opened the door and said, "Well, I'm living here. She wasn't here!"

Did she get pregnant?

She didn't know. It happened two weeks before I met her. She was quite upset. She didn't know whether to fly back to the United States and have a checkup or not.

Do you have any positive experiences, yourself, with Moroccans? Anything? I always get negative stories.

Meet the Parents #3:
The Good Man

Gloria Glenheim

———◦———

Paris, France, 1972. I'm Gloria Glenheim (an assumed name). About two years ago I was traveling around Europe. I had started in Spain and was continuing on my way to Amsterdam but with a change of trains in Paris. As usual, the trains in Spain broke down often and had lots of problems, but really no big hassle; I eventually made it to Paris.

I was traveling alone. I was only 18 and not very experienced with life, in general, and travel, in particular.

I got to one of the Paris train stations — there are a lot of train stations there, and you often have to change from one to another. So, I had to change stations, going between them on the Metro. That was okay, but it was about 12:30 at night and getting pretty late. At this point, I was in the Paris North train station, aka 'Paris Nord,' all by myself and very late at night.

I was sort of lost, because it's the first time, really, that I'd been on the train so much, and where the schedules are complicated, and everything is very confusing.

So, I finally got to the Paris Nord train station and had just missed my train to Amsterdam. Here it was late at night, and I didn't have any sleeping bag or anything. I didn't know really what to do at that point.

There were a lot of bums hanging around, and I was really scared. I guess a 'couple' took notice of my plight, seemed to feel a little sorry for me, I guess, and said, "Oh, why don't you come with us?"

And I said, "No, I can't go with you, that's fine."

They seemed sort of weird like.

In what sense were they weird?

Oh, I don't know exactly; they just acted sort of crazy-like. And I wasn't into anything like drugs or free living. I did not really want anything to do with them or their questionable lifestyle.

These were two men?

Yeah. I was at the time a very straight person, very narrow-minded and very innocent. Not exposed to a lot of things in life.

So, I was sort of wandering about the station, quite upset, because I didn't really know what to do.

This black man now came up to me; he was neatly dressed and seemed like an okay person, and I explained my situation to him.

He said, "Well, you know, I just missed one, too!"

He was very kind to me and said, "Why don't we go have some coffee?"

He seemed like a fine person. And so, I said, "Okay, I don't have anything else to do."

I think I'd have trusted just about anyone at this point. I tend to give people the benefit of the doubt. I always think they're good and go from there.

We sat and had coffee, and everything was really fine. He seemed like a good person.

Then he says, "Okay, I'll tell you what; I'll find you a hotel to stay in, and you don't need to worry about paying for it; I'm glad to help you."

I say, "Oh, this is really nice of you, but you don't really need to do that."

And then he says, "No, no; I want to. This is my pleasure. I'll do it. So, let's go out of the station onto the Paris streets."

I thought that would be neat to see Paris at night, and after all, I had so much time on my hands anyway, so why not?

So, I say, "Okay."

We walk out of the station onto the streets. Of course, I don't know Paris at all. We go way away from the station, and we walk down these little streets, and everything. We were walking quite a while.

And so, I ask, "Are you going to find a hotel?"

He says, "Well, I don't think there's anything open."

I say, "Well, what are we going to do, then? Can you walk me back to the station?"

He says, "No, no. Why don't you just come to my place, then?"

I go, "No, no thank you. Just take me back to the station."

He says, "No, no. Come to my place and you can sleep there."

I say, "No, really, I just want to get back to the station."

He doesn't like that idea at all. So, he next says, "Well, you can just stick around here. I'll just leave you then."

I am getting the idea that I don't like this situation at all because it seems like something's going to happen.

Why did you get that feeling?

Oh, just the way he started to act — seemed a little bit strange to me. It's hard to put it into words exactly. He just seemed like he had some other things in mind.

This part of town was not very good. There were drunks and people — prostitutes and other creeps around this area. I knew that if I would just be left alone there, more than likely, I would be killed. I had that vague feeling because there were just a lot of things going around at that time of night, and I was really scared.

I say, "Well, rather than being left here, I'll just come in, and if you've got an extra room, all right."

So, we come to his place, and he says, "Here, we can eat,"

And so, I have a little bit to eat, and he keeps wanting me to drink some wine.

I go, "No, no, I don't want anything, thank you."

I have the idea that there might be something in the wine. He was going to get me drunk, and the rest, so I say, "No thank you."

He then says, "Okay."

Then I say, "Where do I sleep?"

"Well, here's my bed."

I say, "I'm not going to sleep in that bed with you."

He then says, "Here's my bed; here is where you sleep."

And I go, "No thank you. I need to leave now."

I can tell I just need to leave.

He says, "Oh, I'm a good black man; you don't need to leave. I'm fine." (He's from Africa.)

I say, "Oh, yes, I do!"

And I start heading for the door.

He then says, "No, you don't leave. You're staying here with me."

How did you feel then?

I was scared. It was terrible; it was awful. I started to run for the door, and he had a whole bunch of things cluttering in this hallway, and he grabbed me.

He says, "You're staying here."

I say, "No, I'm not."

I start to run again back to the door again. He gets really mad. He brings out his knife and he says, "Look, you're staying here."

I was helpless. I could not do anything. I knew I wasn't nearly as strong as he was, plus the knife; I didn't want to be killed. I tried to fight a little.

And I finally said, "Okay, I'll stay."

I thought maybe there'd be another chance I could try for the door again because I knew he hadn't locked the door.

He went to the bathroom. Just as he went in there, as soon as he closed the bathroom door, I immediately ran for the door again. But, he must have known what I was going to do, because he suddenly ran out of the bathroom for the door, pushed me down on the bed, and started tearing all my clothes off. At this time, I had never had any sex before.

Never with anybody?

Never, never, any guys, nothing. No one.

He got really mad. He then said, "Look, I'm a good black man."

By this time, I was just hysterical, crying, "Leave me alone! Leave me alone!"

He just had sex with me. I was a virgin.

I said, "Why can't you just let me be? Why can't you just let me go?"

I was so afraid.

I say, "Here I might be pregnant. Now, look what you did. I might end up being pregnant here. I might have a black and white kid, and all the rest."

He says, "Oh no, I know how to take care of this."

But, really; this was just a really bad experience, that's all.

Then, what happened after that?

I was in a state of shock.

Yeah. I looked at the time, and the next train was to go at 6 AM in the morning, and so, I thought, *I've got to get out of here. I don't care if I have*

to walk the streets. I don't really care. I just want to get out of here and get my
mind back together. I've got to keep traveling and everything.

So, I said, "I need to go."

"Oh no, you need to sleep; you're fine."

I say, "No, I really need to go. You already did what you wanted to do,
now just let me be."

I start getting dressed, and he doesn't say too much. He wants me there,
and he got what he wanted and...

So, he didn't prevent you from leaving this time?

Well, he went out with me and we started walking. I, of course, just
wanted to get away from him as fast as I could, but he kept walking with
me. I didn't know where I was going.

I didn't know where we were or anything. Finally, I just ran away from
him and managed to get to the station. It was just a terrible feeling I had
about it all.

You didn't want to call or go to the police, or anything?

I didn't know what to do. It was such a traumatic experience for me that
I didn't want to tell anybody. I thought that I needed to get my head together because I had just bought a train ticket to go over to Europe for a
month.

I decided that I was not going to let it spoil my trip. But I knew from
then on not to trust people so easily, even those who seem on the surface to
be good. And that it's not about just looking good or being well-dressed.

It was a hard lesson to learn, and it took a long time to get over it, but it
was a good lesson. Not to trust everyone that you meet.

Raped and Kidnapped in Milan

Bobbie K.

Milan, Italy, 1976. This is a scary story. I had just arrived on the train to Milan. It was late at night, and I was traveling by myself. An Italian man from Milan on the train befriended me. He seemed very sweet and trustworthy. I had no reason not to trust him.

We talked about that he would help me find a hotel since he lived there. But I suspected that he must have known that the hotels were all closed by then. This is about 10 o'clock. Nevertheless, we looked and looked for a hotel, but we couldn't find a single one that was open.

He seemed sincere about it?

Yes, he did, but, you know, I was very trusting, maybe too trusting.

Then he said, "You know, my roommate is not here; so you can stay at my house in his room if you like. I've got an extra room for you.

I said, "Okay."

And I'm thinking to myself, *Well, you seem trustworthy.*"

I mean, I didn't actually tell him that, but that was my thinking.

He didn't speak a lot of English, but he spoke enough.

So, I went over to his house. We played guitar for a while and then he raped me! I didn't fight it; and, what's more, I didn't really freak out either. I knew that it be would be better not to do so and that it would be best to just sort of go along with it — but there was no doubt about it: it was rape.

If that was not bad enough, he kidnapped me for a couple of days and said that he didn't want me to go!

Was he a nut case?

No, he wasn't a nut case. He was just an Italian man, who I guess convinced himself that he was <u>in love </u>with me, and who decided he wanted to kidnap me!

So, what were you thinking?

177

I was worried that I would never get out of there and that he would have me there forever as his sex slave or something like that. I mean, I've heard that things like that do happen.

But, I appealed to him by saying, "You know, I've really got to get home; my parents are going to miss me. And could you please let me go?"

And, he did let me go after a couple of days.

Did you think about going to the police in Milan?

No, I didn't. I did not. I just left.

He got my address from me. I agreed to give him my address as part of our crazy 'deal' to let me go, so he could mail me letters. I got love letters for about six months afterwards from him.

So, he didn't see it as rape, did he?

No, *HE* didn't; but *I* did.

But, I suppose he fell in love with me, you know, in just those two days.

Did you have any feelings for him at all?

None.

I still have the love letters though; I kept them.

In retrospect, what would you / should you have done differently?

I probably wouldn't have gone to his house in the first place. I probably would have tried a lot harder to find a place on my own there.

But you had no hint?

No. I was so innocent. I just never thought anything like that would happen to me. I should have trusted my instincts in the first place, thinking that he probably might have known that the hotels were all closed by that time. But I didn't. That should have been my first clue.

So, were you too trusting, basically?

Yeah, I was way too trusting. You know, I'm a very, very trusting person, because I'm trustworthy myself. So usually, when you trust and you are trustworthy yourself, you treat people like you expect that's how they will treat you.

But that's not always the case, is it?

Right.

And, after you got free of this guy, did you just decide to leave Milan right away?

No, I stayed actually for another day. I didn't feel any fear. I'm not really a fearful person. I'm not generally a person that hangs on to fear. So, I didn't feel like I had to run from Milan. I'm still trusting. I've never let that experience damage me.

I did get some kind of infection a while afterwards. When I went on to Switzerland, I got something for it. It was just something minor, like a yeast infection, or something like that. A doctor gave me medicine that handled it.

This was not the first time something like this has happened to me, either. The first sex I ever had was when I was 14. I had the misfortune of having been 'date-raped.' I had cut school one day with my 18-year-old boyfriend at the time.

We just went to go make out, but, of course, one thing led to another, and he raped me. I pretty much broke up with him at that point and I didn't tell my mom. Nobody knew. So, I've had that sort of thing happen to me once before.

The Rat Bag Chick

'Janet'

Nairobi, Kenya, the late 1960s. I was staying in a sort of fleabag hotel in Nairobi where the Africans stay and where the backpackers, who call themselves 'rat bags,' stay. I opened the door to my room one day and here was this American chick. She looked like a loser. Not that she was ugly or anything, but she just looked kind of freaked out and a bit nervous. Some people just look kind of nuts when you see them.

This was Janet. She was with this huge African guy. He was very well-dressed.

She said, "I'd like to see your room if I may. I'm thinking of moving to this hotel."

So, I showed her around and spoke with her for a few minutes. And then she went off with this guy.

A few days later she came back.

I said, "I'm on my way to Kilimanjaro. I'm going to climb Mt. Kilimanjaro."

She said, "Oh, can I come with you?"

I said, "Listen, I don't travel with anybody because I don't get along with people very well. I prefer traveling on my own, because that way, when I get tired of somebody I can say "fuck off," and nobody's upset."

She said, "Well, listen, I really had a bad experience, and I really have to come with you to visit the game parks and maybe climb Kilimanjaro."

I said, "Well, listen, you come along, and then if I get tired of you or you get tired of me, we'll fuck off and nobody'll be hurt, all right?"

It was just going to be like a buddy-buddy thing. I was sort of rescuing her.

What happened is that this black guy had taken her home and raped her. A couple of times, probably. They do that. What was strange is that, well, perhaps not strange, but African, I guess, is the fact that she was being raped and she was screaming out for help in this guy's home, which he shared with his sister.

His sister was present at the time, but his sister wasn't about to move to help, because the African woman is inferior to the African man, and she wasn't about to take any risks of getting smashed by the brother.

The worst part about this whole thing is he gave her the clap.

I took her with me to Kilimanjaro, and we didn't last very long. Just a couple of days together, and I sent her on her way. I couldn't hack her. She was really too much of a space cadet.

She had been in the Sudan a few weeks earlier. She'd been in her room while a coup d'état was taking place. And bullets were flying through her room. It seems like wherever she went she was getting into trouble. So, there she was: she got shot at; she was terribly ill; she got raped, and; she got the clap. She was a real loser.

Then what happened to her?

Then she disappeared. She probably went back home. While we were traveling together, her biggest concern was fashion. Whenever she met somebody she'd ask, "Do you know anything about fashion?"

And then she'd go through this whole rigmarole about, "Well, listen, I have to go back to the States in two weeks. I'm going to Kilimanjaro and I'm going off to Europe. Where should I buy all my clothes?"

It was ludicrous. I just couldn't take it. I sent her packing.

Do you think this was all an escape from what she'd been through? An attempt to cope with what happened to her?

No, that's just the way she was. She had enough balls to get on the road and come down to Africa, right? I respect any woman for that, because Africa is very rough, and here she was on her own, making the best of things.

But she wasn't a long-time hardy Africa traveler; she was only there for the summer or something. She wanted to see it, which was fine, but then she was going to rush back with her newly-bought clothes from Europe and say, "Hey, I've been to Europe and Africa."

Bad Things Happen in Threes?

Harriet and Her Mom

Cabo, Mexico, 2014. I'm Harriet (an assumed name). A couple of members of my sorority decided to go to Mexico for spring break along with a bunch of other people from my school.

Now, why Mexico and where in Mexico?

We went to Cabo because it was the sophomore Greek thing to do for spring break, so we decided to join in.

What had you heard about Mexico?

I had never been to Mexico before and that was my first time going. I was a bit nervous not going with my parents, though. I had heard we were able to legally drink in Mexico during spring break, so I'm sure that's part of Mexico's attraction for college students.

And, 'Mom,' how did you feel about this trip to Mexico before they left?

I was fine with it. I mean, she's very responsible and has good values and all of that, and can make good choices, in that they were going with a group. I felt like that was a much safer venue than her going alone just with a friend in venturing down there.

And a couple of members of my pledge class in my sorority and I contacted a travel agent and had them set up everything like the transportation to the hotel, arranging for the hotel rooms, as well as having everything pointed out to us so that we knew what to expect.

Everything was more or less scheduled for us because we didn't have any adults going with us; it was to be just us girls, and we knew that there were multiple boys in different fraternities that were also going and staying in our same hotel. So, that made us feel more comfortable, because, we'd have those guys to hang out with and go out with, etc.

The whole journey there was fine. No one really had any problems, and we checked into our rooms. Everyone was, of course, hyped and excited.

What were your first impressions?

I was a little nervous because I don't speak any Spanish. There were a few people that did, and so, it was a little culture shock, because I've traveled to California with my friend and her parents. But I have never done a big trip by myself, so I would naturally tend to be a little more nervous and had a lot of anxiety about it.

The first day was about getting there and settling in; we had our rooms, which were spread out, which was a bit of a bummer. And the first day, we all went to a welcome dinner for all the people that arrived there together. And there were a couple people coming in on a later flight.

How did the people there seem?

The people in the hotel seemed nice. They tried to cater to us and to make sure we got our rooms okay, and so on. It took a long time to get our rooms, because they needed signatures and credit cards, the sorts of things that we weren't necessarily prepared for.

So, that was a little stressful. It seemed they had us on a schedule. "Okay, we have your rooms for you; these are your plans; this is your transportation, and so on. Soon, with the schedule, things became more hectic.

Were you still anxious?

I was nervous mainly because I had never been out of the country before, besides Canada, so Mexico was my first real venture out, and I didn't have my parents with me.

That's both good and bad, huh?

It was like a good experience, but at same time, I was a bit uneasy. I didn't have many minutes left on my phone or anything. I was expecting not to really use my phone at all because I was hoping other people would have theirs. I was hoping to have Wi-Fi, but it was extremely expensive, so that, as well, contributed to my nervousness, in case I needed to contact my parents. But I just ended up using someone's phone, and then the first day moved on to the worst thing that happened on our journey.

We went to dinner. Then we got changed into our bathing suits and no water in the pool! Later, we were invited to go to 'Mango Deck,' which is kind of like an outside beach bar.

Who invited you to do that?

They were college boys from Yale that had been there earlier, and they invited us to go to the bar with them. But we were at first a little hesitant "oh, I don't know." But at least they were college students, so there was a group of us that went with them. We were drinking at the bar with them.

Is that away from the hotel?

It was probably like a 15- or 20-minute walk down the beach, so we had gone with them.

Was it dark out at this time?

It was still light out. We walked back from the bar when it was dark and had gone to bed fairly early — by ten o'clock. The other girls in our sorority, however, ended up going to the club, 'Squid Row' that was fairly far away that you had to take a taxi to.

Incident Number One: 'Sally'

Around 4 in the morning someone comes and knocks on our door. She is frantic and is shouting out, "Sally got raped! Sally was raped!"

She was one in the group that went into town in the taxi?

Yes.

It seemed like a surrealistic dream that we were woken up from. They then told us the story of what had just happened.

Sally was freaking out, so they took her to a hospital and put her on drugs to calm her down, to keep her sedated, because she was just so freaked out.

What happened is they were at the club — they had girls and boys with them — and Sally was talking to a local Mexican guy. And not once, but twice, her friends were trying to get her away from talking to him, because one of the guys they were with said, "No, this is very 'sketchy.' She should come back over here with us," and so, he tried to pretend like he was her boyfriend. But she went, "No, no, I'm fine."

I don't know if this was because she was drunk or what, but all of a sudden, they turned around and she was gone. She apparently had mumbled something to the effect that the Mexican guy was going to walk her back to the hotel.

Big mistake to leave the group!

Was it 'mistake number one' to even go in the town in the taxi in the first place, maybe?

No, not really. That's what everyone did; they had a group in the taxi with them; they were supposed to all stay together, you know, in a group. So, in their minds they set out to be responsible, and, you know, to keep everyone together.

But, somehow, Sally decided to be walked home. I don't know if it was her level of intoxication that she thought that that was okay. But, for better or for worse, she was getting walked home.

I guess what happened — what she remembers afterwards — is that, all of a sudden, the guy just disappeared, and, somehow, she got hit on the back of the head by two men in an alleyway and passed out. I guess they raped her repeatedly. And when she did manage to get out of her dizziness and disorientation and get herself together, she got up and ran as fast as she could back to the hotel. She was hysterical, and the hotel called the police and the ambulance.

I guess what seemed odd and all messed up to me was that the police only took down her name, and that's all they asked her! After all that, just her name? And it was at that point that I began to notice just how corrupt and inefficient the police were.

They took her to the hospital, and people were visiting her there and making sure she was okay, and so on. Next, they called her mom back home, and her mom flew her home. Sally was gone from Mexico, and the incident set an awkward, unsteady tone for the rest of the trip for everyone who was left.

We got together after that happened and we were like, "Don't be stupid!" Like, don't go off by yourself, even if it's with a college student. Make sure you have at least one other person with you. And we have to move about in a big group of girls. We would hang out together when we were getting ready to go to the clubs at night.

We would go like "okay, we need four or five guys in the taxi with us, because I feel uncomfortable if there's only one guy with us in the taxi. We need some of our guy friends with us.

When the guys heard what had happened, they were like "we're watching out for you; you're going to be protected." We were resigned to be as smart as we could be.

Incident Number Two: The Cops

And then there was the second incident. I don't know what our guys were conceivably doing — but there were cops... (Our guys might have been trying to buy drugs.) Personally, I don't think they would be that stupid to try to do that, but the cops somehow singled them out, right from off the sidewalk, handcuffed them, and put them in the back of the police car.

Then the cops just drove around with them. The cops then were like, "Okay, take out as much money as you can" (and pay 'em off). And so, then they got let go.

My friend said that he was thinking about trying to break his thumb so that he could get his hands out from out of the cuffs, because the doors were open, and maybe they could have conceivably have scurried out and escaped. NOT a very good plan!

The cops were, evidently, extorting them, basically?

Yes.

How'd they know that they were actually cops?

Was it a police car?

Yes.

And so, it was kind of messed up, complicated not in the least by the fact that I didn't have the slightest idea of what the guys were doing that could have gotten them into so much trouble.

The boys said that they were not doing anything wrong. Were they just singled out and plucked right off the street by the cops?

Could it be just that they seemed a little drunk? And so what? Is that a crime? It's spring break, for God's sake. That's what you do on spring break. What's the big deal?

I felt that that was very scary. They were cuffed by the cops. And they just had to be paid off. And the cops made them pay, threatening them that if they didn't pay, they would be taken straight to jail.

How much money are we talking about?

I think they had to take out about 400 bucks each. So, they had to pay them like 800 dollars all together.

There were several accounts of corrupt police happenings.

Was this the same night as the gang rape?

No.

Incident Number Three: The Water Taxi

They also had water taxis there in Cabo, and that's how I heard of another account, incident number three. It was a couple of guys who hired a water taxi, and the guy took them out into the middle of the water, held them at gunpoint or knifepoint and then forced them to give them all the money that they had on them.

And I think, partly, why that happened then was because my friend went a week later and said that no one had had problems. So, it might have been because we were one of the first waves of college students that they thought they could just mess with us. I know that that was kind of scary.

But I think what my group did smart was that when we would go out, we would have a big group of guys and girls together, and, you know, the guys knew us and wanted to make sure we were okay.

My friend and I were dancing at the club one night, and there was this one Mexican guy that was kind of being creepy to us. And so, one of my guy friends came up and hugged me and kind of turned me away from the guy. "Are you okay?"

"Yeah, but kind of freaked out. Make sure he doesn't come over here."

It was kind of nice to know that it was okay. Now we know that scary stuff can happen and that people were watching out for one another. You know, making sure everyone was okay.

I feel like after the Sally incident happened I was way more scared, super monitoring everything that I drank, making sure that I wasn't getting too intoxicated, and so on.

It was as if I needed to know what I'm doing, where I am at, and where my friends are. I had to keep a clear head, above all.

So, from here on, all of the people in my group were being super cautious about how drunk we were getting, because we didn't want something like that to happen again.

Let me ask you this: the guys that were picked up by the police were part of your group?

Yes.

Were they just innocently walking on the street?

I'm not sure what happened. They said that they were standing in line to get into a club. They might have been seen as being riled up or getting rowdy or something like that, though I doubt it. But, they said all of a sudden the cops started talking to them. And they wound up getting cuffed and put into the back of the police car.

I think that happened the second or third night. And a couple nights later we were standing by the taxi; we were trying to get a taxi to go back to the hotel, and there was a group of us girls and guys. And one of the guys said, "There's a cop over there. I can't stand here. I'm scared." He was terrified that this was going to happen all over again.

But Cabo is supposed to be safe!

Exactly!

I heard that Cabo is supposed to be one of the safer places in Mexico, just because it's so touristy. But I almost feel that they thought they could take advantage of us because we're college students there just to party.

Basically, you had a lot more money than the Mexicans were used to. Right? You were tempting targets.

Yes, true. One of their biggest tourist seasons is spring break, especially with all the college students flying in, because it's like week after week, and more and more college students keep on coming.

So, it was the common expectation that these American college kids had a lot of money to spend. So, for a third world country like Mexico, it is tempting to try to get as much from the tourists as they possibly can.

The boys that were robbed by the police, did they go home right away?

No, they stayed.

But they were kind of freaked out, though.

There was a time that whenever they'd see like a cop around — they weren't even doing anything — like, we were just walking down the street — they were kind of like, "No, I'm scared — there's a cop over there."

It was freaky to think that the people who were supposed to be protecting you — the police — were the ones victimizing you. It was kind of all messed up.

Did anybody think about trying to go to the police headquarters and try to talk to somebody higher up? Someone who wasn't on the take?

I don't think anyone seriously thought about doing that because it's the cops, after all, that are the ones, you know, monitoring the area by the clubs. If the cops were doing that, the chances are very good that headquarters not only knew about it but were also part of it. Obviously, the law is not trying to protect us; they're trying to rob us.

Would you ever go back to Cabo?

I think that I would want to go back. I mean, I had a lot of fun there. I think because my friends and I were being really careful, it was all about being smart because we had managed to stay together. I feel it was stupid on Sally's part. But at the same time, it was such a horrible thing to have happen to anyone.

Why didn't her friends get even more insistent that she NOT go off by herself?

They tried multiple times, and then all of a sudden when they turned to grab their drinks, Sally was gone. They really did try multiple times. Like one of the girls that was her best friend went over to her and said, "Hey, come over here."

But Sally replied, "No, I'm talking."

And then she had her boyfriend go over and try, saying, "Hey, come over here."

Her response was, "No, when I'm done, maybe."

Finally, when they both tried to go over once again and try to get her to come back, she just ignored them. And when they turned to grab their drinks, Sally was already gone.

In retrospect, if you had to do it all over again, what would you have done differently?

Personally, my roommates and I never once did anything that could have compromised our situation. I think from the beginning, we all knew that we needed to have our group stay together; make sure we knew where each other was; make sure that we had guys with us that we knew to, I guess, in a sense, protect us. Which is how I felt when we went to the clubs: I knew the guys would make sure we were okay, and if they did notice someone talking to, us they would come to us and say, "Are you okay with that?"

Yes, you did all the right things, actually.

Since you're back, have you heard any more things like that about Cabo?

I haven't heard anything more because when we left, there was another school that also went to Cabo. And I had told them about all the bad things that happened to us when we were there. And she went like, "Oh no! We didn't have anything like that happen to us at all." And she did not even hear of a single account.

Hard to know how often that happens or if it's happening more. So, the colleges are probably not going to do anything differently?

No. I don't think so.

I feel like there are still students that are still going to want to be going to those destinations, you know. I feel like it seems part of the sophomore Greek tradition.

It's like that's what you do — you go to Cabo! And so, I feel like they're still gonna want to go. But I feel like a lot of people have heard of what had happened to our group when we went. And I think, therefore, they'll be more careful.

We can't stress enough that you need to make sure you have multiple people in the taxi with you. Never take a taxi by yourself. Have guys in the car with you. We were telling people when we got back of everything that had happened because they had heard that some bad things had happened. And we told them what happened. We were like telling them, "Don't be stupid."

Were the girls careful about their drinks, never leaving them and walking away from their drinks?

Yes, everyone was holding their drinks at all times. And if they had set them down for a time, they didn't pick them back up. I think that a lot of the times when we are at the clubs, we were 'pre-drinking' in our rooms with people we knew before going out to the clubs.

It's interesting you sensed what these bad people were like.

Yeah, I kind of didn't trust the taxi drivers. I just didn't trust the locals, as bad as that sounds, but I trusted the guys that I came with. I was like "I'm going to watch myself."

I wanted to make sure that I was sound of mind and make sure that the people around me were okay and that they were being cautious, too.

I know that there was one night that my friends and I were going, "Oh, I'm like kind of drunk!" And we went, "Oh, let's get a water bottle."

And so, we drank water to make sure we were fine. I think everyone knew that it was kind of sketchy.

The guys were making sure that everyone was okay. The girls were staying together. The main club that everyone went to, "Squid Row," all the students kind of gravitated to the bottom floor in the same area every night. So, even if we didn't all show up together all at once, it was like the group's gathering spot when they were all there. Like you knew everyone around you, besides the random people that go through there.

These are all the right things for sure. Now, here's a strange question: you had all this anxiety before you got down there, and I wonder if some of this anxiety was somehow related to the feeling that maybe something was going to happen? It's an odd question. But what do you say about that?

I don't really think so. I feel like when I'm stressing out, I have like a very good reason for it. Since I knew that my mom had traveled to Mexico before and she was kind of saying "Yeah, it's like a little sketchy," and so on, I was a little nervous that we didn't have our parents with us. And I knew that we were going to be more of a target since we were college girls. I guess I'm kind of a worrywart, anyway.

That's what kept you safe, anyway. There's no question about it. Let me talk to your mom for a second.

When did you hear about these things that happened down in Cabo?

Not until she got home.

If you had heard about it before, what then?

I don't know that I would have done anything differently; I mean, it's like she was making the right choices, you know. It's just the kind of kid she is.

That's comforting, isn't it?

Yes, it is.

Did you talk to any of the parents of the people that had the problems?

I don't know any of the parents.

Did you talk to Sally after you got back?

Yeah, we talked to her. She seemed like she was okay. But she was having flashbacks of what happened. It was a very scary situation, you know, having to go through all that.

Lucky, nothing worse happened.

Yeah, that's for sure.

I know that when she got home she was back with her mom and she stayed at home for a couple weeks, and the college, obviously, allowed that.

I know that I didn't go back to school right away. I was home because I had mononucleosis, and I had heard that every once in a while, Sally would have her little breakdowns, because that's quite the tragic event to have happened to you, you know.

I don't know how she is affected now, but she seems to be more stable.

And the police did nothing for her, right?

They only took down her name, and that was about it. The people that were there, that were with her when she was getting in the ambulance, they said the cops asked what her name was, and that was about all.

I don't even know if they did the usual rape tests. I'm sure they took samples, though I doubt that they would ever test them. I've heard it said that in Mexico, they have thousands of similar rape test specimens that have never been tested.

I'm glad you got back relatively unscathed, you know, because you've done all the right things.

Finally, anything else?

Be careful of the water (laughter).

That's the least of your worries!

I fear that Mexico is a lot more dangerous than it used to be.

The Moroccans

Iris Inger

———————◆———————

Morocco, the late 1970s. I'm Iris Inger (as assumed name). Confessions of a Peace Corps Volunteer. Did you ever learn to cope with Muslim men in North Africa? You lived in North Africa for a while.

That was an extremely difficult experience. Every day the two and half years or so that I lived there it was intense to try to cope with the men because they are totally chauvinistic. Even the most sophisticated, the educated, because like women are not even mentioned in the Koran.

Women are just considered to be male property and, consequently, that's how you, the Westerner, are treated on every level. From the most blatant wearing of Western clothes, nothing even slinky or anything, just Western clothes, not covered up and in the medina, men would shout things at you like *"kuba"* (prostitute). They'd come by and they would just call you that. They are among the most ethnocentric people I've ever met in my life.

To the Moroccans, if you are Christian, you're an infidel, and you are impure, and you're not a 'saved' people. And, as a consequence, you are always on the outside.

You are never accepted. Even in intermarriage. Even in a conversion, you are never really accepted. They are very, very self-righteous in that respect.

It's very difficult to deal with the Moroccan men. I remember, even in a lot of my dealings with officials and different people — it's their mentality.

You have this French bureaucratic system imposed on the Muslim countries, such as Morocco, and French bureaucracy is very formal and constipated, really. You deal with a lot of petty bureaucratic people. It's all the Moroccans. You might be dealing with a petty post office official, and this person gets off on giving you a hard time because it's like a power trip for them, and plus you are a Western woman, so they like to get off on that trip, too.

If you are assertive with any of these people, they just get obnoxious. I remember one time, I went down to the electric company to complain about a bill, because when the King comes to town, King Hussain [at that time], there's a big fanfare. They have a big parade and everything for the King.

Everybody hates the King. They have been trying to overthrow the King since 1972. He has to do this big thing to make it look like he has all this public support and everything. Consequently, all the lights in the city are all lit up, and they have this big parade and everything.

Well, what the suckers do is they attach all the electricity charges to people's bills. They just put it on peoples' bills to have them pay for it, and they would do it to Christians, as well.

"They're not going to know the difference, anyway; they are just going to pay it. What do they care? They just pay their bill."

But, we Peace Corps Volunteers weren't at all like that, of course, because we lived there, and we spoke the language and interacted with the people.

So, this practice is ridiculous, and we found out from our neighbors that this is what happens. They just put it on your bill, and they figure, "Oh, you Christians will never find out."

So, I go down to the electric company, and I'm complaining about the bill. The guy is acting like a total asshole with me. It is the same initial response that we always get from the people there.

If you spoke Arabic to them, first of all, they would go through a trip of, "Oh, isn't that cute. You know a few words of Arabic." or something to that effect. It's a novelty, because French people, who have lived in that country for 30 years, maybe know about two or three words of Arabic, and that's about it.

The French are so fucking arrogant that they don't even bother to learn how to communicate with the people. So, for a person other than a Muslim to speak Arabic is really something, especially for a white Western woman, so they really get off on this.

Sometimes they'd play word games with you just to see how much Arabic you really do know. We were pretty fluent because we worked in the language. They'd get into talking with you in regular, normal conversation.

Then, if you try to be assertive, or if you are opposing them about something, or you want to change something or try to change the system, first they'll play this game with you that they don't know what you are talking about. And then, if you just keep on talking to them, they'll just get very chauvinistic.

They cannot accept you as an intelligent woman who's trying to present a rational argument. It's all not even something that you could possibly know about, much less argue against or change. It's just incredible to deal with.

Sexual Overtures

It's extremely frustrating, people always making sexual overtures to you. Always. A lot of it is not blatant. Not that many women get raped or anything like that. Actually, I felt quite safe in Moroccan cities any place I went. And I would go even into the Casbah and places like that in cities by myself at night or early morning. Because they have patrols out that protect the areas, so no one comes out and bothers you.

Even when we went to talk to this one Moroccan official in the Ministry of Internal Affairs. We were trying to get money for this particular home for handicapped children that we administered, and this guy had been educated and might have even lived in the United States for a while.

You'd probably think that he was fairly sophisticated and conscious and everything. But he was just as chauvinistic as anybody else. It was weird.

What word of advice would you give to white Western women travelers to Morocco?

Well, really, just make sure you are clothed well. You should cover your hair up, because if you have open and flowing hair, it is considered enticing to men; men accept just that you are trying to come on to them all the time.

For instance, I remember one night when I stayed at my friend's apartment in Casablanca. She used to live with a Moroccan boyfriend, and one of his friends was staying overnight. I was staying in the same bedroom with him. I just happened to be staying in the city on business.

This guy, it was as if he felt obligated to fuck me as if it were some kind of an accepted given. It was as if you are there, a woman, in the bedroom, so it's expected that he would have sex with you.

That's the way it is in Muslim culture?

Yes, exactly, that's what I mean.

Their women?

Oh sure. Yeah, sure. The women are just to procreate with. That's basically it. Even in the palaces: you'd see two beds, the King's bed and wherever the wife was sleeping because he would take the wife only to procreate with. You'll see a lot better relationships amongst the men than the women.

Everything is separate; the parties are separate; the eating is separate, and the women do all the work in the homes. And they don't have any modern conveniences or whatever.

The men, a lot of them, might have a business, and they'd have a little kid or several little kids — the child labor was incredible there — running their businesses in the medina, and they'll just go into the cafes in town and sit around and talk story and drink coffee all day long and pick up the ladies, and shit like that.

Then you'd have the extreme cases, like in the desert areas there, where I was. There would be people that still actually locked up their wives in houses. Well, I knew a lot of men who still had four wives. That was accepted.

Beaten in the Street

I remember one day. This was a very, very heavy experience for me. I was in the medina on a bus. I was just sitting in the bus waiting for it to get out on the street. It was all local people, no tourists or anything.

There was a woman in the street who was getting beaten up by this guy, getting the shit beaten out of her. The guy is kicking her in the head, in the crotch, just beating the shit out of this lady. This whole crowd of people stood all around just watching, and just totally accepting the whole thing. And nobody is doing anything to stop the guy from doing it.

I mean, she might have been a prostitute or she might have just been — I don't know what —maybe even the guy's wife or whatever. But it was perfectly in that guy's rights to just kick the shit out her. It was totally, socially acceptable, and you would never interfere in that kind of a situation; it's the man's right. The woman's his property type thing.

So, I was there sitting on the bus just observing the whole thing. That was a very intense experience for me because I had to practically hang on to the seat of the bus to prevent myself from running out into the crowd and doing something to help her.

I just couldn't handle the situation. It was blowing my mind, and yet, I knew that if I ran out there — if I even *said* anything to people or tried to do anything — they probably would have fucking stoned me right then and there. That's probably what their reaction would have been.

In modern-day Morocco?

Yeah. I don't know if they actually would have stoned me, but people would have likely beaten me up. They would have kicked the shit out of me because this would have been fucking with the white Christian woman interfering in something that was just totally an affair between a man and the woman that he was dealing with.

Not even another Moroccan, either. If another Moroccan got embroiled in the situation, they would just beat him up as well and simply get him out of the way, but a white, Christian woman to do that?

And Marrakesh was much more conservative than a lot of the other towns; it was more traditional, more religious and everything.

It was as if I had to hold myself back, and I was just going crazy. I remember the moment; I could barely contain myself. I just had to reason it out that this would happen, and that I had to be cool and not do anything but just watch it happen.

The little kids were brats. Total brats. Little kids would throw stones at you all the time and yell things at you. Moroccan people are pretty much schizophrenic at this point. They had been perforated by their colonial experience by the French — even though they wanted to emulate Western ways. Like they think it's real cool to dress Western style and things like that.

On the other hand, they don't respect you at all. They think all Western women are whores. There's no doubt about that.

Based on what?

Because of the hippies, all the hippies. I don't know if you know what happened in Marrakesh in the 1960s. All these hippies from all over Europe and the United States and different places came over there to score all the hashish.

I've seen films of people dancing. You'd see a group of musicians from the desert area, who'd get into these dances and everything. It's the black guys from the desert. They'd get into a fast kind of running dance. And I've seen these films of hippies that would get into dancing in those places with those people in the square, and everything.

The Moroccans would look at that, and they'd just say, "Oh, those people are whores. They have to be whores. In the first place, they are wearing these flimsy clothes. Half their bodies are not covered."

An acceptable Moroccan woman wears the veil and covers all her hair and all of her body. Just even exposing your body is obscene. It's not acceptable, and these people [the hippies] are just flaunting their whole bodies, and they're getting wasted on hashish. And, who knows; probably a lot of them did sleep with a lot of local guys that would come around to be their guides in the souks and all that.

The Moroccans just didn't understand... They never understood the true values attached to the hippie movement in California. What really that means — the freedom of living like that. They only understood a part of it. They only saw the central part of it, and that's how self-righteous and ethnocentric the Moroccans are.

So, consequently, the Moroccans don't respect people like that and they swear obscenities at them. I even had little kids, 12, 14 years old, come up to me and pinch my ass or something like that. One of these little kids would even come up and say, "Hey, I'd like to come back and fuck you," and stuff like this.

A Woman Alone in North Africa

Jeannie Kelley

The hippie era, Tetouan, Morocco, the mid-1970s. I went to Morocco. I knew I was going to like it because I'd been to the East before. I'd been to Muslim countries, where women cover themselves up. But, I'd heard stories of people who'd just been in Europe and gone down to Morocco and hated it, because of being hassled all the time.

However, I knew that this wouldn't worry me so much because I know that this is part of their way of life. I think the idea of going to Morocco by myself was exciting. So, I went down to Morocco on my own.

I think why I had such a good time is because I was doing everything that I liked to do and not having to wait around for somebody else to decide what he or she wanted to do. I went where I wanted to go; I did what I wanted to do when I wanted to. However, at times, I teamed up with people when this was beneficial for me to do.

On the way to Morocco, I got down by train to the Spanish city of Granada, where I met an American guy who was the typical sort of traveler who goes to Morocco.

If you were to ask him, "What are you going to Morocco for?" he would say, "Well, all I'm there for is the dope."

And that about summed it up in that era. There's going to be the two sorts of people you'll meet in Morocco. When I got on the boat at Algeciras, Spain for Morocco I'd look around at all the Europeans there, and most of them that I noticed were, I think, the lowest of the low of all the travelers in Europe. They'd all have red eyes because of all the dope they were smoking, and all they were in Morocco for was the dope.

I think these were the people you had to look out for and be wary of rather than the Moroccans. They'd be the ones that'd rip you off. They were the ones that'd just go about five kilometers out of Tetouan and stay there because they'd get stuck there.

And then, there were others pretty much like me: in Morocco for the adventure of it and the cultural experience.

I met these two Norwegian guys on the boat who were heading to Tetouan. We got off the boat at Ceuta, which is the Spanish port city on the coast of Morocco.

Of course, the crafty Moroccans had us all loaded on this bus for three dirham, which normally only costs two dirham. All the travelers were on this one bus together to go to Tetouan.

We got on the bus and straightaway this Moroccan guy sits down right next to me and says, "You come with me when you get off the bus?"

I said, "No, no, no, no!"

Of course, he produces this police badge. And he's one of these policemen that is the first hassle that girls can get arriving in Morocco. I brushed this one off, I guess because I was with the two Norwegian boys. Maybe I would not so easily have done this if I had been strictly on my own. I don't know. Luckily, it didn't happen to me this time, but some friends of mine went through there once and had to deal with Moroccan guys saying such things to them as, "If you don't sleep with us, we're not going to let you through our border!"

Like I said, this didn't happen to me this time, but it can and does happen. I've heard they did it quite a bit. Maybe this happens more when you are coming over Morocco's Eastern borders, but maybe not so much from the ferries coming from Spain.

I heard one horror story about one girl who went back and forth to Morocco a lot who had even been subjected to having her vagina searched! It's the sort of thing that you may have to contend with being a girl alone arriving in Morocco. Maybe these sorts of things happened in an earlier era, maybe not so much these days. I just don't know.

When we got to Tetouan and got off the bus, I met two New Zealand girls. So, I started to talk to them and suggested, "Maybe we should make some plans together because maybe staying together would make it much cheaper for all of us. So, there we were, three girls together and we were in Tetouan that first night.

Of course, we had one of these very learned little boys who knew about 20 languages come and take you around. So, we figured that we would probably save a lot of money and a lot of time if we did let him take us around and give him a dollar or so for his trouble.

Anyhow, that night we went around Tetouan together. Of course, we had our first hassles, because we were such an obvious target — three European girls together. The reason I think we got hassled a lot that night was that we looked so European: we were wearing, of course, our typical European clothes.

That's the first thing that makes you get hassled. I think if you want to avoid it, number one in an Arab country is you don't wear blue jeans; you don't wear shorts; you don't wear suggestive European clothing, but wear the dress of that country. Cover your knees.

When I went overland to India and passed through countries like Iran and Afghanistan, the women there were all covered practically from head to toe. Their whole faces are covered. Moroccan women cover their faces a little. But Iran and Afghanistan, the women were so covered up, that they simply had only these little slits for the eyes. And you had to cast your eyes down every time you'd meet a man. A woman is not allowed to look a man straight in the eye at all unless he's your husband.

I think the next time I go through any of those countries, I'd definitely wear one of those things, a *chador or burqa,* they call it, which covers up your whole face and body, because being a European woman, they won't let you near the mosques.

You'd get continually hassled by men when you are wearing European clothes, and they take you for a European woman. But my being dark, I can almost get away with it sometimes.

Also, the women, themselves, would not trust you. Being a European girl, the women of an Arab country do not like you. They think you are an evil, tart woman who has loose morals, so they don't speak to you.

The men, on the other hand, speak to you only because they think European girls sleep with just about everything.

A "Space Queen" in North Africa

Art Montoya

North Africa, 1963. An interesting event happened to me during a trip to North Africa. I went back again to Egypt. For some reason I didn't make it to Cairo this time; I got to Alexandria instead. It was a pretty cheap passage from Italy.

You get to Alexandria, and it's a pretty wide-open town, sort of like an Arabic Tijuana in a way. It was pretty basic. I'd met a German girl there. Boy, she was really something. She was quite and buxom and she really stood out if you know what I mean.

We hitchhiked and traveled across North Africa together. We went from Alexandria and on to Libya, Algeria, and Morocco. Sadly, she was not very clever. She was one of those early hippie types. She would not wear a bra — and she should have — and now she's in an Arab country! She was, according to their very restrictive standards, asking for trouble, and twice, even, she got attacked. The first time was when we were in Constantine in Algeria.

She had gone up to the room for some unknown reason with a guy who worked there at the hotel while I went out to find a newspaper in English. When I returned to the room, the guy that originally showed us the room had just ripped off her blouse and was literally in the act of attacking her! Luckily, he was a little guy and I got rid of him. He was yelling and screaming a bit, but I managed to get him out of there. We were staying in the place, and he *WORKED THERE,* if you can believe it! And yet, he attacked her right then and there, apparently without any compunction or hesitation whatsoever!

I kept telling her that she should wear a bra. She'd wear it for a while, and then she'd slip back again into her old habits.

202

There were nothing but bad vibes surrounding her. So, I decided that I just had to get her out and part ways with her. We're yelling and screaming in Spanish at each other — and somehow I got her out of there. I took her right to the airport. And all the while she was still yelling and screaming at me.

For her own good, I simply had to get her out of North Africa. So, I went through her money, bought a ticket to Malaga, Spain with it and put her on a plane. I never saw her again. I didn't ask for her name and address because I had absolutely no desire to correspond with someone like that. She was just too much of a space queen for me, so after that, I was on my own once again.

The First White Woman

Colleen Lance

M adagascar, the 1980s. I had a very funny experience once. This sort of thing had been going on for several years, and I had imagined that people were just thinking that I was some kind of wonderful or interesting or curious oddity.

Why is that?

Madagascar

I'll explain. This time, I was in the center part of Madagascar. I was with a guide, and it was on a Sunday, and we were walking through the churchyard just as the people were coming out of church.

And so, it seemed that everybody now stopped dead in their tracks, and they turned around and stared at me. Now, this is nothing new: I've seen this sort of thing happen before — I'm *very* blonde and I am *very* white. So, I was now thinking, *Oh, here we go again!*

How did that make you feel?

They were all looking at me and were all talking and whispering among themselves. And so, I asked my guide, "What are they saying?"

My guide said they're saying among themselves, "Oh, look! Look at that woman. She's so white! She's sick, and she is going to die!"

It suddenly occurred to me that maybe that's what people must have been thinking all along about me!

So, they've never seen a white person before?

Well, probably they have, but maybe not someone of quite my coloring — I'm *SO* white and am *SO* blonde as my hair was — so, no, considering that combination of skin and hair color, they haven't likely ever seen anyone quite like me.

When I was in the Trobriand Islands, too, the same thing happened to me — the children would grab my hair to try to get a handful, a sample!

What did you do?

Of course, I wanted to get out of there.

You tried to stop them?

Oh, I tried to stop them, sure. But, of course, it wasn't all that serious.
You know how children are — they just sneak up behind you and voila, I'd
(just about) get a haircut! Just kidding! (Laughs) They'd grab a sample if
they could!

How does that make you feel to be so different from everybody else?

It's kind of fun, actually.

I'm like the only woman that they've ever seen like me before.

You were somebody kind of special to them. I imagine it could be quite
fun at times.

Well, not *ALL* the time!

Afghanistan

Was that your favorite country in the world?

I thought it was the most exotic place I'd ever been. And going back to
how I looked; when I would walk around the streets, I would get so much
unwanted attention that I couldn't see what I wanted to see or go literally
anywhere without being hassled.

So, I bought myself a *burqa* (a complete clothing, covering my face,
eyes, and body). Supposedly, American and European women, you know,
complain about it, for instance, how it is so repressive and restricts your
freedom, and so on.

But I found it to be very handy.

Oh, good. Can you tell me about that a bit more? You wore that to keep
from being singled out?

Yes. I could walk around completely anonymously among the people,
and they would just keep going and doing their usual things. I could get into places and do things without attracting attention.

And, I just thought it was pretty wonderful, so, I wore it throughout
Afghanistan. However, I didn't wear it so much in Kabul, per se, because at
the time, very few women, actually, had veils on in Kabul.

Does it completely cover your face?

Oh yes; and it has a little-crocheted lace sort of thing that covers your eyes that you can look through, but close out the rest of the world. Actually, *burqas* are very comfortable. Keeps the sun off of you, too.

How did you get the idea to do that?

I saw it one day on a stand, and I thought it was such a beautiful silk *burqa*. So, I bargained with the guy. I never buy anything when I'm traveling unless I can bargain for it. And I got it for only ten bucks!

Every Western woman should buy one!

Just ten bucks?

Uh huh.

Wow!

What was his beginning price?

I can't remember.

So, you always bargain, huh?

Oh yeah.

What's the rough percentage that you wind up paying from the starting prices?

I usually start with at least 40 percent off.

And then wind up where?

Sometimes I get it for what I've originally offered. Other times they don't budge, and then I do my famous "walk away" routine.

What is the "walk away routine?"

The "walk away" is when I turn around and just walk out of their store!

And they usually call me back and accept my final price. (Laughs)

That way you can walk away and say "no thanks," or they are quite happy to get the sale.

No Fear!
Part 1:
The Warnings

Sandra Kessler

Cairo, Egypt, 1968. I'm Sandra Kessler (an assumed name). The way I got to Egypt is kind of interesting. I lived in Rome for a year, and a friend of mine came over from New York and wanted to get married to me.

Rome

That I was kind of running away is how I got to Egypt, because I didn't want to get married, and I thought I'd always been interested in Egyptian art. I love Egyptian art. And the pyramids and such fascinated me, and I had studied a lot about Egypt.

And I said, "Why don't I go to Egypt?" Because I had been to a lot of places already. So, I went to apply for a visa in Rome, and the first thing they said to me was, "You're going alone? You can't go alone; you're a woman."

They gave me 25 things I could or could not do, and "you have to stay here or here. There are only four first-class hotels that are safe for you, and you can't go there, etc., etc."

And my answer to them was simply this: "I'm from New York! Are you crazy? I'm not afraid of <u>anything</u>!"

White Slavery

That is until I arrived in Cairo!

Okay. Stop for a second. Could you go into specifics about some of the other things they warned you about? Anything in particular?

Oh, it was predominantly the white slavery thing. Even at the visa department!

Tell me a little about that.

What they said was, "We don't know if you've heard about the white slavery situation, but we'd like to warn you that in Egypt — especially

Cairo, Alexandria and other parts of Egypt — the situation is extremely dangerous for a woman alone. And they would easily drop something in your drink, or whatever.

If someone gets turned on by you, particularly, you'll be taken into white slavery — and so, it's best for me to be in Saudi Arabia, instead, but definitely not Egypt.

I was amazed to hear this from them. First of all, I said I'm not their type because they already have my type in Egypt. I knew from my uncle, who had lived in Europe 20 years; I had already been warned about white slavery and so on.

Furthermore, I said. "They love Danish women, Swedish women, and women from Texas to Delaware. And that's what I know for a fact."

"Women from *Texas*?" they asked in disbelief.

"Yeah, they love them. They love women from Texas. They love those southern belles with blonde hair."

I said, "Wait, you know they're not gonna look at me because I look like an Italian. I could pass for an Italian," (Which I often did). I had long dark hair, and I was tanned. Nobody would bother me.

Finally, they said, "Listen. Just be very, very careful."

But that was, I would say, the strongest message they gave me — the white slavery situation.

You just pooh-pooed it, huh?

Exactly! You got that right. I don't know; I must be nuts. But wait until I tell you the whole story, what trouble I got myself into.

And then there are other things that I shouldn't go into. (Laughs)

In Rome, they actually gave me a map of Cairo. I mean, it was incredible, and you know like "stay in this district and only stay at the Sheraton, the Hilton or Marriott," etc.

I looked at them in total amazement; I said, "Listen, I've traveled all over the world since I was 16!"

"This is different, this is different!"

And these guys, one was Italian, and the other was Egyptian. I mean, so it wasn't that it was just an Italian telling me this. These two were the real deal!

This Egyptian guy even gave me names of people, like if I ever should happen to meet so and so, stay away from him, and so on. It was amazing. In fact, I still have the names in my book; I'll never forget it.

So, I wasn't really concerned at all, because that's my nature. But having said that, to be very honest, the first time in my entire life that I was frightened was when *I GOT TO CAIRO!*"

Cairo

Why is that?

Well, I arrived in Cairo. I didn't listen to them, of course, so I didn't make any reservations at any hotel. And, I got to the airport — I don't think it's the same now — but when I was there it was a heavy-duty security check — maybe they were looking for a drug smuggler, I don't know.

And so, I arrive in Cairo and I went through, not just me, everyone did; we waited in line to have our bags checked. I didn't get out of the airport for another six hours! They checked every piece of jewelry I had; they checked all my money; everything. It was incredible. As I said, I don't know if maybe at that particular time they were doing that. I never found that out — well, actually I did. I ended up with someone who was actually the general manager of the international airport at that time, and he said that's the way it normally is, but that was 1968. So you know, I don't think it's that way any longer.

Were you getting frightened at that point?

Oh no, not at all.

It's when I left the baggage area and went to get a taxi that I started becoming frightened, because the people — it was almost like in India — I'm sure that you've been to India — It was, well, you know, people, men, coming up to you and women begging, and just aggressive men coming and saying "my name is so and so," and on and on. It was scary. It was non-stop. They were so intense and agitated.

I then got into a cab and said I wanted to go to the Sheraton.

What made them seem scary to you? The Egyptians, when you first went in there?

Their eyes, you know, were very scary. They'd just look at you like you're totally nude. I felt like, *Do I have my clothes on or what?*

Especially if you were alone.

As I said, I keep stressing 1968, because I don't know if it's different now, but I know from some other women who have been there a few years ago, it was still that way. I don't know about going through the airport and the security checks, but they said it was still that way.

Anyway, we get to all the hotels, and they are all fully booked! I get to the last hotel, the Hilton, and at that point it's midnight, and I'm going, "Do you have a room for me?"

And the guy simply shakes his head "No."

I say, "You've got to be joking!"

He says, "I'm sorry; we're all booked up."

I say, "Please, you've got to have a room for me. I've got to stay at this hotel."

And you know, he could see in my eyes that I really was absolutely terrified and that I really needed his help.

So, he goes, "Let me check my other hotel just across the street — also another Hilton, right on the Nile."

He then says, "You're in luck! We do happen to have a room for you; it's first class; it's wonderful, and you've got it!"

So, I go across the street, and I am thrilled because it is right on the Nile River. It doesn't get any better than that. It is just wonderful.

Sandra's story continues next: *No Fear! Part 2* — a tale of unbelievable international intrigue, love, sex, and romance, kidnapping and white slavery in Egypt and the Middle East.

No Fear!
Part 2:
The Arab Middle East

Sandra Kessler

———◦———

Cairo, Egypt, 1968. I'm Sandra Kessler (an assumed name). The next day, at the Hilton I'm sitting at the bar having a drink. Egyptian men of importance, or who have some class, do not themselves come over and personally say, "Hi, my name is so and so." They usually send over people who work for them. An Arabic man comes over to me and says, "So and so would like to buy you a drink."

The Egyptians

And I start immediately arguing with him, saying, "Well, why can't he ask me himself?" One thing, Egyptian men do not have any sense of humor AT ALL! You can forget it! It is incredible.

I look over, and I have never been attracted to that type of dark man before. I have always been partial to blondes and blue-eyes. But Egyptian men and women can be absolutely the most magnificent-looking people. There are not that many beautiful and good-looking ones, however, but this man happens to be very good looking.

And so, I agree to join him for a drink, but the funny thing is, I couldn't just get up and go sit with him or vice-versa; we both had to exit and come back in again. It was the strangest thing. They are very old-fashioned about a woman simply getting up and joining them. So, in accordance with custom, we actually had to actually leave the hotel and come back in again.

Thus, the courier-man says, "Well, no; he will wait for you outside."

Well, we did this ritual and we both actually came right back in.

He wasn't used to a Western woman apparently, especially a business-woman as aggressive as I am. He was involved in politics. He was fascinated with me. I went on and on in our conversation. I would listen very carefully to what he said, too, because I, of course, wanted to learn about his culture.

Next, we were having a fabulous dinner upstairs in the hotel, but he still wasn't used to my being a Western woman. He would stop me and say, "How could you travel alone? How could you do this? How could you do that?"

Anyway, at the end of the dinner, he said to me, "Look, I would very much like to invite you to a very special dinner tomorrow evening. But there are two things: one you must wear Egyptian garb and the veil."

Great! I thought it would be fabulous: sexy and wonderful.

"And the other thing is," he said, "You cannot speak. Women do not speak at these functions."

And I'm thinking, *Oh, my God, now I'm in trouble! That'll be it!*

I said, "Well, of course, I'll do it!

After dinner, we go shopping for the headdress. He said that because I have the dark eyes and am so tan, and so on, and because I have long dark hair and such, I did look somewhat Egyptian.

The next evening, according to plan, he picks me up and we get there. But what he does not tell me was that this dinner was for the then-president of Egypt, Anwar Sadat!

And I can tell you right now; it was *THE* most magnificent dinner I have ever been at. These well-heeled Egyptian people have money and live better than anyone else in the world, even in America!

What was the dinner like?

The dinner was phenomenal. First of all, the setting itself: everything was gold. There were 50 couples — and I remember, because I counted them — all assembled in this magnificent room, which was filled with Rembrandts, Monets, Renoirs. It was a private room that they used exclusively for government functions. It was all Egyptian; there were some French people, though, but there were no Americans. This was very interesting.

And I think that's the other reason that he wanted me to shut my mouth because what if they found out I was American!

I felt awkward. I did not know how to deal with or eat with the veil on. And I really didn't know any of the customs. I mean, I had heard about women being second-class citizens, and so on, but I really didn't know a lot about it and, especially, how to be one!

I am very nervous; I have absolutely no confidence at all. I am worried, thinking, *What if they find out I'm an American — maybe I'll be beheaded!*

You know, things go through your head, right? But, of course, it wasn't like that at all! So, we sit down, and it's like a high school dance: all the women are on one side, and; all the men are on the other.

And there is this one incredibly sexy man at the end of the table (who I will tell you more about later — it was because of him that I spent nearly four-and-one-half months in Egypt!)

So, I, of course, am observing very carefully. The men come in first, and they toast. And then the women come in, and they toast as well. And then the men start to eat, followed by the women. I was so very nervous that, to be honest, I hardly ate and I hardly drank, because I was such a nervous wreck.

Unfortunately, I don't speak French very well, but I do understand a little, so I am able to make out some of the French dialog. There is no English spoken, however, so I really am unable to tell you much of what the dinner conversation consists of.

My friend explained to me later what they were discussing, which was essentially political and what's going on in the world, and so on. In fact, they are discussing Germany and France but not America at all. It is a private dinner for President Sadat, so it isn't some official political occurrence.

What was President Sadat like?

Wonderful. He is without a doubt — fortunately, I got to meet him later on at another occasion — one of the most charming, charismatic men I have ever met in my life. Absolutely fascinating. I cannot keep my eyes off of him as well as this one other man seated at the end of the table.

Where were you seated vis-à-vis the President?

Unfortunately, I was not as close to him as I would have liked to have been. I was about in the center of the table.

You didn't talk to him?

No, not right then and there, not that evening. However, I did meet him at a later time through this man at the end of the table, which I will tell you about.

Anyway, the evening progresses; it goes on for over four hours or so.

I begin playing with this man, with my eyes, who is alone at the end of the table. And he is playing, too. He is an Omar Sharif type, maybe the sexiest man I have ever met in my life. I mean, twice personified! I'm glad this worked out very well.

Anyway, by the end of the evening, the men go into one room, and the women go into another for dessert, and brandy and cigars for the men.

Just before we depart into these two incredible rooms, this man with whom I've been flirting, whose name is "Choekre," now comes up to me and says in perfect English — and is the scary part: to this day I do not know how he found out about me; maybe he could tell by the way I was moving the veil? — he says to me, "I will pick you up at your hotel tomorrow at noon."

That's it. That's all he said.

Oh my God, how does he know, I am wondering? I am really excited, though. This is incredible.

I go in with the women, and we have dessert, and so on. And then, of course, I am taken back to my hotel. The man I came with is very polite and says, "You made a very good impression. People were asking who you are, and so on."

I observed that no one looked you in the eye. Nobody ever made eye contact with you. One Egyptian woman, however, did speak English with me, and I did have a very good conversation with her albeit a brief one. That's when I got comfortable speaking English. However, she seemed a bit frightened or reticent to talk to me, so, I didn't really get much of anything out of her.

I was, of course, fairly expressive, much more than most of the women, who simply sat there and said nothing.

So, I returned to the hotel, and the next day I get all dressed up. It's exactly at noon, and I am seemingly dressed to kill.

And as I'm walking through the lobby — and I'll never forget this — people are looking at me, because they knew who he was. I was wondering why they were staring at me and giving me these odd looks.

"Choukre"

They know that he is picking me up, so they know who he is, but I still do not even know his name! I do not normally take chances like this. And I would not normally even think twice about it, but this is Egypt after all! I've been warned. Anything goes, and; anything can happen.

But, I really want to take a chance, because I am so attracted to this man. It is like; *I'm going to take my chances.*

Of course, anyone who's anyone in Egypt has a Mercedes, so I climb into this fabulous Mercedes 600. I start to say something to him. He still doesn't tell me who he is, or his name or anything. He simply says, "I would like you to listen to this tape."

We're driving. He puts the tape into the player. It's a tape of women professing their love for him. I understand a little Italian and French.

There seems to be a number of languages on it, and I can get the gist of it. It's really hard-core breathing — a sex tape, *NO LESS!* You wouldn't believe it. I'm just sitting there in total disbelief. We're driving outside of Cairo, and I'm going, *God, what am I doing. I'm really getting myself into a situation.*

What's going through my mind is, *Okay, as soon as I get to wherever we're going...*

I had a razor blade that I was carrying around. Honest to God, all I thought about was, *Oh my goodness, I'm getting myself into a situation now. If I have to use it, I'll use it.*

This is the sort of thing going on in my mind at this point. I'm thinking, *This tape, My God; this guy is a real sexual pervert! I don't know, I mean, who plays this kind of a sex tape? Right after meeting you. And he doesn't even tell you his name!*

What is on this tape?

Lots of heavy breathing. And the woman is saying, "I love you, Choukre," and, "I miss you," and, "You are the best!"

One of them is a woman from Australia because I lived in Australia, so I know the accent. I am thinking, *Oh my God, I never knew that Australian women could say things like that*!

It is all very personal.

Anytime I start to say something, he interrupts me and says, "I want you to pay <u>complete</u> attention to this."

We are driving about 25 minutes outside Cairo. We get to this incredible house. Totally empty. Twenty-eight rooms. I went all through it later. I am thinking, *Oh my God, this is it! My life is over!*

I am very scared.

How am I going to escape?

Then he says, "Have a seat." And he puts on this fabulous music. I happen to love Middle Eastern music. Then gives me this strange drink. I am not about to drink it, of course. I am too afraid to drink it. There are plants all over the place, so, when I see that he isn't looking, I throw it quickly into one of the plants.

He comes in, honest to God, with this beautiful, magnificent white silk robe and says, "Take your clothes off and put this on. And I will be back. And drink this tea."

I do.

This is the difficult part of the story. People always ask me, "Why did you do it?"

I did do it. I did take my clothes off, because I guess I was semi-frightened, thinking, *What will he do to me if I don't do that?*

And then, I was also very attracted to him. I thought, *Well, whatever. What can I do?*

I mean, at this point, what can I do? I'm thinking, *Where can I go? There are no taxicabs out where I am. There is not a house within two miles. What can I do?*

He comes back. And, he starts talking to me.

I say, "I want to know a little about you."

I don't want to get him angry that he might turn on me or something.

So, he gives me an approximately 25-minute speech. He is saying he is so and so. He's 30 years old. He's the general manager of the international airport in Cairo. And, get this: he says he will be the best lover I've ever had in my entire life. But, he doesn't want me to fall in love with him. Many women have. As these tapes seem to prove — if these tapes were, in fact, legitimate. But I know they were.

He continues, "I have never loved a woman but my mother. But I love women in a different way. I've never been 'in love' with a woman. I'll treat you marvelously. I want you to spend time with me. We are obviously attracted to each other."

On and on and on he goes.

I'm sitting there thinking to myself, *This is incredible. I can't believe this guy's for real.*

At the end of all this, and, literally, it was about a 25-minute speech, I stop him with all these little typical New York innuendos and jokes. But he does not laugh; he does not like this at all. He didn't think any of it was funny.

For instance, I tell him that I actually went out with Omar Sharif once, and he was very charming.

All of a sudden, the next thing I know... I did not drink; I did not smoke... nothing. I was totally straight. I never met a man like this in my entire life. I have never met a more hypnotic man in my life. He had this sexual prowess about him.

Next thing I know, I am in one of the bedrooms. He definitely is not only one of the best lovers I've ever had in my whole life — he is definitely *THE* best lover I've ever had in my life! He was right! And this is why I stayed with him for nearly four-and-a-half months!

I guess he really knows women. I mean, the man just studies women. He's dedicated to women. I can tell you that right now. He loves pleasing women. The way he treats women. He's incredibly dynamic.

I wound up living with him. I'm a very independent woman; I've always been my own woman; I've always paid my own way. I've always made my own money. The first two months I spent in another hotel, which was less expensive because I didn't have the money I have now.

And, of course, I wanted to pay my own way with him, even though he insisted on paying. But I saw him every night. I ended up with him every night. He worked as the general manager of the international airport.

We went to parties; we went to places that only an Egyptian or someone in a high position could go to. This was approximately six weeks after the night that I met him at the first dinner party.

Some of the homes I went to were magnificent. The homes I saw in Egypt were incredible. I saw Egypt as a queen. I would always wear Egyptian garb when I was with him. Western wear in the daytime. And, even during the daytimes, if it was an important Egyptian function that I was going to, it would be Egyptian wear.

People knew you were running around with him, obviously. Were you treated kind of like an equal? In a Western sense? Were you treated like a queen, maybe?

No. Not at all.

I was treated as a woman in Egypt, which is not as an equal. The men are the kings still. Maybe, I am treated a little bit better than the typical Egyptian women, I will say. Because they got to know me and respect me, some of the men, a little bit better. I could see that they treated me a little differently.

And the men at parties would make a little bit more of an effort to seek me out, whereas they wouldn't be that way with the Egyptian women. I was a little more special, maybe because I looked Egyptian somewhat. They knew me as an independent businesswoman, from hearing stories about me. So, it was very interesting how they did treat me.

Anwar Sadat, *Again*

Again, about meeting President Sadat again... At this one party, which was, again, a private party, also with a number of government officials, I went up to President Sadat during the course of the evening. Unfortunately, I didn't have a chance to speak with his wife. I was very happy that I had the opportunity to meet him, though.

I say to him, "I don't think you remember, but I was at your dinner on such and such date, and I was very honored because I was the only American there. And Choekre brought me to this party as a guest, and so I am very honored because I know that not that many Americans get invited to be here.

And he says, "I definitely do remember you."

And this is very interesting and stunning, actually: He describes the actual color of the dress that I had on! So, I think he must have remembered because I had on this really rich ruby dress. I don't think he was giving me bullshit about that.

I say, "What made you remember me? I don't think that I looked that much different from most of the other women that were there."

He says, "Oh yes I do! It was your eyes!"

I am thinking, *You are some Devil!*

And we continue to have our little conversation. I think he was very interested in me as a person, maybe as a female. I can see that he is definitely into women. And I explain to him exactly what happened and how I met Choekre.

I ask him, "Well, can you tell me a little more about Choekre?"

He says, "He's a fascinating man, but just don't get too involved."

That's exactly what he said.

I say, "I'm not. But, we are having a wonderful time. And I plan to leave Egypt shortly. And while I am here, I am thrilled to be with a man like Choekre."

Again, he says, "I can understand that, but just don't get too involved."

That he says that to me twice, I am thinking, *I had better listen to him!*

I start asking him a question about the government, but unfortunately, at that point, we get interrupted by one of his aides and he is taken away. I never spoke to him again after that. But I was really thrilled to have met him and talked with him. And, when I tried to speak with his wife, unfortunately, this did not work out.

And Choekre later said to me, "You are the only women that I've ever met that actually ever approached him (Sadat) and spoke with him, and spoke to him for such a long time."

But that's not the way you should handle the situation. Choekre thought that it was very improper, but he thought I had a lot of guts to do it! "And I'm glad you did!"

That's why hardly anyone gets to speak to the women at parties because it's just the Egyptian way that women simply would never go up to him like that. He said women would never go up to men aggressively like I did. So, he really got a kick out of it.

The interesting thing is that Choekre got introductions to his mother. And no one ever meets his mother. But that was an honor because I know from what people told me, not many people ever meet his mother, and I was invited to meet his mother. Choekre's mother was very much loved and very well known around Egypt.

We went to Alexandria, which is where she was from. It was incredible. I could just see that she was looking at me and probably thinking, *This is the second time my son has ever brought a woman to meet me.*

I was never in love with this Choekre, ever. But I was very turned on to him physically. From the moment he gave me that speech, I was determined in my mind that he fall in love with me. It was crazy. I can't explain it. It was like because I heard all these women on the tape. He was charming and sexy. Everything about him. And that was one of my goals.

Of course, he brought me everywhere. I went to incredible art exhibits. We went riding camels through the desert, which I'm sure a lot of people who go to Egypt do. We camped out. In the evenings we went to the pyramids. Things like that. I'm sure other people do these things, sure. It was all very fascinating.

The Airline Pilot

Another thing was really scary. About a month after I met him, after three months that I was there, we were at another party. This man came in, 6 foot 2, one of the most handsome, beautiful men I have ever seen in my life. I found out later that he was Indian, and I never met an Indian who looked like that. This man was very light skinned, very handsome, a gorgeous guy.

It so happened to be Choekre's best friend. He was a captain with Air India. The minute he walked in, it was like "holy crap!" And Choekre picked up on this, obviously. Later on, in the course of the evening, he and I made this lunch date.

I knew that Choekre was supposed to be working for about three or four days. He would work and take off with me, and so on. He worked a lot. When Choekre was not available, I would do my own thing.

I usually got followed, by the way. That was another thing. So, we (the Indian and I) had to be very careful with wherever we met, and so on. I had to be very careful, too, that I wasn't followed by one of Choekre's bodyguards.

So, we made a luncheon date, and we thought we were being very careful. I was in the restaurant for only six minutes and Choekre walks right into this restaurant with a gun in his pocket.

And there's his best friend, and he points the gun at him and said, "If you ever... my woman again" — (that's how they are; they are very possessive) — "I will *kill* you!"

We're in a public restaurant; he takes his gun out and points it right at him. The Indian leaves the restaurant immediately. There are no ifs, ands, or buts about it...

I never saw the man again. In fact, I wrote to Air India to try to write to him. He wrote me back once a year after that.

To this day, I am still frightened that maybe Choekre will get that letter and find out and still be after me. It's amazing. After that all, lot of people said to me, "I'm surprised he didn't try to hurt you (me), because that's the way they normally would react. And I was really surprised, too. But I think maybe Choekre had to know that maybe I was a different type of woman. And that I would never ever stand for any man laying a hand on me. Honestly, I don't know if he felt that way or not. I would leave immediately. Maybe he felt that.

So, we went on.

Was he hurt by that?

Yes, but he didn't really show it. But I could tell the difference in him. Yeah, he was hurt. I had lunch with him. We never discussed it afterwards. He never said anything. He wouldn't discuss it. I tried to force it, but he wouldn't talk about it.

And also, another thing was interesting. He asked me a lot of questions about myself. But he never asked about America. He had traveled a great deal in Europe and Asia, but he had never been to America. And he was a very wise man. He was a very politically-involved person and very knowledgeable. He wasn't some idiot.

But he never asked me questions about America or other things. I tried to discuss politics with him, but he wouldn't discuss it with me at all. I think it was because I was a woman, pure and simple. I think he just could not accept that he could sit down and discuss politics or business or anything with a woman. It was that basic.

So, after the restaurant and gun affair, it was a little bit different between him and me; it just wasn't the same for us after that.

I was getting mentally ready to leave,.

No Fear!
Part 3
The Beginning of the End

Sandra Kessler

I guess it was the beginning of the end for Choekre and me. A week or two before I left — because I didn't know I was actually going to leave (which I'll tell you about in a second) — I decided that I wanted to go back to the hotel and stay there. I'm not used to living with a man, which I wasn't. I was always on my own. I was kind of mentally preparing myself to go.

The Saudis

He knew you were leaving, right?

I don't know if he did or not, but I think he suspected I knew, especially when I made the move back to the hotel.

So, he comes to my hotel one evening at about 6:30 and he says, "Sandra, I will send your luggage to Beirut; you've got to get on a boat in 20 minutes!"

I was thinking of leaving, but my God, not this way!

Suddenly, he says, "Get in the car with me right now. I'm sending your luggage ahead. Just get in the car with me right now! Get your passport. Leave your bags where they are."

He goes on and on, and I'm listening to what he is trying to say to me.

We're driving to the boat. And I say, "What the hell happened?"

He said, "Remember the party we were at? (Just the other day) Do you remember the man? He was very old. He was like 77 years old?

I said, "Yes, I do remember him."

"Remember he said hello to me, but he didn't respond to you? Well, that man wants to take you to Saudi Arabia. And I can tell you right now;

the man has the money and the power to do it. And if you don't get on this boat, that's it!"

So, he gets me on the boat to Beirut.

What did he say about it?

Well, to be honest, I didn't say very much for about five minutes, because I just sat there, and for the first time in my life, I was simply dumbfounded and speechless.

I then said to him, "Can you tell me anything more about this?"

I just kept asking questions.

He says, "I can't say anything except just trust me."

He just looks me in the eyes and says, "I think you know me well enough to be able to trust me at this point. I don't want you to go. Someday, I want to meet you somewhere. But you've got to get out of here right now and get on this boat or there's no saving you. I cannot save you with all my power and influence. I cannot save you!"

And that was it. That was basically it.

I got to the boat. I was so frightened because I knew this man had saved my life. And he had. I knew he had.

I said, "How did you find out?"

One of his close bodyguards told Choekre that this was going to happen. They were going to abduct me with a gun. They didn't have to put a mickey in my drink. And that's how he knew that this was going to happen. That's why the only way he could save me was to get me out on a boat. He was worried at the Airport they could have connections with airlines, and that's why I couldn't get on an airplane. That's why he was worried it wouldn't be a good idea to try to get out that way.

I ask, "Why can't I fly out?"

"The boat is the only way you will have to do it. And I will ship you your luggage."

He wrote me a beautiful love note.

We talked since, but I have never seen the man since then. First of all, I would never go back to Cairo alone, because I was really frightened.

I could tell that he did not want me to know anything more about this man.

He said, "You can't get hurt by what you don't know." Something like that. I cannot remember exactly how he put it. "You don't want to know. Don't ask me any further questions."

"Choekre, I don't understand. I am not their type."

"I can't tell you except that the man really likes you." That's all he said to me. "The man really likes you."

"Why?"

He said, "I don't know. He knew something about you because of the parties I've been taking you to."

I know there's another person that works for this older man that had seen you around and asked about you. And he wanted you. Don't ask me what it was. He just wanted you. God only knows why. I certainly don't understand, either, what it was.

I asked, "What would they have done to me, do you think?"

"You just probably would have been one of his many, many women. And he would use you for whatever sexual purposes."

In retrospect, where does that leave you now? I've met many women who travel alone. Especially blondes. They really have to be so careful, because it happens. I know for a fact it happens. So many women disappear every year, and nobody ever hears about it?

I know this from my uncle who has lived in New York for 20 years. Some of these people in the Middle East can find out if these girls have families or if not, or if they are orphans or whatever. And a lot of times when they find out about them — and they can pretty easily — it's the women who don't have families, they can track that down, so nobody is missing. Okay, they disappeared, so what?

From my experiences, from people who have told me about this, they usually find these women in Europe. There are a lot of European women that disappear. You'd be surprised. They find out, like the mafia. How they find out is they have their connections in America.

Choukre kept warning me, "If you don't leave in 20 minutes on that boat, you will probably disappear this evening!"

My hope in relating this to you is that if my experience can help women out there, maybe even if just one woman I can help to save, I'll be very happy.

Even after all this, I would have still gone to Egypt. I would have stayed in a hotel instead of living with an Egyptian man, I guess.

Beirut

What can you tell me about Beirut?

I get to Beirut. I can tell you I was the most scared that I have ever been in my entire life. I was only able to stay a few days. Beirut was such a beautiful exciting city, but I was not there to go around and party. I was, in essence, running for my life! I was just going to stay a few days and think about what had just happened to me.

Were you relieved to be out of Cairo?

Oh, my God, yeah!

But being in Beirut, it wasn't frightening at all. It was much more European and cosmopolitan than Cairo. It was kind of comparable to San Francisco, I would say. Basically, I just wanted to see the sights a bit, to stay a few days, and head back to Rome.

The Libyans

So, I'm there for about a day. And I'm soaking in some sun. I'm walking around the city, and I go to this coffee shop. I'm sitting in the coffee shop having an espresso. A very polite, very humble, very shy guy, a very nice-looking guy comes up to me. He's sitting at the next table and he invites me to have a coffee with him.

Even at that, I really do not want to have anything to do with any men in the Middle East. What I am looking for are American men! Maybe European men, French or German, or whatever, but NOT anything to do with Middle Eastern men! I mean, I was NOT looking for any of that! But still, I do not want to appear rude.

He says, "It's all right! It's all right!"

He chats away, telling me that I remind him of someone, I guess, maybe his ex-girlfriend, or whatever. He doesn't really probe. He's trying to find out about my hobbies, seemingly innocuous stuff. I mean, he is so sweet and so shy.

Then he says to me, "You know, I really don't know you, but I would very much like it if you would come home and meet my parents and have lunch with me.

And I'm thinking, *Oh, God! Just what I need, right?*

And I say, "No, absolutely NOT! Absolutely NOT!"

He asks, "Why not?"

I say, "I've just been through a very heavy experience." (I don't tell him ANYTHING.) "I just want a few days just to be by myself."

But he presses on about what happened to me.

So, he is now about to leave, and he writes down and leaves me his phone number.

The next day, I'm at the pool. And, here he comes, because he knows where I am staying because I mentioned it during the course of our conversation the day before.

And he's sitting there talking. He says, "I just thought *maybe* you changed your mind about lunch."

And I know you are going to think I am totally insane, but somehow, after all I went through, right? There was something so totally convincing about this guy. It seemed harmless.

He says, "Well, look, it would be lovely to meet my parents and have a nice lunch, that's all."

It was like so innocent, so convincing. And so, I go with him. I must be out of my mind!

Wait until you hear the rest of this! It gets worse! (Or better?)

He says, "When we get to the house, if you don't want to go in, we'll turn right back around and I'll drive you right back, I promise."

I get to this house. His parents are beautiful, incredible people! Very striking, very elegant. We're having lunch. We're having a fabulous service. It was a fabulous house. We were speaking English. They spoke several languages. Very educated people. They do not ask me a lot of questions. They are mainly telling me a little bit about the country because I want to know more about Lebanon.

I go into the garden — they had a fabulous garden. His father says, "May I speak to you alone?"

I say, "Fine."

So, we go into a library — a magnificent library. And I swear to you, here's what happened: Americans simply cannot comprehend this. How can this be — one unbelievable thing right after the other?

He sits down and says, "My son would like to marry you!" He looks me straight in the eyes.

I say, "Excuse me, sir, I mean, but I don't want to be rude, but I have to tell you. First of all, I've just met your son. I've talked to him maybe only two hours and including today maybe another two hours. I don't know him at all. I am an American. I live in New York. I'm a career woman. I don't know him. I mean he's a very nice man. I think I like him."

I'm going on and on.

And he says, "I really respect you, but my son wants to marry you. He continues, "My son is a Prince of Libya!"

I say, "Oh, that's nice! That's interesting."

I am certainly flattered.

I say, "Look, I'm an American citizen. I'm on my way to Rome."

He continues, "I will fly your parents in for the wedding."

This is what he's actually telling me. I mean, I can hardly believe my ears!

"My son was in love once with a woman who looks very much like you. She was a woman, and you are a girl."

Evidently, she was not a virgin! They are very strict about marrying virgins. And they test them for virginity.

I am so in shock.

"You would be a very free person. You would have all the freedom. You could go to America. Whatever you want. He is explaining how I would live and is mapping out my future married life with his son. I would be the number one wife, but, of course, there would be other women involved.

Then, at that point, I realized that there was absolutely nothing I could say to him because what only mattered to him was to make his son happy.

I say, "I'm quite shocked and I'm quite honored, but I must go back to my hotel and sleep on it now. I'm very exhausted; I just came in from Egypt. Can I go back now?"

He says, "We will meet you tomorrow. We will have a car pick you up at noon. And we will make plans."

I said, "That's wonderful. That's fine!"

The American

The first thing I do when I get back to the hotel is I'm desperately looking for an American. I go to the hotel desk and say, "I have to speak to an American."

Further, I ask, "Do you know *ANY* Americans who are staying at this hotel?"

He replies, "Well, I have got to look at the guest list."

I say, "This is urgent!"

Why were you scared?

I figured that if this sort of thing can happen to me in Egypt, then this guy can probably keep me in the country. And I knew he would. I had to get out that very night — or even early the next morning if need be! I didn't even want to take a chance. So, I see this guy walking in. I KNEW he was an American.

I say, "Are you an American? You've got to help me. You've got to get me out of here! My name is Sandra. I can't explain it to you."

I am so lucky. He works for the airport in Beirut! He is a mechanic or something. He gets me on a flight to Rome *THAT NIGHT!* A private flight. Not a regular flight. I start to explain the whole thing to him. "I've got to get out of here!"

He totally comprehends. He says, "I've lived here for two years. And I know what you are saying. I am going to get you out!"

Now, this (at the time of the interview) is about 10 years later. In retrospect, what do you think would have happened to you? Do you think you were caught up in a panic of the moment? What do you think the reality of it all was?

I checked with other people afterward. And they said that this guy, the Prince's father, was for real. They said that I was fortunate that I even got out. Or maybe I would have had a good life. I don't know. I don't think I would have been a slave or anything. I don't think it would have been white slavery or anything like that, though. I think I would have just been the wife of this person. But who would want that? I certainly didn't want that. Maybe some other Americans would do that. I could have. But I like to do my own thing.

I would say those two experiences really frightened me.

What was the lesson you learned there?

Well, not really anything specific, except that it could conceivably have wound up being a very positive thing. It all depends on how you view it.

Well, as you look back, what about the warnings they gave you in Rome about Egypt before you went there?

Well, possibly it was true because, knowing some of the people who I met in the four-and-a-half months, they said that these women's lives could have been all messed up.

Right from the start, you put yourself right in the right space, didn't you?

Yeah, exactly.

So, that would never have happened to you.

Right. That's it. You got it. You hit it. That's a good point. Whereas, the other people didn't.

Nope. They fell right into it.

I'd like to go back again one day.

But I imagine you do not use those amazing classic phrases you were using at the outset of all this when you were talking to those guys in Rome: "I'm from New York! Are you crazy? I'm not afraid of <u>anything</u>!"

'Young and Stupid' in Cabo

Vanessa Collier

Cabo, Mexico, 2001. I had a slight emergency situation that arose when I was feeling sick and I left my friends at a bar in Cabo. I was trying to get a taxi to get back to the hotel. I was followed by a man who was trying to sell me drugs or trying to date me, or whatever. And it immediately became a concern to me, and so, I was trying to get away from him.

I tried at first to tell him in Spanish that I had a husband, but he essentially told me he didn't care. So, I started to run down a couple of streets trying to get away from him. And then I ended up getting a cab. I was kind of panicked. I told the cab driver what happened, and he tried to comfort me and he took me back to my hotel. It was a scary experience.

Did he actually run after you?

Yeah, he had literally run after me for a few blocks. Obviously, I didn't know where I was going, but he sure knew where HE was going. I just so happened to intersect with a cab at the right time and the right place and just jumped right in and we drove off. How lucky was that?

What would have happened if there were no cabs at the right time and the right place? Now, in retrospect, how might you have dealt with that differently than you did?

I probably would have just waited for my friends, made one of them go back with me, or tried to catch a cab right outside where I was instead of wandering off looking for one.

But, I guess part of it was that I wanted to look around a bit at some of the nightlife. They have some really late taco stands, and I was hungry. So, I wanted to just wander around a bit, because I'm kind of a night person, and it's the sort of thing I would normally do back in the States.

Was that at the time when you were sick still?

Yeah, I was still feeling sick, but not so sick that it was really an issue for me. I just figured it was 'traveling sickness' of some sort and nothing too severe, but I definitely was still a bit under the weather.

Did you feel like you were more vulnerable, therefore, when that guy was harassing you?

Oh, definitely. And it really became apparent that I was kind of a stupid American tourist, and I had underestimated what I was up against in terms of language ability, and such. And also that their police system is very different from ours. I became very much aware, as a consequence, that I was a very vulnerable young American girl.

And I won't repeat that again.

Two very valuable lessons there.

Another thing: we were walking around the outskirts of Cabo, and the locals were all very much aware that we were American girls, so they were trying to sell us all sorts of stuff. But, the scariest and most depressing thing I saw was — what had to be — probably a seven- or eight-year-old girl trying to sell us drugs — cocaine or marijuana. And she had no adult around her, whatsoever; she was completely off on her own. She was really way too young, certainly by our standards, to be on her own doing that sort of thing. And so, it was a good reminder of the status of the real Mexico, versus the sort of tourist-sheltered Mexico where we were staying. It was a stark reminder to other people traveling that even the so-called 'safe' tourist destinations are not necessarily that, especially when you're young and stupid as we were.

Chased in New Delhi

Jamie Grimaldi

New Delhi, India, 1970. I was in my early 20s and I was walking along a main street in New Delhi. I had just turned right onto another main street and was about to make another right down an alleyway.

Just as I was turning into the pathway, a black car suddenly pulled right up in front of me, screeching to a sudden halt — they were obviously going too fast. I heard two doors swing open and these two men jumped out of the car.

I could see that they were both staring at me with the intent of grabbing me.

So, I started running.

What clued you in on that?

Their very intense staring, their very anxious staring. They focused their complete attention on ME. It was the abruptness of what they did, after screeching their brakes to a sudden stop.

They had very rough, nasty looks on their faces.

What did you do?

I ran. I had, in fact, just come from the Himalayas, from literally running up and down mountains, so I was in great shape at the time.

They started chasing me down this pathway, and I was running to my hotel. They were right in back of me, but as soon as I hit the doors of the hotel they backed right off and ran off.

Did anybody see them?

Nobody saw them. It was amazing that nobody saw them. I didn't scream. I was going to start screaming if they had followed me into the hotel, however. But no matter, they backed off.

What do you think was going on?

Well, they definitely wanted to take me for the slave market. That was high stakes in the 1970s. There were all kinds of stories of white women being kidnapped in India.

In *INDIA?*

Oh, yeah. In India, all right! All across Asia, in fact, from Turkey to India. That's what we were hearing — stories of women being kidnapped. We heard from other travelers, mostly Europeans. We heard from them to be very careful traveling alone, especially as a woman.

I heard stories in Europe even before I went to India. Funny, I was not even intending to go to India, but it so happened that I ended up going there.

I heard all along that we had to be very careful and to watch out where you are going and watch out who you talk to. They could sell you for a lot of money, actually. You're a valuable commodity to them. (Laughs) They sell you, and you can get raped and killed. All kinds of wonderful things!

Did these guys look like they had done this before?

The ones that were after me? Oh yeah, they sure did. They looked like they had done this MANY times before; it was their very high intention of grabbing me. It was all very scary.

Were you wary of leaving the hotel after that?

No. I went out again. But I was leaving India in a few days, so I was ready to leave. I was planning to go back up to the Himalayas.

Have you ever talked to anybody else who had that same problem as you had in India?

I've met maybe three to five women in the last 20 years who have actually gone through that same trek halfway across Asia. There were hardly any women the whole time I was there, mostly European men. So, I didn't see many Americans during that time at all.

Do you think that is still happening today?

Maybe not quite as much, because you can't go across Iran so easily anymore.

I'm sure there are still the slave markets, though.

Abducted in a Russian Republic

Rebecca Rogers

O ne of the *'Stans'* (the former Soviet Asian republics), 1993. My friend, Kim R., graduated law school and passed the bar exam and began traveling around the world for at least six months.

It was in broad daylight and she was literally abducted right off the street, on a side street. Two or three men, like in an alleyway, put a burlap bag over her head.

She had light brown hair and blue eyes. She definitely looked Western in their eyes. They apparently put a bag over her head, pulled it down — I think it was something like a burlap sack or something like that, pulled it down over her, grabbed her and threw her into the back of a truck and were driving her off to somewhere.

Apparently, they did not tie her up, however. In the back of the truck, she knew immediately what was happening. She knew she was being taken somewhere. And she did not think that there was anyone in the back of the truck with her.

Can you describe her emotions?

Actually, she was a very cool person under pressure. So, she kept a cool head and did not panic. She was a law litigator, after all, so she had the singular quality of being able to handle herself on her feet — or not on her feet — as the case may be, in this particular situation! And so, I think she immediately tried to figure out how she could get away.

It was pitch black and she was in a sack in a truck! Probably didn't hear any voices or anything. She assumed that she was in the back of this truck by herself?

I don't think there was anyone in the back of the truck with her as far as I can tell. And I feel pretty confident that she was not tied up and that she was only loosely inside a bag.

The startling nature of that attack was enough to keep her immobilized for a little while, or so, at least, that was probably the thinking of her abductors.

I know that she got away. And the way that I believe that she got away was that she either got out of that sack and rolled off the back of the truck, or even while she was still in the sack she managed to wriggle the sack out and off the truck and onto the street.

In any event, she was quite lucky to be able to do that. I think she said she landed in the street on cobblestones below, so it probably was not very comfortable for her.

I think she then called out for help. I think she knew enough common phrases in Russian or something that she could cry for help, which she got.

She continued on with her travels to other parts of the world, including Europe after that, but most definitely, she left that country immediately.

Did she ever say that she would have done anything differently than she had done?

I don't know. I don't recall her saying anything about that. I don't think we were talking about it as some kind of a traumatic or watershed event for her, either — it was more like something that happened and that she managed to overcome and just went on with her life.

A White Slave in Morocco

Peter Rosti

A tlas Mountains, Morocco, 1968-1969. I had a friend, Ron Laney, who went on a quest looking for a Persian rug in Iran, Turkey and North Africa. At that time, it was before the Shah of Iran was deposed, so seeking out such a rug then was quite the achievement.

He went all over North Africa, including a fair amount of time searching for a rug in Morocco.

He went into the Atlas Mountains of Morocco and was traveling with some Bedouins.

Oddly enough, he came across a young, pretty white American woman who was in her early 20s who spoke English.

She was traveling with the Bedouins, and he was trying to find out why she was there, why she was traveling with them. At first she was hesitant to say anything at all, but anyway, over time, the story emerged that she had been kidnapped in Europe a few years earlier, and that probably would have been, I would guess, in 1965-1966, something like that.

She had been in Europe and had been brought to Morocco in North Africa. Apparently, she was sold to a white slave trader, because, you know, she was young and white and cute — the whole bit. And because she had blonde hair and blue eyes, she had been a target for the white slavery trade.

She had been kidnapped and taken to and sold to some Bedouins, who then took her south into the desert and kept her there for some period of time, maybe a couple of years.

After a time, she had gotten involved with them and started to learn their language. Apparently, she was no longer inclined to run away, and I guess, she had apparently transferred her allegiance to them in some way and was not inclined anymore to run away.

Yeah, she was American, kidnapped in Europe, but I'm not sure where she was kidnapped.

So, by the time he met them, she was already well implanted into their culture and was no longer really a true captive anymore. She was a captive in spirit by that time more than anything else, and apparently, he had asked her why she didn't try to escape or why she didn't run away.

She said that since she'd been there for so long, by then they were now *her* people, and so, she was inclined to stay. He didn't question her any further on that issue, and he traveled with her for some time.

In their conversations, he also inquired, whether, to her knowledge, this had happened elsewhere. Her response was that it wasn't an uncommon occurrence, at least at that time.

So, that's the story, as I know it. Whether she's still there now about 20 years later is anybody's guess.

I think the important thing that stuck in my mind about all this was that she had originally been kidnapped and taken somewhere by force, but by the time Ron had met her she was no longer really staying there under duress any longer.

She'd been absorbed into the culture in a way that she wasn't inclined to leave on her own. I think that was the important point that I caught.

Well, interestingly, she certainly wasn't inclined to use *him* as a route to escape or anything like that, and apparently didn't have an impulse to escape anymore at that time. You know, I don't know, but I think that if she had wanted to escape, I'm sure he would have helped her out, but apparently, she didn't want to anymore. So, because this was a direct contact, you know, I kind of think it's probably a fairly reliable story.

The Orange Man

Cynthia Bronson

Florence, Italy, 2000. I started out walking from the beautiful apartment I stayed in. I would get up in the morning early and I would want to walk. It was so wonderful to walk. And it was so beautiful in *Firenze* (Florence) in the early mornings.

On The Streets

Well, this one fellow on a bicycle would pass me, and he would say, *"Bon giorno!"* or *"Ciao bella!"* (Good day or how beautiful it is!). Innocent enough, it would seem.

But you really have to be careful if you're a woman because you don't look a man in the eye. But me, of course, I did it a couple of times, because I soon realized that all you have to do is kind of ignore them and walk away and get on a bus or something. Ordinarily not that big of a deal. That is, until you get their attention.

I had; I looked at this guy once maybe a bit too long, because, after all, the man was wearing a bright brilliant yellow-orange jacket, and I couldn't help but notice this jacket. It was an attention-grabber! How could you not?

You know, here in Ashland, Oregon, where I live, if you're at all gregarious, you say hello to just about everybody, whether you know them or not. And everybody knows everybody in Ashland. And people do not hesitate to look one another in the eyes.

Did you do that in Italy?

I did that in Italy. I did. And it was a mistake.

I must hear that.

So, I looked at this fellow with the bright orange jacket. He seemed like a nice sort of fellow, but when you consider that you're looking at him, he becomes fully aware and is now looking at me looking at him. It is now bordering on prolonged unwanted attention on my part.

I said, *"Bon Giorno!"*

I mean, how could I not? What else could I say?

At that point, I did not think anything more of it and I just went on my way.

I kind of looked away and walked on until a little bit later, and there he was again.

This time he was smiling at me.

What did you think of that?

Oh, I just kind of looked away.

And then he popped up at yet another corner.

What did you think then?

I thought, *Oh dear; we're in trouble now. This is exactly what people were warning me about, this cultural thing in Italy.*

What did they say?

People said to be careful because men in Italy really think all American women are loose. They think all American women are available sexually and are looking for a beautiful Italian lover.

Well, you know that may be true more or less, huh? Is there a little bit of truth in it?

Of course, there is some truth to it, no doubt. Oh, the rumors, you know... these stories.

It's an exaggeration.

Yes, it's an exaggeration. Because, you know, people are people, and we're really not all like that. But, as Americans, we are definitely more open — maybe a little too open at times. We are willing to make contact with just about anyone.

Which can be a mistake, obviously.

Yes, which can be a mistake.

Back to the Orange man.

Every time I turned the corner, there he was. And I walked for a bit longer and looked behind me, and there he was again — following me. I decided at that point it was time for me to go home, so I just jumped on a bus, and that was that.

In the Hostel

I also had a similar kind of experience on the stairs of the hostel that I stayed in the first night I was in Italy in Florence. I went downstairs to make a phone call. On the way down, I saw this Italian man sitting on the stairs. I really didn't pay him much attention. I made my phone call and came back up.

I saw him still sitting on the stairs, and to be civil I said, *"Bona sera"* (good evening), which, of course, I understood in my basic limited beginning Italian — is one of the simple cordial phrases that everybody knows.

I went up to my room, but I then remembered I forgot to get something else downstairs, and so, I came back down.

He was STILL on the stairs! And this time he looked at me with kind of a sheepish grin on his face.

I thought to myself, *Ugh.* I just didn't have the energy for this.

And when I came back up the stairs he asked me in his limited English, "Are you free this evening?"

I said, "No, I'm going to bed."

And I just grinned and left.

According to Code?

Gabrielle Mylinger

———— ◦ ————

M exico City, Mexico, 1980. I had a sexual harassment experience in Mexico City virtually upon my arrival to Mexico City. I planned to travel also to Acapulco, Taxco in addition to Mexico City. I was traveling with a small group, a mixed group of both men and women. We arrived by bus to the front of our hotel. And already the porter whisked my bags up to my room.

When I arrived in my room, he was already coming on to me and asking me for a date for a drink or something like that.

How did you feel about that?

I was taken aback. And I felt at a disadvantage because he came on so strong.

I'm really not a wimp, you know. I'm really pretty strong. I can say, "No," and all that with no problem.

But his manner was so forceful, and I felt even physically pressured because it was a small room and he's standing right there looming over me.

How did he do this?

He said, "Oh, you're an attractive woman, and I would love to have a drink with you."

I said, "I don't think so."

And he pursued it! It wasn't enough that I said, "No thank you," but he kept on going. It was probably almost five minutes before I finally got rid of him.

I absolutely said to him, "Definitely not, and I'd like to be alone now!" And he left.

That was fairly innocuous, huh? Did you feel threatened?

I didn't feel threatened as such, but I did feel that it was so inappropriate for an employee of a major hotel to do that. I thought that the young man must have been out of his mind that he would break the 'code' of, you know, how you treat guests to the point that he could probably not be trusted.

Do you think that there was such a code in Mexico or in Mexico City? That they were bound by 'normal' Western standards?

I certainly hoped so. But, in my heart of hearts, I guess they didn't adhere to our first-world standards of hotel etiquette and hospitality that we are so used to.

Hitchhiking in South America

Amanda Carnahan

Lima, Peru, 2011. I will tell you about my hitchhiking adventures. I was staying on the coast near Lima at *Eco Truly,* which was a Hare Krishna ashram and sustainable farm at the time. I was staying there and was meeting a lot of really awesome travelers who were passing through from all over the world, and I teamed up with and traveled with whomever I could find.

There was one girl, Katie, in particular, that I was starting to form this really awesome bond with. She arrived with her boyfriend, but they weren't getting along so well; she'd only been dating him for like a month, and he was like, "Oh, come to Peru with me." And she said okay, but now she was kind of freaking out because she didn't want to be around him anymore.

And I told her that I had already been there for a month and had a couple of extra months remaining. So, I said to Katie, "Let's do some traveling; let's just go."

We were thinking at first of just going to Cuzco, but then somebody was telling us about a festival that was down in Argentina, the Rainbow Gathering.

"Well, we don't really have the money for that; how would we even get there?"

A girl we'd been talking to, Marnie, said, "You could just hitchhike down there. It's sort of normal; people do that all the time."

Katie and I really had very little hitchhiking experience.

How old were you and Katie?

Katie was 25 and I was 22.

You were kind of young to be out there traveling by yourselves, huh?

Totally.

So, Katie and I started planning it all out, figuring out where we're gonna start out. What we ended up doing was taking buses through Peru down into Bolivia. Going on buses in Peru is not that big of a deal.

Our first bus was pretty nice — a kind of luxury bus. Nonetheless, it wound up breaking down after only two hours for about five hours.

Was it one of those famous (in Central and South America) chicken buses?

No, it wasn't. This was one of the luxury ones with recliner seats, a meal — not very decent meal — but a meal, nonetheless. And so, it broke down and we were waiting for a while, and we finally got going again.

We made it to the Bolivia border. We were trying to get a bus there, and as we were walking out of the building, Katie suddenly realized that she didn't have her visa or any of her money on her. She had either left it somewhere or it got stolen. So, since she didn't have anything, I then became the financial carrier for the rest of the trip.

She lost how much money?

It was like her debit card and her credit card, which she canceled it immediately, so she didn't lose anything really. But, she just didn't have any money to speak of. She ended up paying me back, but at that point in time, I was kind of the one and only person with money.

We got into Bolivia finally.

Ride 1

We found cardboard boxes, tore them up and created hitchhiking signs. We actually went to the wrong side (south) end of town and were waiting there for about three hours. People were looking at us like we were crazy, like, "What are you doing?"

And we were like yelling, "Hey, pick us up!"

Did anybody else have these cardboard signs in South America?

No, not around us. We were the only ones hitchhiking, pretty much. We didn't see anyone else hitchhiking.

And finally, this little family came along, complete with their kids just kind of crawling all over them in the car. And they like went, "Where are you going?"

This is all in broken Spanish because Katie and I were just awful in Spanish. We said, "We are going to Argentina."

And they all were like, "Well, you are on the wrong side of town!"

They put us in the back of their car and they took us to the correct end of the town.

So, this was like totally insane. Were the kids crawling all over you?

Yeah, pretty much.

Was it like these people wanted to take care of you?

Totally insane, but, yeah, it was pretty much like they wanted to take care of us.

They were kind of concerned for us, because, apparently, most people don't hitchhike in South America.

But, you two were cute as can be. And maybe a bit dirty, too?

Yeah, cute and dirty.

Ride 2

So, they took us to the right end of town, and we waited there with our cardboard signs for only a matter of minutes. One trucker came by and saw our sign, so we shouted, "Hey, are you going in this direction?"

He said, "Give me a second."

And the guy gathered together his coca leaves, made room for us and he said, "Okay, come on. You can come with me."

So, we got in his truck and it was just awesome. The back of his truck, you know, was all decked out: a nice bed, a fridge; it was pretty awesome, actually.

But, I was really sick at this point in time — flu maybe? Or maybe I just had a really bad cold, but it was like body sickness too.

You didn't have diarrhea or anything?

Not at that point.

So, was this a good thing to do, just jump into his truck?

You've got to play it safe. It was all about using your intuition and just playing it smart. Just making sure you're not hitchhiking at night. And if you look at the person and they seem a little sketchy, don't get in the car.

You said this guy put a whole bunch of coca leaves in his mouth?

Oh, yeah.

I think Americans have the stereotype of South America about coca leaves being some kind of a drug. But they put it in all the teas, and I drink plenty of it. It never made me feel like I was on cocaine or anything.

It's supposed to help you with altitude sickness; they give that to you before you go to Machu Picchu.

Exactly.

And so, he was chewing on his coca leaves. And, after a short while, he picked up another hitchhiker, a South American guy this time, who was sitting in the front seat with him.

And we were driving along. I fell asleep.

After a while, I wake up and I see this new passenger is taking a swig out of a fifth of something. So, they're speaking Spanish the whole time, getting along, and then I notice that the hitchhiker's handing the fifth over to the driver. To the *DRIVER!*

How did that grab you?

It made me more than a little uncomfortable. I had really no idea where we were. All I knew was that we were in the mountains easily at 11,000 feet. So, we kind of just went along with this for a little bit. The hitchhiker finally left.

And the driver kept turning around and looking at us while he's driving. I was thinking, *Oh, my God, you need to focus on the road, focus on the road, Stop looking at us!*

Was he driving straight at least?

No, no; he was swerving, but since we were very close to our destination, we sort of hung in there.

Was the alcohol getting to him?

Definitely.

Were you getting a little worried?

Oh, yes, more than a little worried.

And we had been talking with him about going with him across the Bolivian border to Argentina the next day. At least that was the plan.

Finally, we pulled up to a truck stop; thank God we made it at least to there!

Next, we were going to pitch our tent. I always bring a lock with me when I'm doing this, so we can lock the tent from the inside. I suppose it afforded us some protection.

And all night long we hear a party; our driver's across the street, and he's over there in the bar getting pretty wasted.

Were you a little worried about him?

Oh, yeah, *VERY* worried.

I mean, was he making gestures at you?

No, not at that point. No. Actually, he pretty much kept to himself. But, later on, we could hear him playing music really loud in the truck.

Basically, the plan was that you were going to go with him across the border?

Yes, early in the morning, but we knew he didn't get any sleep. It was very worrisome.

And your tent is still locked up?

Yeah, but we didn't get any sleep at all... barely. And I'll note that there were no problems to speak of during the night.

But, at about 5 in the morning, the truck driver comes over, and he's trying to get us out of the tent. He goes, "It's time to go over the border!"

I go, "Nope, we're sleeping here. Sorry. You need to go on."

Did you no longer want to go with him?

No. He'd been drinking all night, and we knew that wasn't a good idea. So, we're like going, "No, you go on ahead."

He is really angry. He tries getting into our tent. He's laughing and getting angrier.

Now, why is he getting upset?

I think he really wants us to go with him. He was excited to have a couple of American women with him

Did you think he was going to be a problem?

I'm not sure. I don't know that he would've been a problem, but we definitely didn't feel safe.

Was he insulted then that you didn't want to go with him? Was it a pride thing?

Yes, exactly. We knew that he hadn't gotten any sleep, and it just didn't seem like it was a very good plan.

What happened then?

He finally left

Rides 3, 4 and 5

We ended up having to take three more cars before we got to the Bolivian border, where we had to walk over, which took us a little while.

They wanted you to walk over the border, the drivers of the car?

Yeah, we had to.

We don't even know how trucks really got through the area. It was like everybody was on foot going across, and you had to go through security and everything.

So, we went over there and then we waited on the side of the street for about five hours that morning.

And this kid, kind of looking like Pauly Shore, but with a South American twist to it, with these really crazy dreadlocks, comes over, and he goes, "Oh, you need to go over here; it's a much better place to hitchhike from."

And so, we go over there and wait for another few hours. But everybody passes us by pointing and signaling like, "You need to go up there; you need to go up there!"

Did you have dreadlocks at the time?

I did, but they were a lot smaller, and I usually wore them under a hat.

There was that immediate bond — that guy with the dreadlocks. He recognized you and there was that immediate bond.

I was a hippie. He knew it.

Are there still hippies?

Yeah, totally. Totally!

But I think there's a new twist on what the hippie idea is. I think the old-school hippies still exist.

Totally. And it's huge all over the world, basically.

Ride 6

We were making our way to the Rainbow Gathering, which is a huge hippie gathering basically.

So, we finally got to the right spot and a security guard there got us into a truck. "This guy will take you to where you want to go!"

So, we start driving down. We pitched our tent that night, and we woke up the next morning at 6 o'clock. We're going to start out early and get to where we want to go. We're right on Highway 80, I believe, and we just needed to get to the other end of that highway, which was about an 8-hour drive. We waited there all day, and we didn't get any rides.

And finally, two girls come up. They're also hitchhiking, but they're local Argentinians. And five minutes after they come up a truck comes by, and we are waving, and it is obviously stopping for us.

But just as we're trying to grab our big heavy bags — and we're sprinting over there — the two girls see us taking our time, and we're kind of slowed down by our bags, so they take off sprinting, too.

They were going to try to beat you to the truck?

Yeah. And they did.

They got there before us. They got in the truck. And then they just laughed at us and were pointing at us.

I was so angry. We've been waiting all day and I just wanted to be in a freaking truck right then. Katie said, "You know, Amanda, everything is going to be okay; everything happens for a reason. The next truck is going to be so much better."

They just drove off laughing and pointing.

Did you signal anything to them?

I kind of just glared at them and stomped my feet and threw a little hissy fit, but then I got over it pretty quickly.

Ride 7

After about five minutes, another truck comes along and we get in. My God, it has a flip screen TV and really good surround sound. I'm thinking, *Where does this guy get the money for this stuff?*

What's the driver like?

He seems relatively nice. He's drinking a lot of *yerba mate* (a South American tea-like brew), which he shares with us. I'm thinking this is great. However, there is just something kind of strange about him, and it's not anything that I can really remotely pinpoint.

You cannot say what was strange about him? Because these intuitions are important.

Yeah, totally.

We kind of slough it off. We're going, "Well, nah... Maybe this is like an Argentina kind of thing."

Maybe a little bit of a macho kind of thing?

A little bit, but also a little bit of weirdness that I can't really put my finger on.

So, we are driving along and we don't really speak Spanish very much. But by now, he's making all these phone calls telling people that he's got these two girls in his truck that don't speak Spanish, and so on. It kind of sounds like he's making some kind of plans for us, but as our Spanish is so bad, we don't really know.

We're going along, and he pulls out all these American Girl CDs, like Backstreet Boys — these weird CDs. And I'm thinking, *Where does this Argentinian truck driver get all these American CDs that girls listen to, and why does he have them in his truck?*

And why does he have such expensive stuff in his truck?

It's interesting that you have these thoughts.

Exactly, it's like there are all these little things that are not necessarily normal and that do not add up.

We keep going along and it's getting darker out. And by now, he's seeming to get really anxious and excited and oddly agitated — it's really weird. He's kind of like bouncing up and down, just getting like really riled up.

And he next says, "I've really got to go to the bathroom. So, he pulls over to go pee.

And I turn to Katie and say, "We really need to get out of here!"

At this point, I'm feeling like I'm having like a really bad trip of some sort.

What is it that's clueing you in on this?

It's all the subtle things that I'm picking up on that just don't seem right. I'm feeling that something is very, very off. It's hard to pinpoint any one thing in particular.

It's the mixture of all the things that I've said earlier: like the phone calls and also the weird giddiness at this point. Like, *What is he getting all excited about?*

What was coming together in your mind about what was happening?

Well, you know, I've heard stuff about the sex slave trade and also about people in South America getting captured and getting like body parts taken out of them.

You are thinking these things?

I'm going like, *Okay, am I going to be part of this?*

Okay, this is a fear is starting to well up in you?

Totally. It's like really starting to take over me. I'm really not doing very well.

That's when I turn to Katie and say, "Katie, we need to get out of here."

And she is also saying, "I'm feeling the same way like something is really not quite right."

And we are in the middle of nowhere

"Amanda, where are we going to go?" asks Katie, "We're in the middle of nowhere; there's nowhere around that we can even feel safe at."

I go, "Well, I think there's a town a little bit farther back that I saw. We'll walk back and go camp in front of a house or something."

And she goes, "Okay."

The guy gets back in his truck.

And we're going, "We're going to get out here."

He goes, "Oh, no, no, no, don't worry. The next town is really close; I'll just take you there. And you can get out there."

"Okay, if it's that close, then we might as well wait."

Do you trust him at this point?

Well, we were in the middle of nowhere. There's not much we could really do.

You had very few degrees of freedom at this point. This is not good when you have a minimal amount of freedom of choice. That's troublesome.

Exactly.

I think what was adding to the anxiety and this feeling of helplessness was like, *What am I getting myself into?*

And you have no options.

Yeah, and so we're sitting there and driving along and I'm thinking to myself, *Amanda, in two weeks, what if you wake up from being drugged and are now some sort of sex slave that you've been traded into. What will you be thinking?*

My answer to myself was: *Well, you know, I would be really pissed. I do listen to my intuitions when I have a chance in the choice.*

I then say to myself: *Okay, Amanda, you still have a choice — right now!*

And just as if on cue, he pulls over and starts doing — *of all things* — *CLEANING* out his truck: vacuuming, washing the windshield...! And it's still the middle of the night!

And it's just before the so-called 'town,' right?

Yeah. It's before the town.

He didn't even go very far before he stopped the truck to do this ridiculous thing at this ridiculous time of night!

He could have waited until he got to the town to do that.

Exactly. It was that close.

I thought, *Why do this here when the town is so close?*

And so, I turn to Katie and I say, "Let's get out, *NOW!*"

We throw our stuff over us to the ground and are out the door in a flash, and are going to find somewhere to camp.

And he is very, very angry as if he was somehow maybe about to lose some money over this. He doesn't move while we're walking away. And the truck stays there for a little bit longer. We walk back to the town that I thought I had seen earlier. When we get into the town, we are very afraid, and so, we hide behind some houses. We see all these different trucks coming through. We are that scared and that paranoid that we do not know if it is that guy or even "one of his men" maybe looking for us. We didn't really know what was going on.

Very soon, after a little while, we go down the street, take a left and we come to a police station. We then ask, "Is it okay if we camp outside? We're hitchhiking and need a place to stay."

They are very upset that we were hitchhiking, being such young girls. They go, "This is not a safe place to be hitchhiking!"

They said that to you?

Yep. They are saying this in broken English. They are trying to communicate to the best of their abilities, but it doesn't work out all that well.

But you get the message?

Yeah.

Did they let you camp there?

They not only let us camp there, but they brought us some yogurt and some other food and fed us. We woke up the next morning and continued on.

So, you never saw that truck driver again. So, what's the moral of this story?

Be smart!

You really were in some danger, weren't you?

Yeah, I think really that we were.

I think this is interesting that you did seem to pick up on all the cues. You are not understanding the language, in particular, but you apparently are adding it all up. And you had only one option, and that was to get out.

Do you think, on the other hand, that maybe it was your imagination?

I'm not sure because Katie and I were both feeling it. It wasn't just one of us but both of us, you know. We turned to each other and went, "What's going on here?"

Like something just doesn't feel right, and I'm also very intuitive; Katie's very intuitive, too, and so the energy itself that was present with both of us was just very *off*.

I don't think South America is such a terrific place, after all, for young girls to hitchhike.

Yeah, it was a good experience, and I think that we learned a lot. And I think that's why Katie is one of my sisters now because we went through these experiences together. I know that she's going to be a sister to me for the rest of my life.

I have a number of stories of how some girls got themselves in trouble hitchhiking and could not, unfortunately, exactly get out of it like you did.

More Untenable Propositions: Hitchhiking in Algeria

Unknown

Tamanrasset, Algeria. Tamanrasset is an interesting place and we were enjoying it. We decided to take a camel trip. We ended up doing that with two other Europeans.

But when it was time to go, we had a hard time hitchhiking out of Tamanrasset. Said one truck driver when looking us over as hitchhikers, "I've never slept with a Japanese woman. I hear they're really good. If you let me have her for a couple of days, I'll give you guys a ride to the next big town."

Of course, we didn't agree to do that. In fact, you don't want to be a woman, either traveling alone or maybe even with a single male in Algeria, like us. In North Africa, you are virtually guaranteed to be hassled, so be prepared for that.

It's a heavy hassle, but it doesn't usually necessarily get physical. But the women really do get hassled. Even with my Japanese woman friend sitting right next to me in cars and trucks, people would be trying to hustle her all the time saying, "Well, we can stop and have a little fun and then we can continue."

The Elevator Guy #4:
The Russian

Vittoria Abercrombie

A ustin, Texas, 1994. It was the MUFON (Mutual UFO Network) annual symposium, a group meeting. And everybody was having fun. This time, we just happened to be hosting a gentleman speaker that was visiting from Russia, Vladimir R. It was very unusual to get Russian speakers in those days, but because, in the climate of political change, the Soviet Union had just collapsed, and the new Russian Federation was just now getting started. And, Russians were beginning to venture out.

So, we now had ourselves a Russian guest-lecturer this time. We were getting to know Vladimir a little. Maybe we were too accepting and maybe even a little overly friendly, and interested, not necessarily in him, per se, but where he was from and what he had to say, and so on. He was one of the first Russian speakers ever to attend one of our symposia. We had some lovely chats between us, and so on, during the evening and earlier.

And there I was, part of the hospitality committee. I should say, it was almost a part of my personal duties to make him feel good (Laughs) — I mean, *comfortable* and *welcome* as one of our guest speakers. But, of course, that was as far as it went! (Laughs)

I recall we were having a late evening drink at the bar with a group of people.

Finally, we all decided to call it a night and retire to our rooms. Three of us then made a move towards the elevator. As a matter of fact, I got into the same elevator as the Russian gentleman.

It was one of those open glass elevators, not exactly what you would call a private space, but the ones you usually see rising up from the lobbies of big hotels.

Not a minute after we got on the elevator, Vladimir next declared how much he really, really liked Italian women above all!

Who else was in the elevator with you?

There was me, the Russian, and my friend Linda C., also a speaker at the conference. We were now about to say our "goodnights." And for my part, I gave the Russian, a very friendly sort of hug and a light friendly kiss goodnight on the cheek, like you normally do among friends and acquaintances, that sort of thing.

He and I are by the elevator door at this point, and this evidently, in some way, had gone to his head in some way, whereupon he immediately pounced on me and decided to give me a REAL hug and started wandering about to places he shouldn't have and was quite aggressive about it, actually, yeah.

Right in the open glass elevator and right in front of Linda, too?
Yeah.

How many floors were you going up?
Three floors only.

He didn't waste any time, needless to say.
This happened as soon as the door shut?
Yeah.

With three people in the elevator?
Yeah, indeed, with the three of us in the elevator!

And the interesting thing about this is that the Russian appeared to be a gentleman throughout the evening, but on the elevator, he actually became somebody else, as is often the case.

Did he seem to be drinking a lot?
I'm not sure.

I'm not much of a drinker, myself, and I wasn't really keeping tabs on the Russian or anyone else, for that matter.

He wasn't obviously drunk.
And obviously, you weren't worried about being raped.
No, of course not, no.

But, the thing that startled me most is that he and I had been relating to each other normally, you know, as equal human beings, talking and exchanging information about all sorts of things and whatnot, like everyone else. That is, until you are now in this semi-private space together. And then, all of a sudden, the person becomes almost justified in asserting himself over you in an unpleasant way.

What went through your mind at that point?

I guess I had sort of humored him more or less all throughout the evening. I now had to place myself in his situation a bit: here's a man who's lived in repressive Russia all his life, you know, a certain kind of limited, restricted lifestyle compared to the rest of us in the free world. And this was his one chance to go out in the world and have some real experiences.

I'm sure he probably had his own fantasies of what it would be like to go to America and be in a conference — and even be a speaker there, no less — meeting and interacting with all these interesting people.

And now, he probably just took the opportunity of a lifetime to maybe try to get something going with me. But, I thought it was absolutely inappropriate, though not, by any means, particularly surprising at all.

So, what did you do?

Well, I pushed Vladimir away and told him that was not the deal.

Was he angry at this point?

Yeah, I'm sure there was a little bit of anger, yes. He clearly wasn't pleased by my refusal. You know, men who evidently feel entitled to cross over the line are, as a rule, much angrier than I would ever get over this sort of thing.

When the door opened, did he just run off?

No, no, not at all. Actually, I was getting off first. So, I did that and I made a very hasty retreat to boot.

Did Linda remain on the elevator after you left?

Yes, poor thing. And, what's worse, I understand, that he attempted the same thing with her as well, who was still on the elevator with him after I left.

He evidently did not know, however, but very quickly discovered that women from Brooklyn are not easy pushovers, either! And Linda was also a tough, no-nonsense lady of Italian descent as was I!

Needless to say, this Russian was never again invited to be a conference speaker at a MUFON event!

The Elevator Guy #5:
The Arab

Natalie Fleischer

Waikiki Beach, Honolulu, Hawaii, the late 1980s. I'm Natalie Fleischer (an assumed name). I entered an elevator in Waikiki Beach, Honolulu, a tourist mecca in the South Pacific. I was on my way to visit a friend's apartment. I recall, I had just finished a pleasant jogging run because I had my jogging clothes on.

The elevator I got onto alone stopped to pick someone up, and when the door opened, I would say, a Middle Eastern-looking man, very aggressively entered and suddenly began to pull me by the arm and drag me out through the open door of the elevator into the hall, I suppose, towards his apartment he was staying in.

I don't remember exactly what I did or said at the time, but he did let me go on the promise 'that I would come to his apartment.'

I, of course, told my friend about this, but she had NO idea who this person was, where this person lived or stayed or even if he was in that building at all.

Within a few days, while going down that same elevator again, this same person stepped in. There was complete silence. We exited and that was that. That was very scary.

The Cloud of Unknowing

Margot Dodds

Yugoslavia, 1968. I was on my way to Greece, but I never got there, because I ended up falling in love with Yugoslavia. I was in a small town on the Dalmatian Coast. I was 19 and traveling alone, and I had met two English girls. In those days we were 'girls,' not women, and accordingly were very naive.

The Road to Greece

We were all staying together in a youth hostel. One day we went out in the evening. I had made friends with one of the men who was hanging out in the coffee shops in the main square. He invited us out for the evening to his beach house — well, we thought it was a beach house — but it turned out to be way in the middle of the woods at the end of the only road on the island.

Now, was he driving you?

A friend of his was driving. There were actually six of us in the car; there were three men and the three of us women.

How did you feel when you saw that you were going out into the sticks?

At first, I wasn't disturbed by it, but things began to get a little weird, and there was a lot of pressure on us. It was clear that they were not intending us benefit.

Okay, when you say things are getting weird, I'd like you to describe that.

When we were at the "beach house" it was fine; we were drinking some wine and talking, and then they began to become more physical with us.

We told them we wanted to go back. There was only one who spoke English, and we told him that we wanted to be taken back to town, and so, they started to drive us back to town. But they were going extremely slow, and they were all talking in Yugoslav and were kind of cozying up to us as much as they could.

How did you feel about that?

Well, it was very frightening.

And I was also very angry. I had a knife with me. I was sitting next to the person, the only person who could speak English, and I told him that I had a knife and that I wouldn't hesitate to use it.

And he said, "Well, don't let *THEM* (his friends) know; Do *NOT* show them the knife!"

Because then he got scared; he was afraid it was going to turn into something very bad.

Was this a good thing to say?

I don't know; it probably wasn't! It sort of upped the ante. And I don't know if I would have used it or not, but I was really frightened. And I just might have used it! Because I had had other experiences in the past, and I wasn't going to let those experiences happen again, if I could help it.

But, I also didn't want to die on a little side road in the middle of nowhere in Yugoslavia, either.

Anyway, they pulled over to the side of the road; they couldn't get off the road because it just wasn't wide enough. So, they pulled over to the side and were trying to kiss us and whatever.

We got out of the car and then they tried to run us over. And we had no idea where we were. So, reluctantly, we ended up getting right back in the car again, which, no doubt, wasn't a very good idea, but we didn't really know what else to do. What choice did we have?

Anyway, all of a sudden, as things were really reaching a point where the men were starting to get angry and pushier. All of a sudden, we heard a loud noise. Behind us was a huge garbage truck coming down the road. There was no way they could pass us — it was really a one-way road — and we were, of course, right in front of them, blocking them, on the way back to town.

I then, literally, threw myself out the window screaming and waving my arms, and, in response, the garbage truck came right up behind us. So, the driver of our car just took off and took us back to town. They were all really mad!

And ever since then I've been very fond of garbage trucks!

Now, in retrospect, how would you have done things differently?

I probably would have drunk far less and not taken the first step out of town.

So, in other words, "do not go with strangers" ... You do not know where they're going to take you!

Yeah, yeah, it's like that basic. But I was young and foolish and maybe a little stupid. I don't know. I also want to be able to trust people, but I think it's possible to be intelligent about it at the same time.

So, how do you know who you can trust?

What a wonderful question!

The Road to Oregon

In 2003, I had another experience that might shed some light on this. I was driving a very small car from Vermont to Oregon. I don't like to take the main roads; rather, I like to go on the little roads. I let everybody else go on the highway, and then the little roads are empty and you can go 65 or 70 miles an hour, and every 15 miles you'd slow down to 30, go through a little town and enjoy it. And then there're no medians, dividers on the roads, so you can see everything.

Anyway, I got to Montana and stayed with a friend. I had been reading a mystical book from the 14th century called the *Cloud of Unknowing*. It was a spiritual teaching about the practice of being in the 'cloud of unknowing,' and instead of fighting things in life, you should just go with the flow more — and that it's okay to be in the 'cloud of unknowing,' and that things can turn out to be all right.

And that was exactly it: I had been in Montana and not seen a single mountain because it had been foggy and raining. It was sunny when I had left in the morning, but by the time I got gas and got back on the highway, I could not see a thing in front of me except the sides of the road just ahead to my right and left.

In fact, I could barely just make out one sign if it was right in front of me; I could see only about 30 feet ahead. And so, I was crawling along at about 10 miles an hour, and suddenly I had this epiphany: I realized as I was driving along that road that I was literally traveling in the 'Cloud of Unknowing!'

And why could this be okay? It was really beautiful; I didn't have to fight it; I didn't have to be afraid of it. I just couldn't go any further than I could see, and that was all right. It was okay.

I never did see a mountain, but after a couple of hours, the fog lifted and I was safely on my way. But, just to see it as a 'cloud of unknowing' made all the difference between fighting it and accepting it.

Okay, if you accept that philosophy and apply it to your Yugoslav incident, I'm not so sure that that would have been a good thing, no matter any philosophic point of view. What do you think?

That's a good question. I think that if I had been in a place where I had known about the 'Cloud of Unknowing,' everything might have turned out differently. I might not have been in such a fearful, needy space and might have been more available to other forms of interaction.

So, do you think that might have changed the outcome of that misadventure?

I'm sure it would have.

The Road to Kopan

Samantha Tavares

Near Kathmandu, Nepal, 1989. I was going to the Kopan Monastery on the outskirts of Kathmandu. It's a beautiful place where they have lots of Tibetan monks that speak and teach in English. Anybody can go up there and study. They have weeklong, three-week-long, and ten-week long courses that you can go and take there.

What happened to you there?

I arrived in Kathmandu alone. I was only 19 then.

Isn't it pretty brave to be traveling by yourself as a young woman in places like this?

I guess you could say that, but I also think that if you don't put out the fear, you don't attract the danger.

Okay, now I've heard this and I'd like to hear more about that because I want to know if it is true or it isn't true. It's not always true; I know that it's not always true.

Right. It's not always true because of the story I'm going to tell you, right? (Laughs)

But it's usually true.

I was born in Brazil, the crime capital of the world, right? So, it is pretty dangerous there. I was raised there, and so I know that danger truly exists there, even if you don't put out the fear vibes. But I think overall, my personal experience is that if I go to places and I present myself and put out the clear energy, that I'm okay and that you cannot mess with me, and I go for what I want to do, and I'm not just wondering, for instance, what is this? What is that? In other words, I'm clear what I'm doing; I've never attracted too much trouble in my life except only a couple of times, even in Rio.

And you know your way, you avoid certain areas, and you're alert all the time. And as long as you're aware and alert and you're putting out that clear energy, 90 percent of the time I think it works, even in Rio.

You know, what I found out is the Americans who travel, but who do not have a lot of travel experience, they didn't expand their alertness because most were kind of asleep and didn't pay much attention to the need for surveillance.

For instance, when you get to a place like the main train station in Rome, Termini, you really have to all of a sudden be much more aware of what's around you than just merely being half asleep.

But, you growing up in Brazil knew to do that more than a lot of people.

Right, so I got natural training, and that's something that travelers should always be aware of and to respect the 'laws and lay of the land' so-to-speak, wherever you go.

So, in Kathmandu, when I arrived at the airport, I guess I was somewhat lax: I simply assumed that I was going to be able to get a cab quite easily to drive me up the many hills around Kathmandu to where I needed to go.

But I arrived kind of late in the afternoon, which was a bad idea, too. I usually am careful with that, in that I usually try to arrive in places earlier during the day. But at that time, I couldn't avoid it. So, I got into this one cab, but I had a nagging feeling that this just wasn't the best cab to get into.

What were the clues?

In the face of the guy, for one. He looked like he was restless and anxious and just meandering around. He pulled up and I got in. His cab, apparently, was the only taxi available to me, because four planes all arrived at virtually the same time.

It was not the biggest airport, either; it looked like it was one of those small country kinds of airports stuck out in the boonies. So, when four planes arrive at the same time at such a place, needless to say, there are not nearly enough cabs to go around.

So, I grabbed the only one that I could, and I just thought that since the sun was already still up, I'd get to Kopan before sundown, anyway.

Well, it didn't quite turn out that way!

The people at the Temple had told me it was going to be about a 40-minute ride from the airport to the Kopan monastery, and like an hour later we're still driving.

So, I started feeling a little restless, about 50 minutes or so into the ride, it still looked like we had a ways to go.

What are your options at that point?

None. I'm virtually in the middle of nowhere, right?

I had, however, a *knife* — a jackknife! And THAT was my only option!

So, the thought occurred to you that there could be trouble, huh?

Of course. And that's why I had the knife in my hand at the ready.

So, he could see that?

No, I was in the back of the cab, so I had it out of sight.

He started stopping in a couple of little villages, because there are many villages on the way, seemingly running *HIS* errands, apparently doing whatever he needed to do without much concern for me.

So, I'm thinking we're running behind because he is making all these stops. At that point, I am becoming very frustrated; I was travel weary, and it was getting dark.

So, I tell him — and, of course, his English was badly broken — "I don't think we're going in the right direction."

At that point, I know we're not going the right direction.

And he says, "Oh yeah, I know where we are. We're going there by a different route because I need to drop this off and do this or do that."

And I am saying, "No, we're not going in NO different direction!"

He then starts getting really angry at me. He turns around, looks at me and says, "Hey lady, you think you are from America. And because you guys are rich over there, you think you can just come here and run our country. Not here. We do it my way! I'm going to take you to a place you're not going to like," or something like that.

It wasn't clear, but he seems threatening and menacing.

So, that's when I get my knife out, made it very visible and say to him, "I'm going to get out right here! Stop the car. Let me out!"

So, he gets even more angry. He does stop the car, and he gets out and starts yelling at me. I just had a backpack, so I get my backpack out, and while he is yelling, ranting and screaming, I tell him to keep his distance —

to stay away from me. He surely does see that I have a knife in my hand and that I am not afraid to use it.

He wasn't much bigger than me.

And you obviously hadn't paid him yet.

Oh, he wasn't going to see any money from me, that's for sure!

I started running towards where I thought it looked like a village not too far from where we were and I saw some kids playing and asked where Kopan was.

They pointed to the top of a nearby mountain.

Was it on the way where you were headed in the cab?

It seemed like a different direction, but I'm not really sure.

The hard part for me was that it took a long time to regroup — to pull myself together. My adrenalin was running on overdrive, and it was getting darker than when I left. And the people were not especially friendly, even the kids.

They kept pointing that Kopan's "over there," so I started walking, and then the climbing began. My adrenalin rush had subsided by then, and I was really getting tired and running out of steam.

So, it's getting late at this point? So, what did you do?

I finally got exhausted and just stopped in place and sat down. I was actually quite close to Kopan at that point; I just didn't know it. I was just exhausted, carrying a huge backpack after traveling from Taiwan to Nepal... you know, a long flight and no food... just my water and some nuts maybe.

So, I decided to set my pack down and just sit and wait it out, to take a break. I'm thinking, *God, I'm here to come to the Temple. If you want me to go, come get me. If not, I'm going to spend the night here.*

Then I heard the kids in the distance suddenly yelling and calling out to someone, and then as if out of nowhere, this monk just appears — manifests out of the blue — and comes up to me and asks. "Oh, you're coming to the temple? Are you coming to Kopan? We've got to keep going up; you've got to keep going up!"

So, he snaps me out of my momentary daze, gives me some more water, and then I follow him up to the temple. It turns out; it wasn't more than some 15 minutes more up the hill from there.

So, you must have felt absolutely relieved and happy by that time, huh?

I got there and they even had a candy bar waiting for me! And, boy, did it taste good!

I stayed at Kopan for a month.

In retrospect, if you had remained in that taxi, would you have ultimately wound up there?

Probably. But who knows for sure?

Do you think he had any sinister plans in mind for you?

It's hard to say. I think he may have, but I think he was trying to test me, to see what kind of personality I had — if I would succumb to his plans. You know, if I was a weak female or not.

But, once he saw that I was confronting him, and he wasn't going to bend me any, then he let me go, I guess. I simply do not know that I was in any real danger.

But I think, that maybe if I kept on being afraid, he might have probably just taken my money and my bag and stuff. I don't think that he was going to do anything much more than that, though. But again, you just don't know. It's better to be safe than sorry.

But, once he saw that I wasn't going to give in to him, he gave up on me.

You know, you succeeded because you basically followed your instincts. Did you feel good about that?

Very much so, and that's the story that I tell people. I remember it often, because when I finally let go, when I finally said to myself, *I'm a very strong person; I have a lot of stamina; I can go for a long time; I can climb mountains,* I became a survivor and overcame any danger.

In reality, of course, I was really exhausted. I could hardly even take one more step! I could not move.

So, when I said to myself, *Okay, I surrender; I give in; I'm just going to sit here... if you guys want me to go up there, come get me, or I'm going to wait until tomorrow morning...* the monk suddenly appeared as if out of thin air!

Raped in Mexico

Lorraine Bonner

Quintana Roo, Mexico, 1994. I am Lorraine Bonner (an assumed name). This is my story of a little side trip in Mexico. I was going to Tulum on the Yucatan peninsula from Palenque. I had already had a string of bad experiences with Mexican men harassing me in southern Mexico on this trip earlier.

Quintana Roo is very barren, very scrubby, a kind of desert terrain. Nothing much happens there and you only go *THROUGH* there to get *TO* somewhere else.

I hitched a ride and was driving for an hour in this big dump truck. I had my pack between the driver and me. I looked over at the driver; he was very sleazy looking, creepy, with darting eyes, and so forth. I just did not trust him at all. But at least my pack separated us, and so I didn't feel all that threatened by him at that point.

You looked at him when you first got in his truck, and now you're looking at him again. What's going through your mind?

I'm thinking, *Oh boy; you really did it this time!*

But I wasn't thinking about it all that much because I was suffering from sleep deprivation and was not nearly as sharp or alert as I might have been otherwise.

We are going for about an hour, and all of a sudden he makes a sharp right off the highway onto a dirt road. And I know that's wrong. He now pulls off this road to the side. I speak very little Spanish, and he's got this little Mary hanging from his mirror. So, I am now pointing to this Mother Mary and shouting at him *"Mal hombre, NO! NO!"* (Bad man!)

It's now obvious to me that he is up to no good. And, I manage to talk my way out of it, and am feeling pretty good for now! I somehow changed his mind. And so, we're back up onto the main highway again and I am relieved for now.

But sadly that relief is only short-lived. We go on for maybe an additional half hour, and then he suddenly turns left off the highway — apparently the same scenario as before. And I think, *Oh, shit!*

Do you think you maybe should have gotten out right then and there?

Well, I wanted to get out of his truck, but I couldn't; the door wouldn't come open. I don't know if it was broken or not, but it just wouldn't open. And, as much as I tried, I just couldn't get it to open.

I did try to get out at the first place we stopped, but the door wouldn't come open. I don't know if he rigged his truck door shut like this on purpose or not. But, of course, there's so much poverty in Mexico, it's no surprise that cars or trucks can be broken and don't work.

But, I do have a knife on me; a sort of pocketknife that every lady has, you know. And I bring it out, which is really stupid. I bring it out just to let him know that I have a weapon. It's stupid because he can easily overwhelm me and grab it away from me in an instant and then even turn it on me.

And that's exactly what happens! He has it in an instant away from me! This is a skinny little runt, who, even so, is stronger than me and there is not even a contest there.

We stop on this dirt road by what must have been a church, because it has a cross on it. It looks abandoned, and somebody has evidently painted a cross on it.

Once again, I try to talk him out of it and did what I did the last time. But, unfortunately, it does not work this time.

He raped me! Pure and simple. I didn't have much choice. I couldn't resist him for fear that I could get hurt or even killed. He had my knife, after all.

There's a part of you that doesn't even know that it happened, but you do KNOW it did. You go out of your body! I went out of mine; I had an OBE — an out of body experience!

You did actually have an out of body experience?

Yeah, I did; I was gone! I did not experience it at all, but I knew that it happened. But I just wasn't physically and psychologically there!

What I've found out since then is that women say they do go out of their bodies when they are raped. They say they leave their bodies when it happens, and it's kind of like God just spares you from it, the details that you do not need to have.

And I was gone from my body, thank God, because, fortunately, in a way, I was able to dissociate myself from it. I've been told by other people who have been raped, that that's what also happens to them.

Then I get out; he let me out. I don't know how he gets the door open for me in the first place when I was hitchhiking, but this time, he simply reaches over to the door and somehow just dumps me off there. I guess he feels sorry for me: he gives me a warm bottle of Pepsi Cola with the cap still on it, so it didn't do me very much good. And he leaves. And that was it. I was on my own again.

I had my pack by me. He didn't steal anything. So, I sat by the abandoned church and started crying, feeling sorry for myself, and feeling bad about what had just happened to me. But now I am much smarter. In an instant, I was now far smarter than I had ever been in my whole life. I cried for a while. I thought, *You know; you're not a virgin. This is a good life lesson for you. This is going to help you a lot!*

No woman ever deserves to be raped. And this is certainly something you wouldn't want to have happen to you again, and so, you put it out of your mind and you just move on. It's not the end of the world.

I then pulled myself together thinking, *You still have got to get to that party in Tulum!*

And so, I get back out on the highway again, and this man picks me up in this car. He's Mexican, and I try to tell him what just happened to me in my limited Spanish and his limited English: but I am worse than pathetic at this point.

And after a couple of hours, his car starts to 'cough.' I mean, this is the most unbelievable trip you can imagine. And he starts looking at me with that certain look. And I am going, *Oh no! Not again!*

It's a look like you know you are in trouble because this man's starting to look at you like — the sympathy is now gone, and he has already forgotten what just happened to you, if he even understood it in the first place.

And now the new truth is that he's probably going to rape you, too. Or maybe not; maybe at least just some kissing and fondling, and things like that. Nevertheless, it was stuff I wasn't about to do.

At that point, we pass some Mexicans along the road who look just like your stereotypical guerrillas, *bandidos* (bandits), you know, with the big huge belts of bullets draped over their shoulders and with their big rifles and sombreros. They were very scary looking, to say the least.

Meanwhile, the car slows to about 15 mph and is coughing away worse than before, and I am going, *Oh, is it going to be this amorous guy with his coughing car OR the scary guerrillas that are going to get me? I am going with the guerrillas!*

So, I let the car cough until it slows to only 5 miles an hour, And suddenly I yell out, *"Adios!"* and I jump out of the car as quickly as I can.

And since I am a runner, after all, I just start running, trotting, along the road with my pack.

He is now completely stopped about a quarter of a mile ahead of the guerillas at this point. And as soon as they catch up to him, they help push his car, to try and get it going again. At this point, they are still behind me, and I am splitting out of there as fast as I possibly can. I can hear them catcalling to me all the while they are pushing his car down the road.

Did you think that they had the same idea he had?

I am going, *"Adios amigos!"* (Goodbye friends), and I am laughing at them as I am running down the road at a good clip. I only know that I am going to get out of there as fast as I can!

Did you have any idea where you were?

Just that I was still in Quintana Roo! It didn't matter. Just get me to a city — any city! (Laughs)

I finally get to what seems like a gas station and I end up in this little town. It's now getting to be nighttime. This trip began early that morning in Palenque and now is getting to the point where I am in this village where they've never seen any Americans before. There doesn't seem to be any police around, and the people do not seem all that friendly.

I am regrouping at this point, and I don't have my thumb out yet. I'm am just sitting there with my pack, really tired after having had a very long day of one misadventure after another that I really didn't need.

I'm getting a little scared that I'm not going to get a ride out of there. And I have no idea where I am going to sleep or anything. But this one young teenager comes along and he speaks a little bit of English. He asks me where I am going. And I say that I am going to Chetumal, which is right on the border of Guatemala and Mexico.

Amazingly, he says, "That's exactly where we are going! Hop in! We've got this one old lady whom we've got to take first up to her home in the mountains, and then we'll go on from there."

And I take a look. There is, indeed, this old lady there and some other people in the back of the truck. So, it seems safe. He's just this wonderful little teenager, a good little soul, and a guardian angel who has just happened along at the right time.

We arrive in Chetumal very late at night. Since I have to get up very early in the morning, I don't want a hotel. So, I figure I'll just stay in the bus station all night long because I have to catch the bus at 4 AM to Tulum.

There are also these two ladies from Italy there as well. They speak some English and I tell them what happened to me that day. And, I really do need them, really bad.

They're going on an early bus, too, and they also don't want to spend any money on a hotel room, either. So, together we all decide to sleep in a schoolyard. And so we scoot under a fence under the watchful eyes of the Federales (Mexican National Police) right close by. We know it's okay because they don't do or say anything to stop us.

Did you think there would be any point at all in telling the Federales what happened to you?

Nah. Not at all. No way. It's out in the middle of nowhere. It's lawless where it happened. What could anyone really do about it?

I remember that night going to sleep — I haven't slept for, gosh, two days. The two Italian women slept on either side of me, and they both cuddled with me. I felt really nurtured and taken care of; I felt like they were kind of guardian angels, too.

I never did make it to Tulum, because we heard from an American writer also in the bus station that apparently a big shipment of marijuana came in from Colombia, and so, I am warned not to go to Tulum, because he said that backpackers were being framed for drug possession and then thrown in jail, and it was, therefore, very dangerous to go down to Tulum.

They would simply slip marijuana into your pack and then go, "Marijuana!"

Then they'd throw you in jail and either throw the key away or extort some kind of a bribe from you in order for you to get out.

Are you extra cautious now because of your experiences in Mexico?

I'm still not 100 percent careful these days, either, because I love adventure. And I love to just explore and see new things. I get rather bored in the States because there's simply not as much adventure there. I travel alone a lot of the time. Sometimes I don't have enough money. And, a lot of times I don't go to hotels and just sleep in my vehicle. I do set myself up at times. But it's like I can't let it stop me from traveling. I love to travel.

So, you are not too terribly afraid?

I'm just not.

Are you afraid of being raped again?

I'm not afraid of it. I just think if it happens to me again, I'll just have to let it happen.

Were you not afraid of disease or getting pregnant when this happened to you?

No, I couldn't get pregnant. And, in those days disease wasn't much of a problem. But these days, yes, it is definitely a consideration.

Giving Me the Asshole Pill

Eleni Papakakis

D id you always have this accurate insight and soul connection with the people who were giving you rides while you were hitchhiking?

Well, it depended on how desperate I was for a ride, how long I'd been waiting.

So, you mean, did I ever get a weird driver?

Hitchhiking in Europe

Well, this is a loaded question, because I have lots of hitchhiking stories, and I know that you expressed some wariness, and I noticed that you are a good judge of character when you are traveling, you know, you have this intuition, this soul connection in a sense. I want to know if there were times when you didn't make such great judgments. You say it depends on how desperate you are. I mean, are you willing to let down your guard?

No, I never let it down entirely.

There were a few times where I just waved trucks on even though it was pouring rain and I was freezing.

We need to know what was that insight?

It's a feeling I can't even describe; it's like I am, I guess, a walking bundle of emotion because there are times when a car would drive up and I would just feel happy. I would just feel like the world is right, and I'd get into the car, and I'd usually meet some really interesting, wonderful people who had great stories to share.

And then there were times where the car would pull up and it would feel dark and icky, and I'd get really panicked and my right chest would get tight.

Can you describe the person in the window?

It was different. It was mostly men but sometimes women. And I can't even describe it; I would just get this feeling, and they wouldn't even need to come right up to me for this to kick in. I would get this feeling when the car was coming down the road, and so, when I'd get the feeling that this was not so good, I'd look like I was just walking down the road. But, if I had the feeling that it was all good, I'd put my thumb out.

Did it always work for you? Were you always accurate in these intuitions?

It's funny. There's one time where the guy was a very nice guy, but he couldn't drive. I mean he was just a horrendous driver, and it was the only time I felt like I was going to die on the road. This was in southern England. And he was weaving in and out of traffic, going under trucks — I mean, he even came right up under a truck and started honking his horn. Now, the front part of his car was just under the back of the truck! Because he had to go! He had a place to go! And it turned out he was just crazy!

So, how did you extricate yourself from that?

When we came to a stop sign or a red light I said, "Oh, there's somebody I know," and then I ran out of the car.

Was there anybody where your intuition or your emotional feeling was to go with this person, but it was a mistake? Was he one of those mistakes?

I didn't get anything from him one way or the other, so that was a weird one.

Mexico

Mexico, 1986. I needed to get to a boat in a hurry, so I didn't hitchhike this time. Instead, I hailed a taxicab. And, as you know, cab drivers in Mexico all kind of drive crazy, so this one guy didn't strike me as being any different from any other cab driver, except that he first asked me if I would sit in the front seat with him,

I said, "No, I'm more comfortable in the back seat."

He then said, "Well, if you don't mind, I'm going to pick up another fare, because they're going to the same place you are, and I will make more money off of this ride."

I went, "Okay, that's good."

(I mean, couldn't the new person sit in the front seat?)

But I still didn't feel quite right, and I thought, *I don't feel right just about EVERY time I get into a Mexican cab!*

Why is that?

That I didn't think anything in particular about this one cab driver is because they're all crazy really; they all just drive crazy. Cab drivers all over the world have this other sort of culture and demeanor, although I usually do really well with cab drivers and make some good friends among some of them, and I do occasionally get some great stories from cab drivers.

So, this guy, it seemed, was pretty much like just about any other kind of cab driver, except that I did have sort of a weird feeling about him. But, again, I was late and I had to get to a boat in a big hurry that was about to leave. And, what's worse, I had to stop at my hotel first on the way to the boat.

Desperation may get you every time!

I'm thinking it does always get you, now that I look back at this. That's why I got into the cab in the front seat because of the boat.

Against your better judgment really.

Yeah!

So, anyway, wouldn't you know it: He pulls off into a little wooded area and accosts me!

And so, I hit him!

Where?

In the face with my fist.

And?

He looked surprised and he said to me, "But you're American; you *WANT* this!"

So, I hit him again and I said, "And that's for all Americans!" (Laughs)

He was little. So, I guess I convinced him that I could take him.

Next, he yelled, "Get out of my cab. Just get out of my cab!"

And, of course, I'm in the middle of nowhere, in the middle of the woods in a place I didn't recognize.

So, I said, "No. You are driving me back to my hotel!"

Really? That took guts.

Yeah! I get a little like that when I'm in these situations.

He knew you were in control at this point.

Yeah.

But he says, "No!"

Well, I automatically put myself in control. I get really bold, you know. Usually, I'm kind of a wuss, but when someone does this to me, I call it *'giving me the asshole pill.'* Once someone gives me the pill, it's like, "Okay, don't mess with me."

So, I now say to him, "You are going to take me to my hotel, or I'm going to boot you out of this cab, and I'm going to drive the cab back to my hotel myself!"

He panics and screams, "No, no, Lady, I'll do it!"

And he did just that; he drove me right back to my hotel.

Did you sit in the front seat?

I sure did. I did because I needed to make sure he was going to take me to the right place. And then, you know, because I'm a decent person I paid him for the cab ride. I did.

Well, Kill ME First!

Joyce Alexander

Cabo, Mexico, 1996. I went with my boyfriend at the time to Cabo. One evening we decided to go dancing and were headed towards *El Squid Row*, a very popular local place in Cabo that was just full of cafes, bars, and nightclubs.

But to get there we had to walk through this relatively unlit and off-the-beaten-track area, and two men appeared out of nowhere who wanted to apparently attack me and rape me, it seemed. They were very menacing and seemed intent.

So, tell me how did you feel at that moment? What went through your mind?

I was very scared; I was completely thrown by it — it was all happening so quickly.

You were with your boyfriend then, right?

Yeah. What happened was he got right in front of them, between them and me. And he's a bit short, not a real tall man — he's 5-5 or 5-6, but he's a real aggressive New Yorker, and he's like going, "If you touch her, you're going to have to kill me first, because there's no way in hell you're putting your finger on her, unless you kill me!"

And they just backed off. And they're like "Okay, sorry," and they just left!

Wow! Was he normally like that?

Oh, he had some wonderful qualities and some challenging qualities, as well. But this was definitely one of the times that he had this amazing quality that he was such a charmer. It was incredible: he just like looked them in the eye and said, "You will have to kill me," and then they just backed down.

What did he say about it afterwards?

"Let's go get a drink." (Laughs)

And I'm like going, "Oh, my God."

He then he goes, "You know what? I love you. I'd never let anything happen to you. You should know that. You should know me better than that."

And that was it.

Was it very surrealistic?

Yeah, and they were absolutely serious. I mean they were there and very intent. But what I think happened was that they understood there was some kind of code between men going on — a kind of respect of one man for another man, that had I been alone, there would have been no question about it. But, that it was a man that was saying "No," they had to respect that.

That's pretty amazing. Was Cabo generally a reasonably safe place to go, do you think? You just wouldn't think of it being a dangerous place, right?

Yeah.

I think a lot of places in foreign countries, you, as a woman, should be wise about and not just assume that it's like anyplace else if you don't actually know. Don't just feel that you can simply go out at night like business as usual or walk down dark alleys or places unless you're with a group of people.

And that's why I'm really an advocate of going on tours with other people.

In going to El Squid Row, you kind of had to walk from the mainland off down through this sleazy area. We were walking down a certain street. So, I think what happened was we just took like an alleyway or something off the main drag, and it was just like that two-minute walk that made all the difference.

What time of the night was it, would you say?

It was not late; it was like 10 o'clock.

Did you report it to the police?

No. We didn't think it would do much good. So, no, we kind of just accepted that that's what happened.

If we had reported it to the police, what could we really tell them? So, where did they go? What did they look like? And so on.

Did it bother you that it might happen to some other woman?

I think it's easy to think that, "Oh, if I don't report it, it could happen to some other woman."

But, no, that's not like it at all. No. Unfortunately, this happens here a lot. Some are just unluckier than others.

How did you feel about Mexico?

Honestly, I'm not really that thrilled about going there without at least one or two men with me. You know, I prefer going with a group. It feels better to do so.

Well, Fuck ME!

Joyce Alexander

Arab Middle East, the early 1980s. Now, you say you've also been to other places in the world, including Israel and Arabic countries, for example? Anything you can think of that happened there?

Yes, I did go to some of the Arab countries.

Once, a man came over to me and simply said to me out of thin air, "I want to fuck you."

I couldn't believe my ears — that I actually heard this. And so, I said, "You must not speak English very well."

At first, I thought I must have misheard it because I thought there's no way he could be that rude and abrupt. I thought this guy just didn't know what he was actually saying.

And so, I asked, "Do you really know what you just said?"

He went, "I do! Yeah!"

So, I said, "That's rude."

And I then I slapped him!

What's that like slapping an Arab man?

I didn't care that he was Arabic or anything else; he was just a man being a jerk! How do you just walk up to a woman and say, "I want to fuck you?"

NO! (Laughs)

What was his reaction to that?

"You don't want to?"

I didn't actually slap him that hard. Just enough to get the point across — _NO!_

I was just, like, besides myself; I simply could not believe it!

Accosted in Athens

Lynn deBeauclair

———— ◦ ————

A thens, Greece, 1985-1986. My ex-husband had gotten into some trouble with the Athens police. He just kind of was a street person and would tend to get himself into trouble at times. He was of Middle Eastern descent, Egyptian, but that's as far as I want to go with this one anyway.

He'd got into some trouble, and I'd gone to the police station with him and was sitting in the lobby of the police station waiting for him to straighten out the situation. And there's a cop sitting in the corner at a desk.

So, anyway, we're sitting there, and there was one other guy that came into the waiting room, and he was kind of a young early 20s Arab guy, Middle Eastern, anyway.

He comes over and he sits right down next to me in this totally empty waiting room. And I'm thinking, *Okay, this guy's going to bother me.*

Were there any sorts of armrests separating the seats at all?

No, it was a bench-like thing with no seat separations and he sits right down next to me. And I look at him and I go, "Don't even start with me."

And I flash my wedding ring right at him. I just narrow my eyes, and I'm sure he gets it. But that's not apparently what he wants. He isn't hitting on me, apparently.

He rummages around for something in his pack and he says, "I need to talk to you about something."

And I'm like, "What? There's nothing you need to talk to me about."

And he speaks English. Meanwhile, the Greek cop sort of picks up on this and is kind of looking warily over at us, you know.

Anyway, he rummages around in his knapsack and brings up, of all things, his *"Watchtower."*

The Watchtower is a little flyer that the Jehovah's Witnesses hand out when they come to your door.

"Where are you from?" I ask.

"Cairo, Egypt," he says.

I don't know quite what to think, so I ask, "You're an Egyptian and you're a Jehovah's Witness?"

And he's waiting there for what? I have no idea. I guess it is some kind of police business that he has.

I then say, "Well, I'm not interested. Thank you."

I continue, "I have my own spiritual beliefs and they are not that."

And I now move away from him to the other side of the room, which has got to be pretty obvious to him.

What does he say in response to you when you say, "You're an Egyptian and you're a Jehovah's Witness?"

He simply says, "Oh, that's because we are everywhere."

Anyway, "So, I'm not interested. Thank you."

I am not nasty to the guy because I'm not nasty when they come to the door, either.

So, I go over and I sit on the other side the room nearer to the desk where the Greek cop is sitting.

But he cannot seem to leave me alone. He just doesn't get my direct response, let alone any hints. So, anyway, he now comes over and sits down right next to me *AGAIN,* but this time he puts his hand on my leg.

He actually puts his hand on my leg! I just cannot, for the life of me, believe this!

I'm wearing blue jeans. I waste NO time. I haul off and whack him on the side of the head with the back of my hand so hard, it almost knocks him right off the bench.

He kind of looks up and half-smiles, sheepishly.

And I say firmly, "Get away from me or I'll have you arrested!"

And, wouldn't you know it, the Greek cop is just sitting there and is now taking an interest. He puts down his paperwork this time and is just watching this unfold. I wonder to myself, *What's it going to take for him to intervene?*

Was he likely to intervene?

Ah, who knows? Maybe, yeah. No, actually, probably not.

Did the guy leave you alone after that?

He went and sat on the other side of the room at that point and minded his p's and q's after that.

Truth be told, nothing more happens. It's over.

I've been seeing those Watchtowers for years. He had copies of them in Arabic and in English. I don't know if he had any in Greek or not. But Jehovah's Witnesses can be quite aggressive and assertive. And on top of that, what goes on with men towards women?

In 1984, before I got married, when I was in Egypt, you'd get on the buses and you are slapping hands off of you like flies. They are groping you just non-stop. I even made a mistake once of giving a Bedouin woman my seat on the bus. So, I'm standing up hanging on to the thing. Just hands all over you. You're just being groped and just slapping hands off like flies. It's unbelievable.

Did the older woman see this?

Nah, she just stared straight right ahead. Couldn't care less.

Do you think this is a typically American kind of thing, to give up a seat to somebody? But they would never do it there, do you think?

She was older and had a bunch of stuff. Men don't give up their seats to women over there.

So, you set yourself up there and it doesn't even cross your mind.

But you see, I've had women even sit next to me on the buses and, somehow, the men still try to grab and grope you. You see, it's all over the Middle East.

Accosted in Paris

Jennifer Swatez

Paris, France, 2001. We had been in Paris for about three days and we had gone to a string of pubs earlier in the evening that are really nice. It was fun.

Anyway, my son had this dream of sleeping out all night under the Eiffel Tower, and I was not real thrilled about it, because we hadn't had much sleep anyway, and I didn't feel real comfortable sleeping outside; I just didn't feel like it.

So, anyway, at about 2 o'clock in the morning, he had met a young woman who was going to go to the same college that he was going to go to in southern Sweden. And, I didn't want them to know that we weren't going to stay there. I guess what happened was we couldn't find a hostel that had room.

So, we got to the Eiffel Tower and found that there were several other groups of people partying there, young people partying, speaking various languages, not English.

My son was very tired, and so I said I'll sit up and I'll keep watch. I'll just write in my journal. I thought it would be safe and sound under the bright lights of the Eiffel Tower. But, I soon learned that the lights basically didn't stay on all night. They shut off at a certain time. I learned that all too well.

You thought it was going to be bright all night?

So, who knew that all hell was going to break loose under the Eiffel Tower on this particular night? Least of all, ME!

Anyway, the first person that approached was a man on heroin who did not speak English, but we communicated enough with, you know, very good gesturing. He wanted to know if we wanted some heroin, if we wanted to buy it or not. And because he was so high, I didn't quite know how best to get rid of him.

What were your choices?

Well, my choice was to sit there and be patient, because he didn't appear that he was rational. And his movements were so jerky, that he appeared that he had considerable strength behind him as well. And so, I just decided to ride it out with him and let him talk until he got really bored with us. And, anyway, my son was getting irritated with this as I was very carefully watching this whole scenario unfold.

But I felt this man had a potentially violent type of strength, even though he wasn't a big man. I just picked up on his energy.

Anyway, fortunately, finally he was gone, and my son found people to play soccer with, you know, at 3 or 4 o'clock in the morning and I watched.

Finally, just before dawn, you could begin to see the outline of the Eiffel Tower appearing, and my son was still playing soccer with people from different countries, and so on.

I thought that I wanted to do something, however, it was still too early, and none of the coffee shops were open yet.

It was just about dawn, and I wanted to see Paris from a different perspective. So, I decided to start to jog a little bit.

I jogged along one of the green lawn areas below the Eiffel Tower and checked it out. And I felt, *Okay, I'm pretty safe doing this.*

My son is still playing soccer. And it's getting a little bit lighter, so I thought I would jog up another of the open green lawn areas there, the grassy park spaces. So, I do that. There are two or three people in this next lawn area, so I thought this green was essentially okay and felt pretty safe.

I could now see a little bit more, and I could still see my son down there playing soccer with the other people. I was kind of just biding my time until I could maybe find a coffee shop that would finally be open. I do that every morning.

I decide to jog, yet again, this time up along a third grassy area. In front of the Eiffel Tower, you know, there are these lawns — these green grassy areas — like you see in front of the White House, and so on.

So, okay, now the third lawn. I jog up to a military building at the far end of that grassy green. And, now, there are no people at all.

I am about to start on my way back, and I notice that there still are no people around at all, and I can now vaguely make out the gray shape of the Eiffel Tower, which is, of course, simply spectacular.

I decide I will now jog back this time by way of the middle grassy pathway. I don't care that I am alone; at this point, I feel quite safe.

However, I suddenly notice on my left that there is a well-dressed man who is making a beeline quite fast right in my direction.

What went through your mind then?

Well, I begin doing my affirmations again, because I am not going to be a victim on this trip, even though we are living a lifestyle on this trip that I realize is a little bit risky. And so, I reaffirm my affirmations again that, *No, no; I am not a victim. I am not in agreement with being a victim!*

I thought I would be positive about myself and that would give me some added inner strength perhaps.

And I see this man making a beeline right for me.

What was in your mind right then?

Well, this man comes right up to me; I don't have much time to even think about it.

I don't run and I just keep on walking as if I have a purpose and a place to go. But, unfortunately, I know that this is not deterring this man at all from making this beeline towards me. He continues to move right for me.

Can you describe him a little?

Yeah. He was well-dressed.

Be wary of well-dressed people! You can't rule them out!

He was middle-aged, very attractive, French, and professional-looking, and was making a beeline right towards me from apparently out of nowhere.

I knew I was out here all by myself; I knew I was taking chances.

He just comes up to me, gets up real close, starts talking to me, and then grabs me.

Where?

Well, he grabs me and puts an arm lock on me.

I do not resist. I am not going to resist: this guy's bigger and stronger than me.

I figure, *Instead, I'm going to talk to this guy and try to communicate with him without acting scared, because, there's just not a damned thing I can really do.*

Could you have kicked him in the groin?

No, not from where I was and how he had me. Uh-uh. No.

It was 'checkmate.' He had me. Game over.

All right, so you know he knows you know.

Yeah, he knew what he was doing. And I just realized I'll need to just psych this one out, because, physically, this guy has a complete direct lock on me if I resist in any way.

I knew, therefore, that I needed to psychologically connect with this guy somehow and just go along with this guy.

I can actually get back alive, you know? Who knows? I don't know exactly what this guy wants. Basically, you know, he is very sexual. That was probably his entire motivation. He is going to rape me pure and simple

I tell him that my son is just down the field. And I also tell him I have a boyfriend. I am just trying to talk to him very quietly.

But he's still grabbing at you and all this?

Oh, yes. He still has a lock on me

But, for some reason, I am basically able to talk my way away from him. What did it?

I don't remember exactly, but miraculously, in some way, I just manage to talk my way away from him. It takes a while.

I don't know. I guess basically you use your God-given gift of intuition how to gradually be able to get yourself out of the situation.

This is really important, please go on!

I kept reaffirming in my mind, *I am NOT a victim! I am not a victim.*

I guess I must have mustered up some inner personal strength as a result.

I'd like you to be very explicit — as much as you can remember.

He just has a lock on me and he is very sexual.

Can you be any more specific about that?

Were you talking to him in English?

It's curious. You know, I don't know. I don't remember. I seem to have understood him in English. I don't know French, and he didn't *seem* to know English, and yet we seemed somehow to understand each other. Maybe it was more an emotional than intellectual kind of thing. I don't really know. It might have even been a psychic sort of thing.

Once you got away from him, did you just walk away?

Yeah, but I walked fast, you know, and with purpose. Yes, you know, I went... "Bye!"

Just not to attract him in any way, shape or form, and I did not run.

You did not run?

No, I did not run.

I was moving very carefully so as not to upset him. He then moved back directly to where he was in the first place. And, after he was gone, I, in turn, kept moving steadily back towards where my son was.

You knew you shouldn't do that, go to a dark, unpopulated place in a Paris park area alone and by yourself. You knew better. You intuited that maybe it wasn't such a good idea to jog where there were no people. And yet you did. Why?

In the beginning, I did have a sense of the risk, but I guess I didn't think it was very likely to happen. Who knew?

But, on my way back, I definitely had a sense that there was still a continuing risk. The guy could have certainly changed his mind and come after me again.

And, on my return, I was certainly keeping my eyes open both on my left and on my right, as I jogged along that middle empty green.

The reality was, that there wasn't much of anything that I could really do right there and then when the incident happened. And I certainly wanted to avoid any repeat on my return back while getting closer and closer to the Eiffel Tower itself.

Had you been running along the lawns at the sides rather than in the middle, might he have gotten you on the side and dragged you into the bushes, and then that would have been it, huh?

And, I told him that my son and his guy friends were there and they should be coming up and they would see him.

What did your son say when you got back?

I didn't tell him right away.

Does he know about it to this day?

Yeah, he knows a little of it.

Let me just tell you what somebody else did in a similar situation in Egypt.

It was a couple of Western guys and two girls who came across two Egyptian night watchmen in some area where they definitely should not have been.

The guards said to the guys that they could leave but only after they had sex with their women. And, the Americans were trying to talk them down just as you did. Finally, they did manage to convince the Egyptians that the women had HIV (AIDS) and that they would catch it! Like, the women were saying, "We don't want you to get AIDS, because we have it!"

Yeah, that's a good idea!

Well, the Egyptian could have said, "Wow, so do I. That makes two of us!!"

But that's a risk that the four foreigners had to take.

You knew the possibilities but not the probabilities.

Well, I knew what the possibility was, but I really didn't know the probability, or it didn't seem like it was all that likely at the time.

But, in the end, you intuited the right way.

I wouldn't have gone down that isolated green, really, in the first place, not at that time in the morning, if I really had thought it was that risky. The simple truth is that I didn't.

You know, you're a confident person; you have a lot of self-confidence about dealing with situations. You've gotten out of more than your fair share of horrible situations.

Well, yes, I've dealt with a lot of situations in life, and so, I figured that I would probably psychically be safe, in a sense, I guess. But, I was safe, after all is said and done. I'm here to talk about it. There's your proof.

It was a very interesting trip that tested my confidence and ability to overcome some horrific situations. It was all really intense. People really need to be more careful, though.

Raped in Soviet Georgia: Aftermath Nightmare #1

Donald Rauly

Aftermath nightmares are what often happen overseas after a rape is reported to authorities, whether they be the local police, military authorities, secret police even, or embassies or consulates.

One could and would expect that such reports made in the aftermath of sexual assaults to the proper authorities might conceivably lead to the desired results, such as jail convictions for the perpetrators, and so on.

But actual events in these circumstances suggest otherwise, that the aftermath of a rape overseas is often anything but simple and clear-cut! It is often the case that the proceedings and outcomes are so unbelievably complicated, convoluted, at odds with competing rather than cooperating authorities and interests, and are wrought with virtually any other hindrances that you can conceivably come up with!

It is no wonder then that rape victims overseas (as well as at home) often opt to dispense with the reporting of such events and to simply learn the life lessons entailed and get on with their lives, instead.

Several accounts of rapes overseas are presented here along with the complex aftermath nightmares that ensued.

The first case in point concerns what happened to a group of American tourists visiting the former Soviet Republic of Georgia, in its capital, Tbilisi, during the Cold War. It smacks of the need to exercise good judgment — perhaps at least as good as or <u>better</u> than one might normally exercise at home.

To go to the police or not to go, to report a crime or not to report a crime, has always been the question — but, especially even more so, when it comes to such iffy places as one of the former Soviet Republics, not only under the yoke and chains and control of Mother Russia, but also all wrapped up in a complex mix of almost indecipherable shenanigans, ruses and subterfuges that often take the form of what can only be described as a 'living nightmare!'

One almost does a double-take when, under such circumstances, the rule of law is often juxtaposed against the notion of 'frontier justice' as a potentially viable solution!

Much goes on in the normal, typical pursuit of 'American' justice when such justice back home is demanded, even during the most normal of circumstances. However, when such an episode takes center stage overseas in a supposed three-ring circus — such as these stories represent — there are further risks to contend with in pursuing justice — and all bets are off. If the pursuit of justice and the American way is what we aspire to at home, then be not surprised by its absence overseas.

The Rape in Soviet Georgia

Tbilisi, Soviet Republic of Georgia, 1975. My wife and I were responsible for our group of American students visiting several of the former Soviet Republics during the Cold War.

A girl in our group was raped. It happened on top of a mountain just outside Tbilisi. And the guy responsible got out of his car not knowing that our women drive, which their women barely can do. She simply drove the car back down the mountain to the hotel. The rapist's identifying documents were in his car.

Then she found me in the hotel and told me what had happened to her. We decided to go to the police. Our Russian guide said, however. "No, I had warned them all."

She had warned them, but exactly how so and to what extent was not clear.

"What do you mean, you had warned her?"

"I had warned the group that Soviet Georgia had a reputation for men who are very eager to attack Western women."

Western women, or any woman for that matter, but Western women, in particular.

Here's what had apparently happened. Apparently, a Georgian couple was having dinner next to our group in a restaurant, and they were very hospitable. They're known for that. They were very generous. I saw them giving out fruit to the students, and one of the students who knew a little Russian went up to them to thank them. I noticed then that they sat down together.

All right, fine, I encouraged them to meet people. So, the next day the student said that this couple had invited her out to show her the city. And when she went to meet them, the woman wasn't there, for some reason. The guy told her that they were going *TO* the woman and that they were going to pick her up on the way. He was very well-dressed and seemed educated, etc. So, the girl went with him.

If she would have asked me, my advice to her would have been, "I don't know the situation. You need to be the judge."

Knowing the situation in this particular country, I, personally, would have been more cautious.

Our guide kept on insisting that I did not give any warning, but I guess I did, and I didn't. I felt after the fact, that maybe I could have perhaps been clearer on this one point.

On the other hand, I'm sure I did say to the group, "Look, I don't know the situation, and I wouldn't do anything here that I wouldn't do at home. I don't want you all to be afraid of going out with people who you meet, by no means, but just size up the situation and react to it. But, here is the reputation in this particular country..."

And then this was something that came up?

Yeah, that, essentially, women should be very careful.

So, the student was only in first year Russian, so she knew very little Russian, and this guy didn't speak any English."

So, it became clear they were not going to pick up this girl. And they went to a restaurant on top of the mountain above Tbilisi. In the restaurant the guy drank; she didn't. And he asked her, "How about vodka champagne?"

She said no. Next, he apparently came on to her.

She apparently understood that but didn't want any part of it. Agitated by his behavior, she said she wanted to go back to the hotel. But what he did next was stop the car and rape her.

She could not escape. And she, of course, was very frightened.

He then got out of the car to urinate. And not expecting that she knew how to drive a car, she just jumped over, left him with his pants down, drove down the mountain, and found the hotel. It was around midnight. And apparently, all his personal documents were still in the car.

What happened at that point?

She knocked on the door, found me, and was really upset. We went out together to a semi-private corner of the stairwell, and an older Russian or Georgian woman, the floor guardian and overseer of the room keys, was also there.

She saw the girl crying, and first thing thought that there was some foul play going on between the girl and me, seeing us standing there in the hallway together, what with the girl crying. So, I had to tell her essentially to get lost, to just leave us alone. But she kept on insisting, "What's going on? What's going on?"

Aftermath Nightmare #1

We went straight to the nearest police station. The girl at first did not want to go. Our Russian guide insisted, "Don't go to the police; she got what she deserved; she should have known better?"

So, she sort of was forewarned?

"Yes."

The guide said, "I warned them all on the bus."

Your feeling about that?

I'm not clear about the warnings and admonitions. But in retrospect, we probably should have had more of a discussion of such matters. But, I say this in hindsight.

Walking into the police station was amazing, the seriousness of it all. On the wall was an immense portrait of Stalin, the leader of the Soviet Union who was from Georgia. He was not Russian; he was a local boy who made good. And they're so proud of him down there. It was a giant portrait of Stalin with a smile on his face lighting his cigar (or his pipe), whichever it was.

At first, we were intimidated a bit by it all. It was all so very bizarre and immense. They tried to, I think, play games with us, to frighten us. They showed us the laws. Everything was very clearly spelled out including some of the punishments, unlike here in America, where the judge usually decides the punishment. Here they were saying, "If you do this; then they'll do such and such to you. It was all simple and straightforward and clearly spelled out."

Why were they trying to scare you?

"Well, they kept on telling us, if anything is perjury... If there's anything wrong with the accusation... Are you really sure you want to go through with this? "

That sort of thing. Apparently, we'd be liable to up to maybe five years imprisonment. But that didn't faze us because we weren't doing anything wrong.

So, the tone then changed a bit when they realized they weren't going to scare us easily. But at that point, though, too, I think at first the local police just wanted to scare us until they, themselves, could figure out exactly what they were supposed to do.

Oddly enough, it ended up that the head of the KGB (the Soviet Secret Police) for the whole republic of Georgia ultimately got involved in the case and came there. And we spent that whole first night, literally *ALL* night there. We began about 1 AM and finished at 8 AM in the morning.

Everything had to be handwritten; they wouldn't use tapes. At first, they just wanted us to just sign the document. But we demanded that it be read back to us. And then, when it was read back to us, we discovered that it was full of mistakes. Every page had mistakes! It had to be re-written; they couldn't just correct it."

This was the head of the KGB?

Yeah. And the whole thing was more than 10 pages in all, so it took all night, literally.

Finally, we demanded a medical exam. And they brought in this grody-looking, greasy, slimy man with a big beer belly and a cigar. And I said, "You're so proud of the fact that 80% of your doctors are women, find one now!"

And they did just that, and that, too, was a farce, in a way, it seemed. Yes, it was a medical exam, but it wasn't very sophisticated. It was just very basic.

"I don't see anything here," said the lady doctor, and that was basically it.

We were given about two hours' rest.

I got back to the hotel in the early morning just in time to meet up with the group at the bus, just as they were all getting on the bus for the morning tour.

The big deal of the day was the complaint from our group that we had tongue for breakfast three days in a row! The group didn't want tongue AT ALL, and we had told them in the first place *NOT* to give us tongue. But they gave us tongue, anyway. So, the group gathered the tongue from everyone's plate and reassembled all these slices to make up a single, complete tongue out of it all, garnished it, and then wheeled it back into the kitchen in protest.

So, I had to deal with that, talked to the kitchen staff, and calmed everyone down. There were far more important matters to deal with than the breakfast meats!

I then got on the bus and told the students briefly about the more serious issue at hand: "There's a problem that may become intense, but it doesn't look like it will. It looks like the person is fine now, but the Soviets do not want that person out of the hospital quite yet. I just grabbed the nearest student on the bus, put him in charge and said, "I'll see you later."

At noon, we went back to the police station. I demanded to call the American Embassy, but the number I was given, the "in case of emergency" number by our organization in New York that sponsored us overseas, was out of service.

I kept on insisting to the KGB guy that they could find a number if they really wanted to, and he asked me how. I said, "The KGB! I cannot believe that the KGB cannot connect me to the American Embassy."

So, we played this game for a little while.

We were in the regular city police station at this point, but someone from the KGB had apparently shown up in person to oversee the case.. Everyone I talked to I asked for their documents, and he (the KGB guy) presented to me his documents as well. I had to assure him that it wouldn't get back to our FBI, and so on!

We sort of liked him, by the way. We called him "Kojak" (after the famous likable bald detective sleuth of TV fame in America). But this Kojak was really ugly and sort of looked like a Georgian version of Kojak.

Meanwhile, the person who committed the crime also came into the police station to report that his car had been stolen by this American girl. So, we spent the whole afternoon sort of playing games back and forth trying to get evidence together to make a case against him.

I tried to get hold of the Embassy again. Finally, I just threw a temper tantrum, and they took me to someone who had a phone number of Air France. So, I called that number, which just happened to be Air France in Moscow.

I read French but could not speak it. The French person, in turn, did not speak Russian or English. However, I did manage to get the number to the American Embassy. I called and got a marine on duty who took everything down and said to me, "Call back in half an hour."

Which, I, of course, did, and they seemed as if they could care less.

So, here I was with all these people, far away from everything, and by this point, I think the student group was beginning to wonder what all was going on.

Nobody else knew?

No, no one knew any of the details.

We then went back at 7 PM to the police station and began a marathon session in the same room with the rapist! Our girl told her story; the rapist told his. And both stories were written out verbatim.

Was he nervous or anything?

No. He was brazenly nonchalant about it all. He, of course, said he had no idea why she did this to him (stole his car and drove away), and that he was the typical, hospitable Georgian, and this strange American girl who stole his car should be the one being prosecuted, not him, and that she obviously had made this whole thing up.

It began in the early evening, and by 3 AM in the morning I was already about to pass out from exhaustion.

Oh, when we sat down to do this, they told me at first that I couldn't be in the room, on some technicality. So, I said, "Okay, then this session simply will NOT take place!"

They argued in Georgian for a while, which we could not, of course, understand. They then agreed to swear me in as the translator, so that I was essential and could, therefore, be in the room. By about 2 AM I was completely fading,

Then a most extraordinary thing happened. Our Soviet KGB Kojak said, "Everyone, please step out of the room." (Except the rapist)

And Kojak next said to him, "Except you. Sit here, you son of a bitch!"

The rest of us walked into the next room, and to our total surprise, the wives of the city police had brought in grilled chicken and *shaslik*, (grilled meat), cognac, and bread. None of us had eaten anything for a long while. And so, we all just pounced on this delicious food. We gobbled up chicken, all the meat, and even drank some cognac and made some toasts to our mutual friendship.

Except for the rapist, of course, who was still sitting in the other room with Kojak, the KGB officer.

You were drinking toasts?

Right. Thinking that, *Are they doing this to get me drunk so I can't talk?*

Because it really wouldn't take much, since I was so tired. But it was all very sincere.

We got done at about 6 AM, and our group was about to leave at 9 AM for the next city on our tour. We parted actually with hugs and kisses from the police, including the head of the KGB, Kojak, himself.

By this time, however, our local guide, who was not involved in all of this, of course, knew about it and told one of the students who she spent a lot of time with, who, in turn, told some of the other students about it. So, our group knew, and we, for obvious reasons, wanted to keep it all very private and personal.

In the next city, we decided to clear the air a bit more. We told the students, "Look, we all know this happened..."

We carried on a 10-minute session and decided that we weren't going to let this ruin the rest of the trip. And that was it. This really tense brief meeting cleared the air.

What was the outcome of it all with the police?

The end was that they dropped the charges that the rapist raised against our student, altogether. There were no charges; they just said it was ridiculous. And since there were no witnesses, it was her word against his, so they told us that it would all depend upon the results of the medical examination, which were not back yet, and which we never ever did hear about.

We knew what that meant. As soon as we left town, we were sure that that would likely be the end of it all.

The only interesting thing that came out of all this was the admission that the guy, the story he had told her, that he was a dentist, was not true at all. He was a plumber from a local state farm who seemed to be a real wheeler-dealer. And I sort of got the feeling that he may have been a troublemaker before because the police were a little rough on him.

In what sense? Were they slapping him around?

No, nothing like that, but they were a bit crude to him. Well, not so much at first.

I guess one of the things that really stood out when I was alone with the local police — not the KGB guy — was that they were saying things to the effect, like, "Oh, typical woman, she asked for it, and you didn't satisfy her, and now she's bitching."

And I really objected to that and gave them a hard time about saying such things, and they sort of backed down a bit off of that position afterwards.

Oh, that first night I demanded that they take his underwear as evidence and do an analysis to see if they found any semen.

And these police were real crude in what they told me regarding that. They said, "Big deal, he's gonna say that she wouldn't put out for him, and he went and he beat off, or something like that."

This is what they told me literally in very crude language.

You speak Russian, so you understood it."

"Oh yeah."

And the KGB's point of view?

The KGB guy, of course, had to play it all a bit more seriously. Meanwhile, when I got to the next city and I talked to my Soviet friends there, they all said to me, "Look, this would never have happened in Russia proper, not with a foreigner."

Furthermore, the Georgians could care less who it was, and that, if anything — if it were a Georgian woman involved — her brothers and father would kill the person right on the spot, and nothing more would happen to any of them for doing so. A type of frontier justice in that part of the world!

So, the police would probably go through the whole charade, and as soon as you'd leave the country, that would be the end of it; they'd simply forget all about it."

So, what do you think Kojak's attitude was after all was said and done?

I got the feeling that this guy, the rapist, had probably caused some trouble in the past and that something more might have happened to him this time, considering his former behavior and reputation.

Kojak was basically on your side, wasn't he?

Oh, he at least pretended to be, and it was very convincing.

But in the end, you just think nothing much happened and that perhaps the guy got roughed up a bit?

No, probably not. Because we cabled several times more and never really heard much more about it.

Oh, I had mentioned that the Embassy at first couldn't care less. When we got to Leningrad, all of a sudden the Consulate was now looking for *us!* Now, for some reason, they were suddenly interested in the case.

Why was that?

They were interested because there was this Soviet KGB couple, a British woman and a Russian husband, an alleged Russian "Journalist named Victor Louis." They were infamous. They'd have lunch in Paris and dinner in London, that sort of thing! They're always suspected of being involved in training spies, that sort of thing.

For some reason, they became interested in this case. So, they apparently called the American Embassy and said that they knew about what had happened.

They asked the Embassy, "Are you intending to give a news release?" (Because they were evidently intending to beat us to it.)

And they said, "Well, we want to get our facts straight because we're going to have to tell foreign correspondents about it."

The U.S. Embassy's reaction to Victor Louis was typical: "What business is it of yours?"

Your reaction to this might be, why? Why would the Soviets be so interested in this?

It's because the Soviets felt that such an incident would not put them in a very good light, and so, they wished maybe to pre-empt any official re-action by the United States.

People were not normally shocked that this rape had happened, know-ing how common it is here in the U.S. But what does shock people, I think, is the apparent hypocrisy of the Soviets liking to point out that they don't have this sort of thing. "We don't have crime," is the typical Soviet response to this sort of report. In other words, they were very much concerned with their public image.

So, in Leningrad, the likely reading by the U.S. Consulate was that THEY (the Soviets) were wondering if WE (the Americans) were going to get publicly involved with this case as some sort of a propaganda thing, like a U.S. versus the Soviet Union sort of thing.

The U.S. Consulate really had no intention of doing anything at all, but if we were going to, the Soviets were going to try to beat us to it, perhaps.

What the Soviets were doing was merely trying to see what our reaction was to it all. And, of course, we, ourselves, didn't want anyone to know, par-ticularly because all we only really wanted was to protect the girl's privacy.

So, in other words, nothing was going to be done about it. So the Con-sulate just told the Soviets that it really was none of their business, and so the Consulate had called us in to tell us that this sort of thing was, after all, a distinct possibility.

Of course, we neither wanted nor did we, conduct any sort of press conference at all. It was the farthest thing from our minds at the time. None of us needed that, and, of course, nothing ever came of it from either side.

The Soviets, for their part, never held a press conference, either. So, it was this Soviet Victor Louis couple's interest in the case that prompted the U.S. Consulate to be so nice to us. At least the Soviets threatened at first to do a press conference if they thought the U.S. was going to trump up the case on its own. I think that all the Soviets really wanted was merely assur-ance from us that we weren't going to make a big deal out of it, either.

Would they have presented us as this wild group of Americans who came here for a good time? As a result of having no press conferences on either side, that crap was now out of the picture altogether, and we were re-lieved.

There is probably little question that the Soviet Union may have less crime than perhaps we do in the West. But rather than being able to deal with it squarely without all this reluctance, that embitters people more than the particular rape occurrence itself.

Victor Louis was allegedly involved in trading spies. Ostensibly, Victor Louis was a Soviet 'journalist.' There's no doubt that he obviously had very top KGB connections, because he lived high on the hog, in a mansion villa, and he traveled whenever and wherever he wanted to back and forth. He was always involved in exchanging of spies and all sorts of things like this. The case of the Georgia rape of an American student was beginning to attract attention and could have expanded worldwide. It's clear that Moscow, at the very least, was involved in every step of the way and knew everything that was going on.

Raped in Nepal:
Aftermath Nightmare #2

David DiPietro

May Sakai. (an assumed name) was a Japanese-American physician who worked in Oakland, California at the time that I knew her. She came to visit me and my friend who was living in Bangkok, Thailand for a couple of months. We were working on doing relief work for the Cambodian refugees there.

May — The Woman

May came to visit because she was a classmate of one of my friends. She was doing an around-the-world tour all by herself and had been all over. She had just flown in from West Germany and said that she was en route to Nepal.

At that point, I had just been doing a lot of work, which was just slowing down and I wanted to join her in Nepal.

What is she like as a person? What does she look like, and what was her stature?

Well, she was a spunky young woman, about 29 or 30, fairly short, about 5' 2". She was very pretty, maybe a tad stocky, but she was very active. She was very intelligent, very witty and always had a keen laugh. She had pretty eyes and very pretty Japanese features.

I'd say she was very modern in her outlook and perspective. She was not held back by typical Japanese-American traditions. She was raised in Hawaii. I'd say she was more the typical American, maybe a San Francisco type of person.

Her father was a physician, very traditional and very stern. He was dedicated to raising his family. And he put his kids through medical school. He was a very strict, stern Japanese-American male who had done everything for the family and worked very hard all his life. He was an incredible physician and he worked virtually all the time. His whole life was dedicated to his medical career.

May was a pretty good student, first in her class in high school and won all sorts of debating awards, and such. She went to Stanford as an undergraduate and then got into the University of Hawaii Medical School. She wanted to be an ophthalmologist. She did get into the Mayo Clinic, which is like the number one residency in ophthalmology.

Nepal — The Trek

I decided to go to Nepal, and so I was in Nepal with May. She wanted to go trekking, and I wasn't sure that I wanted to go trekking to quite the extent that she did. We decided to do the Annapurna Range, a beautiful mountain range. It's not the one with Mount Everest; this is on the other side.

May had prepared to do this trek for about five months. She was in good shape: she had been weightlifting and jogging for about five or six hours a day. She was in very good physical condition. Very strong.

We contacted the Annapurna Trekking Company, a very reputable outfit. It cost us quite a lot of money, $35 a day, which was very exorbitant by any standards at that time, especially by Nepali standards. So, we signed up and paid in full in advance.

May had planned to do a 16-day trek, and I only wanted to do an 8-day trek, because I wanted to get back to my work in Bangkok. I didn't really want to be that long in Nepal. We hired two Sherpas, which are guides who show you the trails and tell you all about the mountains and the different peoples along the way.

Nepal is a country of about a million people who inhabited the villages. There are not many roads as such. It's all mountains, and you have to do everything by footpaths and donkeys. Houses are dirt huts. Not much in the way of windows. And people are poor, but they're healthy poor.

They're self-sufficient in their own foodstuffs and have a very good diet. Even though they probably only live to be 40 or 50, they are fairly self-sufficient and no one gives them handouts.

So, I was to do an eight-day trek. And May wanted to do a 16-day trek. She wanted to go to the top of Mutinah.

May's sort of Buddhist in her philosophy of life. She said that she had read up on all of this, and studied the mountains and the tradition and culture. Mutinah is supposed to be a very holy place, and therefore she wanted to go there. A kind of special thing in her life.

Was she really into Buddhism?

I don't know how seriously she practices it, but I think Buddhism is a philosophy of life, and she knows much about it. Being a Japanese-American, she did study Japanese and probably had gone to a Buddhist temple as a younger child and all. I don't know how seriously she practiced it, but she was definitely attuned to the culture and what was going on in Nepal.

We hired two Sherpa guides and four porters who carry all your bags and luggage. And it was quite nice. All you had to do was just walk. They set up the tents; they cook the meals, and; they set up your place to sleep.

It could have been cheaper. For instance, you could do all of that for as little as $15 or maybe even $10 a day if you know the right people. But the Annapurna Trekking Company was a very reputable firm, and we were able to arrange it with the ease of using American Express, and all that.

So, we started our trek. It was beautiful. It was in November. It was peak season for the rice harvest. The mountains are just golden with rice, and you have the people in the fields harvesting the rice, and their vegetable gardens are full.

There are incredibly beautiful mountain streams. It was really all so picturesque. I love high technology, but Nepal is such a change because you can't do that.

We were trekking, and the people were so very nice, very pleasant, and very friendly, and they would all come up to you and they'd sing songs and ask for a few rupees, which are the Nepali money.

They'd say *"Namaste"* which is "hello" and little kids would run up to you and sing their songs, and they'd play their traditional instruments. And they'd be running around there all barefoot. It's poor but very pretty.

The guides were very helpful and very cordial to us all the time. I had my tent and May had her tent, and the Sherpas, of course, had their tents as well.

Wherever we'd go, they'd buy their local vegetables and they'd cook us Western-style vegetable meals.

Stark Realities

I, being a physician, however, was very much aware that I was not going to eat any cold, uncooked vegetables because if you just looked at their gardens, they had their outhouses right over their gardens. Not good. All the excrement would be right there by their gardens. I spoke to some Peace Corps people, who told me that on the average, 95 percent of the Peace Corps Volunteers in Nepal come back home with one or two intestinal parasites: mainly embyosis, giardia, and hookworms.

Can you get rid of them?

You can get rid of them, but you have to stop re-infecting yourself, and they said some Peace Corps Volunteers come back with as many as 10 different intestinal parasites.

It's incredible. Here they are feeding us these really nice Western-made salads. However, they'd go pick cucumbers and lettuce and tomatoes, and all that, which they've grown there with their gardens and their outhouses. So, I'm saying, "I am not going to eat this. No way."

Our Sherpas, however, are eating their boiled vegetables and their rice and I'm saying to them, "I want that."

But May's going, "No, no. They prepared this for us. We have to be polite, and it's a way of acceptance. You just accept."

Well, I told them, "No, I don't want any more of this," but May made us eat one or two meals of this, anyway. Fortunately, I didn't have any problems, and neither did May.

So, you started eating their food?

Oh, yes. But I told Rodna, one of our guides who spoke English and was very knowledgeable — he was a cook in the British army. I told him, "No more. We want to eat your cooked food, too, just like the Nepalese. I like the Nepali kind of food!"

So, that was a good culturally sensitive way out, huh... "Like the Nepali?"

Oh, yeah. We were trying to be very polite when we said this.

We went to all these different places. We were running up and down the hills. May was laughing and joking and having a really merry time. We were really enjoying ourselves. We got along very well, which is surprising, considering that we'd only known each other for four or five days. It was working out well.

I ended up going as far as Tatopani, which is about 3,135 meters altitude, about 9,000 feet. It's very beautiful there. You go to Ghorepani first and then go down to Tatopani. From Ghorepani you get a spectacular view of the Annapurna range: Dhaulagiri, Annapurna One, Annapurna South, and Annapurna Two, simply beautiful. You walk way up to the top of the hill where they have an observatory.

Along our way, we met many foreigners: Western Europeans, including French, Scandinavians, West Germans, and Italians. It was a very international group and everyone was speaking English, and I couldn't believe just how much tourism there is and how popular Nepal is among the Western Europeans. Oddly, we were some of the very few Americans that we had seen there.

I Leave May

I left May at Tatopani. We parted really happy. We said our "goodbyes" and she continued on with her two guides and three porters.

That was after five days together. I had yet to do my three-day trek back, a much shorter trip back. May, however, had 13 more days to go, but only three more days up and then eight days back.

Her final destination was Mutinah. She left with two Sherpa guides and her three porters. She had five Nepali men with her and herself. She had her own tent and she was left pretty much alone. They never bothered her, and they were very polite.

The Fateful Night — The Incident

I never had any fear. Never had any inkling that anything might happen as it ultimately did.

And there were foreigners all along the trail all the time. When she first decided to do this trek, the Dean of the University of Hawaii Medical School told May that Nepal is the "safest place in the world" and that "we'd never have to worry about anything."

It was the only place he could conceive of that a woman could walk alone and have no fear, or anything like that.

We had been given no reason to think otherwise, in that the Nepalese people we had met were always so friendly and kind and everything really seemed to be encouraging tourism in that respect.

Who'd a thunk? Boy, did that turn out to be wrong!

At this point, let me ask you, how much later was it that you heard about the rest of May's trek?

Just three days after I left her!

I continued my trek alone back, and May continued her trek up to Mutinah. From what I understand it was very uneventful going up to Mutinah until the night she got there.

I had made it back to Kathmandu, and I was preparing to leave that night.

Then all hell broke loose for May.

The Sherpas had pitched her tent up on a hill above a hotel, which was down a little bit lower, maybe a couple hundred yards below. What they did was, every night they'd put a candle in the tent so you'd be able to see. You could see the tent and you could get there easily and have no problem in the dark.

What they ended up doing was the guides and porters slept in the hotel below, which you could get for about 50 cents a night. They probably could do it much cheaper being workers, guides and porters, and such.

She wanted to stay in the tent?

Well, you have to understand that Nepal is not a very clean place. The beds, I would say, are perhaps infested with lice, maybe not. I don't know. But you saw lots of animals, say lots of chickens up and down, and everywhere. You don't know what kind of excrement was around, so it's not a very clean place. And everything is dusty and dirty. There's dust simply everywhere. You just have to adjust your whole mindset traveling in Nepal.

However, the tents were very clean by comparison.

They provide you with warm sleeping bags, so things are very comfortable in your tent. So, you get the picture: the tent is up on a hill. The tent was a golden-orange-red, so it's like a beacon. I'm sure you can see the shadows of a woman in there. May was in her tent and told me later that someone (a Nepalese soldier it turned out) was scratching on the tent from the outside, making noises.

May shouted out, "Get out of here," in her best Nepali. She was really scared and she called to her Sherpa who was now bringing stuff up to her, "Rodna, there is someone at my tent. I'm really scared. I want you to stay here with me."

How far away was he at that point? Was he there when the scratching was going on?

No. She called down to him. He was on his way up the hill to bring some stuff to her when she heard the scratching on the tent and then she screamed out to Rodna. He came to the door, so he couldn't be very far away.

So, apparently, whoever it was split at that point?

I guess.

She said, "Rodna I'm very scared. I don't know. But someone's bugging me at my tent, and I don't want to be left here alone."

So, Rodna ran down back to the hotel and got a knife and came back to the tent and stayed with May there.

Shortly afterwards, some Nepali guy came back and started screaming outside the tent, calling May all manner of names like, "American whore" and other vile obscenities. And he's yelling, calling Rodna "a very bad Nepali," and "What are you doing with an American woman?" and "What's are you doing in the tent?"

All these things, including, "You shouldn't be there."

At this point, it was a drunken Nepali soldier and Rodna became very scared. To him a soldier represents authority and the soldier wanted in, and he said, "I want to see your papers. What are you doing here? Do you have your trekking permit?" (You have to have a trekking permit to trek in Nepal.)

May said to Rodna, "Don't open the tent. I don't want to see him in here. I'm really scared. Just tell him to go away."

But, Rodna was very cowed by all this and said to May, "I've got to leave... He's the police. He's a soldier."

So, Rodna opened the tent. As soon as he opened the tent, the Nepali soldier then grabbed him, pulled him out of the tent and started strangling him. Now this man is off his gourd or whatever, I don't know, but May is watching in horror as this man is hurting her Sherpa. And she's a very spunky, independent woman who's taken karate before, and who has dealt in emergency rooms and seen lots of very tough people come in with knife wounds and bullet wounds. She's dealt with this kind of crowd before.

So, she sees all this happening and knows full well what it means to be actually in threat of losing one's life. So, she saw him strangling her guide, and she thought he was in really a lot of peril.

So, May, being the spunky woman she was, went out there and started beating on the Nepali soldier. He then slapped her and she fell backwards, and he went back to strangling Rodna. He sure seemed really intent on doing something to this Sherpa.

May next goes back to the tent, grabs the knife, and starts stabbing the soldier. She stabbed him about four or five times. She's short, remember. I don't know how tall this guy was, but she was only able apparently to get the lung. She did not mortally get him, but I think she might have known where she was stabbing. I don't know.

Trying to avoid stabbing him where it might kill him?

I'm not sure, but I think that must have been going on. I don't think she really wanted to seriously hurt him; but she just wanted to stop him from killing her Sherpa, which she really believed he was doing.

At this point, he now let's go of Rodna and turns on May and starts grabbing her. Rodna takes off. He just runs. He's scared. He doesn't want anything to do with this. I don't know what was going through his mind, but he obviously wasn't staying around to help.

May sees this and then screams, "Rodna, don't leave me. How can you leave me like this?"

She sees Rodna running down the hill. She panics. This is a Nepali soldier. She's in no condition to handle this man who's a lot bigger than she.

Was he bleeding at this point probably?

I don't know. She had stabbed him a good five times. She then dropped the knife and started running herself. But, as she was running she tripped. It was a dark path. She'd fallen and she saw this Nepali soldier coming after her. She looked up and saw this guy with a knife coming down at her, and she just kind of turned really scared. She got hit several times, including a couple of hits on the head with the knife.

Aftermath Nightmare #2

She lost consciousness at that time. She woke up, I don't know how much later. I think it couldn't have been more than five or ten minutes later when she came to. She then regained consciousness and discovered that her skirt was torn and that she had semen over her abdomen. I assumed that she was raped. And she, too, assumed that she was raped. She didn't tell anyone about that.

She saw her wound and saw the blood gushing down her head. She quickly regained her senses, gained control of herself, and ran down to the hotel screaming for help.

You have to realize now, Nepal is primitive, and in Mutinah there are no roads; there is no transport at all. She's far away from any doctors. She's a physician, herself. She knows she's the only one that's going to save her if anyone is going to save her, so she tells them to "boil some water and get me a mirror." And she just starts. She cleans her hair, cleans the wound, and inspects to make sure that there are no fractures because she's done this a hundred times.

No anesthetic?

No anesthesia. What she does is tie her hair. She takes her hair and approximates the exit of the wound by pulling it tight — she has long hair. She could do that. So, it was very good. She cleaned the wound and kind of stopped the bleeding by applying pressure.

Was it a superficial wound at that point?

No, no. There was a laceration to the scalp, a gash, and she felt some of the edges of a bone, so she knows she has some type of skull fracture. She wasn't quite sure, but she apparently felt some ridges. I don't know how good her clinical assessment was at this point, but she knew that she wasn't going to go to sleep. She knew she had to get to some kind of a hospital, to some medical care, because with any type of wound to that area — you worry about a hematoma, a subdural hematoma.

That's like bleeding under the scalp that can compress the brain, and it can depress the respiratory centers in the head and cause the brain to herniate through a hole at the base of the skull called the *spirana magna,* which can cut off your breathing and you die. That could happen in 20 minutes, an hour later, or a week later. So, she's saying, she's got to maintain, and she's just watching all the neurological stuff, making sure she doesn't vomit, as well as making sure she doesn't start seeing double, not having clear speech, blocking of the consciousness, or blocking of her awareness, and such things. Anyway, she's trying to keep clear of all of these bad things.

She next tried to get some people to try and find out if there was a doctor and stuff anywhere near. Two hours later they found a German doctor, who during that two hours had been suturing — the Nepali soldier, who he assumed had been involved in a fight.

He had some problem with his lung. I'm not sure if his lung was collapsed or not, but he sutured up the knife wounds and he used all his anesthesia up, used all his antibiotics up, and all his suture material on this pathetic, despicable character.

The doctor had no idea of what was going on. He thought that the guy was involved in some heavy fight because of the nature of his wounds. But, never in his wildest imagination did he have even the slightest idea that this was the soldier who had assaulted both May and her Sherpa guide and raped May.

He finally came to May's aid and, of course, did not have any anesthesia left — no Novocain and no lidocaine. What he did was he got a thread and needle and sutured the wound with no anesthesia.

Rodna, at this point, had all but disappeared. He was gone, but the other Sherpa still remained, and he was really very nice, very helpful, and very capable and gave May a lot of kindness and support.

May said she was only one day's trek away from an airport, and it was a $28 flight at 10 AM. They hired some mules, but she didn't have any money to pay for it.

What kind of a flight? $28 to where?

To Kathmandu Airport from there. She didn't have any money — after all, she had been robbed as well. Her tent had been ransacked and her jewelry and all her money were stolen. She did have her passport, though.

The Authorities — The Red Tape!

What did she do next?

They hired mules. They got everything ready, packed up and got ready to go.

She didn't allow herself to go to sleep because she was afraid she'd never wake up. They got on the mules. They traveled all morning, and they got to the airport area, which just had flights and helicopters, and such.

The Nepali authorities, however, wanted a full description of what had happened, and they delayed her. They caught the soldier and made her identify the soldier, which was all very good, but she had to catch the plane to get out to get back to get urgent, desperately-needed medical treatment, and they had delayed her so long that she missed her $28 flight, which she had had all arranged.

However, they were apparently able to contact the Annapurna Trekking Company, which was now really concerned about their reputation, so they had a flight arranged for her to get her back to Bangkok. But, of course, May was delayed and missed the $28 flight from that area to Kathmandu, which is like a 20-minute flight.

Meanwhile, May asked, "Contact Dr. DiPietro and have him meet me at the airport."

She knew I was going to be at the airport. She knew when my flight was going to be leaving and all that.

But she missed the trunk flight?

She missed that day's flight. She'd been up all night. She was really upset at this point. She started feeling woozy, not sure of her balance. She was almost starting to faint and she started vomiting at this point after she had missed the flight.

The German doctor got very scared because these are the signs of a herniation of the brain, the temporal lobe herniation, meaning that there might be some type of subdural hematoma going on and that she had some serious brain injury. She had vomited once already, and she was seeing double.

All these symptoms are a sign of an ongoing subdural hematoma, which means that you only have a matter of hours to save someone. What that means is you have to put holes into the head to ease the pressure, so that you don't crush the brain stem and stop her breathing apparatus.

The German doctor panicked, and May knew something was going on, and they had got to do something urgently.

They said that we needed a medivac immediately. What they had to do was have the Nepali authorities contact the Nepali army. The Nepali army, in turn, said they would medivac her out if the U.S. Embassy guaranteed the payment of the cost to do that — I think, around $4,300, something like that.

May did not know about this yet. All she knew was that there was a flight ready for her and that the medivac helicopter was coming to pick her up.

Unbeknownst to her, the U.S. Embassy okayed the loan, okayed everything, and arranged to medevac her out.

But, as soon as May got to the airport, the U.S. Embassy Consul took her passport and they brought it to the hospital at Kathmandu. She didn't want to give up her passport but she had to. Then, when she was finally put into the hospital, they told her, "You have to contact as many people as you can to try to raise $5,000."

She said, "What do you mean?"

"Well, you have to pay for the emergency helicopter flight out of there. We guaranteed the $5,000, but you cannot leave the country until you raise that money; you need to find someone right away to guarantee the payment."

She again said, "What do you mean?"

At this point, they had her passport. She felt desperately at odds that they had taken her passport away and that she couldn't leave the country. She had a flight out that day to Bangkok. They wouldn't let her go. For whatever reasons.

She's pleading with the Consul who has no medical background. She's saying, "You don't understand. I'm a medical physician. I know what a brain injury means. I know that I could be talking to you right now. I can be perfectly normal and in a half hour, an hour, I could be dead. You have to understand that I have a ... "

She had this big gash. It was sewed up.

The Consul had no right, and the Embassy doctor was on a trip to Burma, so he wasn't here for any counsel.

What happened at that point?

They put her in the Kathmandu hospital. She had this 70-year-old American physician, who didn't even get her history and physical, took an x-ray and May saw what looked like a suspicious skull fracture, which can lacerate some arteries. You just don't know.

Anyway, she was saying that it wasn't enough. They had not done a complete thorough enough physical. They had not ruled out that she had anything going on and her skull wasn't that bad. Anyway, there was no medical authority making any clear-cut diagnosis on her, and she was apparently being kept in Nepal against her will. And she had a flight out and they had her passport. They wouldn't let her leave until she paid the money. So, she had to fill out all these different forms. So anyway, they just kept her there.

She had flown into the airport. I was waiting there for my flight. She had asked the Consulate to go and contact Dr. DiPietro (me) to give her some help. I would have most certainly stayed on to help her. All they had to do was walk just 200 yards to go over to the international flight area to find me. But they would not do that; they just did not do it.

So, you knew nothing about this?

No, not at all. And I was <u>right there</u>! We were both in the airport at the same time! I could have helped May so much, but they didn't do it.

Why not?

They kept saying to May, "You're exaggerating. You're really upset. Just calm down."

And she was, indeed, really upset. This was all the American Consulate would do, who you would expect in a time of need would really be of help.

They did put up the $5,000 though, didn't they?

Yes, but they're keeping her captive when she was in dire need of medical attention. I don't know exactly what her needs were at that point, but whatever it was, there was no one competent enough there to decide, and on that sheer basis alone, someone who's had a significant laceration, big gash, should have been medevac'd to an area that could really give her the medical help she needed — in this case, Bangkok. And then solve all these other problems later on.

May felt like she shouldn't have had to pay that since it was a Nepali soldier that was responsible.

But, anyway, the U.S. Consulate wasn't going to be stuck for the $5,000, and they were going to make sure that she paid it. They confiscated her passport. Now she didn't know how legal that was to do, but anyway, it prevented her from leaving, because you can't leave without your passport.

She was put into a Kathmandu hospital. The conditions of the hospital were so terrible and deplorable by any standards. May saw someone being overdosed on an anti-asthmatic medication. And she had someone coming in and out of her room all night long with acute gastroenteritis, excreting on the floor for a bathroom.

They also wanted to give her morphine, which you should never ever do with a head injury because it can mask the signs of an ongoing subdural hematoma. They were trying to give her medication. Since she did not know which medication that was — they wouldn't tell her — so she just tongued all the medication, ultimately spitting it all out.

The next day May left the hospital. She thought, *I'm better off by myself.* So, she simply walked out the doors, went to a hotel and got herself a room.

She then went back to the Embassy, and they made her call all these people that she knew. She made a list of people and they contacted them, and that's how we found out.

I had already flown back to Bangkok. Two days later we got a telegram from May saying, "Been attacked while trekking. Please help!"

I thought, *My God! Attacked by what? A Yeti monster, which is like the Abominable Snowman? Who'd attack her? Why? This just does not happen!*

Anyway, we wired back for more information. She needed $5,000 right away. A Dr. Dan Susa put up the money, backed up by his father. He wrote out a check.

Was he a friend of yours?

Yeah, he was a classmate of May's at the University of Hawaii.

Once the money was put up, they gave her her passport back. But what they did was, she had to have a 10 AM flight. She went to the Embassy 8 AM that morning and they still made her fill out five different forms with four copies each. This is at the Embassy and she just kept having to fill out these forms.

She said, "I can't, I've got to catch my flight. I've got to be there."

And they just kept her there, making her fill out all these forms.

Did she know what she was signing?

I think she was signing releases saying she would not hold them responsible or anything like that, but they said she couldn't leave until she did this.

They were even going to make her take a taxi and pay for it herself. They did, finally, however, give her a ride to the airport, but at this point, she had been signing since 8 AM, so many forms, that she said, "I know I'm not going to make it. I know I'm not going to make it."

She broke down at this time crying and she was getting hysterical.

They said, "All right, stop. You are just getting hysterical."

She said, "Look at the time. I'm not going to make it."

They called the Embassy physician who had finally returned from Burma, and he looked at her. He took one look at her and saw the seriousness of her condition. She should have been evacuated immediately.

He said, "What is going on here? You get her right to the airport right now. I don't want to hear anything else."

So, they brought her right to the airport.

Needless to say, she missed her flight. And she was delayed yet one more day. She was just beside herself. She felt like she didn't have a friend in the world really, but the doctor was very nice. The doctor took her home overnight and really treated her royally.

The Vice Consulate woman was just very impertinent to May. Just callous and exaggerating, "You're okay. You'll be able to leave the next day."

In all, they had made her stay needlessly an extra five days in Nepal.

So, anyway, we met her at the Bangkok Airport. We met her and she was just crying and stuff. It's just so heartrending to see all this happening to her. We admitted her to the Seventh Day Adventist Hospital in Bangkok, which was under the direction of the American Embassy doctor.

He examined her, assessed her neurologically, and determined that she was fine.

He did an x-ray. There was some questionable skull fracture, but he said, "We started her on apisone and Keflex, which is administered to prevent any venereal disease and any other infection that may be due to the lacerations that she had,

As it turned out, it wasn't too serious for her after all, but there were a very significant laceration and a questionable fracture to her skull, all of which could have caused a subdural hematoma but, fortunately, didn't, and we were very thankful for that.

May stayed in our apartment for a couple of days after we took her out of the hospital after a day or so because I think what she needed more was just a lot of moral support, but she was fine neurologically.

Once, while taking a bath, May hit her head on the faucet. The wound opened up again and we got a look at it: It was just all the way down to the skull. It was just so massive. Anyway, we got very of it. She had a bruise on her cheek, on her chin, and her hands and stuff and her knee at a couple of points. We tied it all back up and kind of steri-stripped it, and it was okay after that. We haven't heard anything else, so we assumed that May healed all right after that.

Then, after all that, we contacted some news people that we knew from Reuters and the Associated Press (AP).

There were a lot of news people there, because of the Cambodian refugee situation and the Vietnamese and all that, so they put the story in a couple of newspapers. It hit, of course, the Bangkok news, and of course, we went to the Embassy in Bangkok and tried to get redress for all this.

They started some type of investigation. The Japanese Consulate even called May and said they were outraged that that had happened to her.

May next contacted people in Hawaii and also people in Washington and San Francisco. She knew a couple of lawyer friends in San Francisco who could help her. She contacted columnist Jack Anderson and I think there was an ensuing investigation. I guess, from what she told me, what they determined from the American Consulate in Nepal was that it was some form of a cover-up. They said they had never taken her passport. They also claimed they had never prevented her from leaving Nepal. They never said that she could not leave before paying.

I don't know the exact details since this is all second hand. This is what May was saying, but she had a lot more detail, a lot more to report.

But after all was said and done, it didn't sound all that good. I guess the U.S. Government was doing some type of investigating.

What do you think the status of May's situation is now?

I don't know. I guess they're working on it.

She says she earned the money and paid it all back. She's a New York physician now and she's got a job. She picked up her job, earned the money as fast as she could, and paid off the five thousand dollars. Other doctors in Hawaii put up a fund for her as well and helped pay off some of the money, too.

Do you think they are suing the Nepalese Government for the money?

May looked into that, but it would have been so much of a hassle. She would have had to go back to Nepal, which she did not want to do. She would have had to fight it in their courts, and no one is going to pay for this. It's going to cost her a lot just to get back there. She's got to get back to her life.

Well, she wired her dad but he just wouldn't send any money. He felt that this was all her fault. At this point, he didn't know that she was raped, but just that she was attacked. His attitude was that, "It's your fault for being there. What do you think you're doing, a single woman all alone in Nepal? You asked for it; you deserved it! Goodbye!"

And that was it. He didn't give her any money, and this is after having all this happen to her. You would think, your own daughter, you'd certainly bring her back to a civilized country, and you would help her!

And then you can rant and rave at her afterwards, if you are so inclined. I guess this was Japanese tradition. Accordingly, she'd disgraced her family for doing this. He just didn't want to have anything to do with her, and she's just left.

I think that was hard for her to accept, as well as it was that we were saying earlier when we had to accept the food that was offered to us, even though we knew it would give us an intestinal disease. It's just to save face.

According to May, they (the Nepalese) are really trying hard and stuff, and the only polite Asian way is, you just accept it. You just save face. So, that was May. She was always very polite, very sweet and willing to accept other people.

But I think she just came to us. And she had some friends back home, she had us in Bangkok, she went to us for help and that's what it was.

When she got home, when the father found out that she was raped, he was mortified. The Japanese are conditioned to commit suicide. His thinking might well have been, *You (May) have disgraced the family. The only way you can bring honor back to your family is to commit suicide.*"

I believe that was May's father's way of thinking. I don't know how serious he would have been about wanting her to do such a thing, but I surmise it wasn't that far off the mark.

What was her response to that?

I think she said "no way was she going to commit suicide."

It's not that I think she told her father off or anything; it's just that, well, okay, she just left and realized that nothing — no love, no support was going to come from her father. She had gone through a lot of this in the past. They had been reconciled at different points, however.

Her parents were very hard to deal with. Her father was divorced from her mother and to the father medicine was everything and he just worked all the time. Ironically, he was the greatest doctor to his patients, and even May'd be the first to admit that. People felt that he's was a super guy. He'd bend over backwards. He'd come home late at night. He'd do anything he could for his patients.

But for his family? Well, that was a whole different matter. It was they who had to support HIM. Not the other way around. She just had to reconcile that fact in her life.

I don't know how well May's done that. She's very quiet about this. You don't present these types of things to people. You just deal with it yourself, I guess. She did talk a little bit about it, but even though I had been really close to her, she never really spoke of her father in that horrible way. She just kind of, in her own objective way, just said, "Oh, you know..."

She's definitely of the modern era.

Let me ask you a couple of final questions.

Why didn't the soldier kill May when he had the chance?

Well, I don't know what the soldier actually wanted. He hit May a couple of times. She was unconscious. How much more do you want him to do? He was drunk from what she could assess earlier, so he might have just been in a violent drunken rage, out of control, but not necessarily with any intent to actually kill or rape anyone.

Choking the Sherpa?

I think that was just to get him out of there. Obviously, he (they) robbed the tent. I think there may well have been a couple of other soldiers involved, too, who robbed the tent. But I don't know what the culture is. May was an American Japanese woman out there. There may have been some animosity between tourists and some Nepalese.

Maybe, because she's not with a man, didn't have protection, then, therefore, she's open game for any man. I don't know if that's what it is. I know that's the macho Latin type of culture to think that way. Maybe it's the same in lots of other places. Any American woman, for instance, traveling alone is a whore. Now, I don't know for sure if that's the way they think there.

Okay, you started off saying that this guy at the University of Hawaii was saying that Nepal is safe.

Oh, yeah. The dean of the University of Hawaii Medical School said that at the time. And I think that was the thinking in common among lots of people.

Okay, but in fact, it's not all that safe, is it? Or is this just an isolated case, do you think?

I don't know. May said as she was coming back, people she met in the hospital and stuff, were telling her all types of hair-raising stories that they had gone through.

So, maybe Nepal isn't really all that safe these days?

Finally, whatever happened to the parties concerned in May's situation in Nepal?

May did say that the Nepali soldier was convicted and received two years in jail.

Any remorse on the part of the Nepalese government?

She tried to talk to the Nepalese ambassador to Bangkok in Thailand but he wouldn't talk to her. She called several times.

And, did she ever hear any more about Rodna?

Rodna was fired.

For running off?

I guess for running away. Well, I kind of blame him for that. I don't know what would have happened if he hadn't done that. Rodna was sent off. He had never done that trip before. He was new. The only reason why they had him there was because he could speak English, and the other guide who was the other Sherpa couldn't speak very good English, but he knew the trails very well so they kind of combined the two talents.

But there were no complaints about that. The only thing is that you travel with five people you trust and yet this still happened.

But in a life/death situation, you never know. You don't know who you can count on. You better be able to just be able to count on yourself.

May was, in the end, not absolutely sure that she was actually raped other than the after signs.

She only supposed so from the aftermath. Obviously, there was some sexual goings on there, but it was a seriously violent attack.

It's a very heavy story, but one that must be told.

Raped in South Asia:
Aftermath Nightmare #3

S. Johnson

This story is of a tall athletic blonde, a beautiful Swedish girl with all the physical and mental attributes I think of a woman in her early 20s. She goes off to India. She goes off to a remote part of India, somewhere near the borders of Afghanistan and Pakistan, traveling alone. For whatever reasons, she was evidently kidnapped and raped repeatedly by a whole gang of men.

She stayed a captive for about a month. She finally freed herself and got back somewhere to get help.

She was in such a bad state, and being in India, the only thing that they could treat her with was morphine or some derivative of morphine, and she became addicted to the morphine or heroin, whatever it was.

She finally got back to Europe after becoming a drug addict and having to support her habit. I picked up this story when an old boyfriend of hers came and lived with me in London.

He came to London because she was then in prison. How she got in prison after all this rape and ordeal out of India was that she started smuggling drugs into the country and into Europe from Asia, and the curious part of it was that in smuggling the drugs into England, she was stopped coming through customs.

Because she was an addict or because of some guilt she had about what she was doing or some guilt of being mistreated by all these people, all these men, for such a long period of time, she just about gave herself away.

They did not, however, find any drugs on her this time, but in being questioned — not even interrogated — going through customs, she sort of just broke down and told them where all these drugs were on her person, who was involved with her, and everything, else.

And now this specimen, this superb specimen of a person, is doing a number of years in a London women's prison, and it all happened within a period of one year of her life.

I've not seen her in prison. I've not seen her since it happened.

I did meet her a year or two before it happened, and there's no reason to deny that she was exceptionally beautiful; she was exceptionally talented; she was exceptionally intelligent.

Languages, everything.

The money from drugs — the money for her to be cured of the drugs — she meant to go to a special hospital. That's why she was smuggling drugs, to become cured by going into a special hospital in Switzerland. And that was her last trip.

She had the money. Her life had disintegrated in the aftermath of being raped in this God-forsaken India-Pakistan area of the world. Too bad.

The Camel Chronicles:
A Camel Ride into Oblivion?

Linda Rollie

N ear Eilat, Israel, 1986. At a time just before my adventure to Israel, I
was an independent, invincible 26-year old American woman exud-
ing self-confidence. I decided that I was already burned out on the reality of
having to work for a living and was going to escape and travel somewhere.

I was convinced that I would be very safe if I traveled alone to Israel.

My very loving father was fearful about his youngest daughter traveling
to Israel all by herself and had even heard some horror stories about such
adventures. He decided before I left that he would take me fishing and do
some father-daughter bonding with me and maybe talk some very needed
sense into me.

I remember before I left on my trip to Israel, he grabbed me and hugged
me. And this man, who normally didn't show much emotion, was now literally shaking, even though he was a strong burly timber feller. And me, I
was so naive, that although I glimpsed his love and concern and fear there
at the time, I couldn't really grasp it.

I decided to go to Israel because I didn't know anything about another
culture. I was a young Christian woman from Jacksonville, Oregon who
hadn't so far been exposed to very much in life.

And somebody had suggested that, in my denial of having to work for
a living, Israel might just take me in and let me work in exchange for food
and board in a kibbutz there, a typical collective working farming com-
mune. That certainly was a life lesson for me.

So, I arrived in Tel Aviv with only $11.50 in my pocket. I then went on
to a kibbutz just ten minutes short of the Lebanon border and worked there
for a few weeks doing such things as picking cucumbers, doing kitchen
work, plucking chickens, making lasagna for some 600 people, and even

cracking open some 600 eggs a day, and so on. I did this for a few weeks and it got old very quickly. So, I decided I didn't want to do so-called 'women's work' anymore, and I was ready to move on.

Among the other Kibbutz volunteers, about 30 of us from all around the world, who having heard of my plans, were nothing less than horrified at the notion that I would not only consider venturing out alone but that, in particular, I would travel in Israel going south all alone.

They took me aside and said that they just heard that a blonde woman was traded for some sixteen hundred camels somewhere down there and that it wasn't such a terrific idea what I was about to be doing.

Where this had happened, I guess I didn't know and nobody else knew. It seemed conjecture and overblown — at least considering my level of self-confidence. And come on, 1,600 camels is a bit much! It had to be an exaggeration. I really had a hard time believing this sort of thing.

But again, this naïve, invincible, strong-willed, stubborn young American-educated woman, *ME*, from America, could not be dissuaded. My mind was made up, and off I went.

By the time I was making my way south, it became more apparent to me that men were becoming, in general, more assertive and aggressive the further south I went.

I was traveling, however, making myself look as unattractive as I could: for instance, I dressed in a pair of navy blue wool pants left over from somebody's military days, a blue jacket keeping a hood up over my blonde head, my hair in a ponytail, no makeup at all, with my nose to the ground, so-to-speak, and walking straight. *This should make a difference,* I was thinking.

I remember coming to the end of the road at the southernmost point of Israel, which is Eilat, a wealthy seacoast resort town that, of course, I could not at all afford.

As I looked out in front of me, I noticed six Bedouin Arabs, who looked pretty authentic, coming right out of the really harsh desert in southern Israel. I think it might have been a father-son combo and maybe a few others, as well as a camel or two.

Then they asked me if I wanted to 'take a ride on their camel.' It seemed innocent enough, kind of just to have some fun, and so on. However, I was in no mood for that at all, given how shocked and horrified I was, on seeing the poor animal's condition. I loved animals, and this poor camel had sores all over its body, probably having marched for miles and miles under the hot desert sun to get to where they were now.

So, there I stood, in all my self-righteousness, self-indignation, and over-assertiveness — and maybe even a dash of Israeli *chutzpah* (guts) even — and said, "No, I don't want to take a ride on this camel! And, in fact, that camel could really use some *CARE* from you!"

So, now the man who had made the 'kind' offer seemed to retrench and pull back a bit, I think, out of being shocked at my over-confidence, apparent verve, misplaced assertiveness, and maybe even insolence in his eyes.

Then they started to laugh, seemingly mockingly at me, and kind of spoke among themselves, sequestering for a moment probably, maybe about to have a "Well, what have we here?" kind of moment. At this point, I suppose it was all conjecture on my over-imaginative part, after-all, how much world- and desert- savvy could this naïve and inexperienced traveler really claim?

I happened to look over to my left, and standing there not far from these Bedouins, and seeming strangely very out of place, but apparently observing the goings on, I saw a young Caucasian man, dressed in minimal desert garb, staring very intently directly at me. I think this was his way of trying to get my attention.

I then seemed to hear his voice INSIDE my head saying to me — and it *HAD* to be telepathic — (I swear he didn't actually speak to me; I'm absolutely convinced of this) — as he looked me right in the eyes conveying, "Get out of here *NOW!*"

What was so odd about this was, rather than speaking to me in English, his message seemed telepathic to me. It was the first and only time in my life that I think I experienced anything like telepathy!

And, I looked at him, and I just shook my head and thought, *Okay.*

I then promptly turned around, reversed course, and simply walked away from these men immediately. And I remember feeling a little sick right then at that moment, maybe as the result of some emotional start over all this. And momentarily, and without any fanfare at all, I was promptly out of there.

Who was that Caucasian man? Was he really there? Was he a figment of my imagination? Was he a guardian angel? Was my reaction to these Bedouin men maybe all a figment of my imagination?

Then, I remember thinking to myself, *Just look at the color of their skin, Linda. They're dark; they're Arab. And you're a white Norwegian-Swedish blonde out here in the desert all alone by yourself. You don't belong here at all, and you just pushed your envelope as far as you can push it.*

After I left, I found a small hotel and stayed there for about two days, recognizing that I was getting heat stroke and that I needed some fluids in me and I just needed to recuperate and regroup a bit.

Two days later, I was out of Israel altogether and landing in New York's John F. Kennedy International Airport. I remember thinking it was so beautiful in the women's bathroom there. Such opulence! The gold and the brass handles and the tile; everything was so bright and shiny. I literally dropped down and kissed the floor; I was just so glad to be back in America.

So, my loving father was right, after all, and has now forgiven me for my travel indiscretions. I had to eventually write him a letter of apology.

My whole interaction with the Bedouins lasted probably only two minutes. So much happened in that brief space and time. But in thinking back, I feel they must have been a little conniving and manipulative. I think they were presenting themselves to me as being gregarious and friendly and 'what a fun time this would be for you to take a ride on a camel'... I mean, after all, the tourists do it elsewhere, such as in Egypt, don't they? While having, all the while, more sinister intentions in store for me.

And when I responded so confidently and shared my feelings so freely about the lack of care of the animal, which, of course, they didn't care at all about, and which was in conflict with their own values, maybe I had been quite naïve and vulnerable after all.

Their rubbing shoulders together and communing among themselves for a minute or two about me, "Well, what have we here? This is different from what we expected."

I think I must have caught them all by surprise as some sort of a fortuitous unexpected find.

My guess is that had I not have gotten out of there right there and then, it wouldn't have taken too much longer for me to be merely grabbed and taken off. But, in the end, I guess I'll never know. And I'll never know how much this near-desert traveler would have been worth in camels, either.

How do you know that you can trust certain people? These people even?

That's probably a question of just darn good common sense that you're a single woman all by yourself, 26 years of age, and that you've been fore-warned; you've been cautioned not to do this. You've already heard the alleged outcomes of similar situations, and it's a matter of just using your head and your common sense at that point.

When you feel you had that so-called telepathic experience, did you think that that was a bit strange?

Oddly, not really. He just connected with me; and however he did that, it just resonated perfectly with me. And I guess when I responded, "Okay," I suppose it was in recognition, on some subconscious level, that I had better take heed, that I would be getting myself into a very precarious situation, and that I should get the hell out of there post-haste.

Maybe it was just his look that said it all? Maybe it was just my imagination? Maybe I projected all this onto him? Or maybe it was telepathy with a guardian angel? Who can say?

It certainly looks like it might have been a close call. And, no doubt, I learned a serious life lesson on that day. Just two minutes might have changed my life!

Geeky, Disabled Girls in Italy

Have you had to fend off any other male advances in other countries?

A girlfriend from Portland and I were recalling stories one day, and she talked about how we two blondes were so fatigued with Italian men pursuing us that we decided to pretend we were really geeky disabled people, and we were walking down the street geekily and spastically just so we wouldn't be attractive to the Italian men.

Did that work?

Yeah, it did while we were acting geeky and neurotic, yeah.

But, nonetheless, I do remember getting pinched several times from Italian men on other occasions, and I believe I think I actually liked it!

Your Daughter for Camels?

Selina Delafield

Jordan, 1981. I was traveling in Jordan with my father. I was about 17 years of age. We were traveling around the Holy Land. An Arabic entourage stopped by near to where we were to pick up our travel belongings and accouterments.

Since I have unusually clear blue eyes, which they like, of course, and dark hair, and fair skin, which seem to be valuable to men in that region, in Jordan and elsewhere in the Middle East, my father was offered a fortune in camels for me right there on the spot.

Like, how many camels?

I don't remember the amount, but it was a considerable amount, the offer that he was given.

So, what was he saying?

He started laughing. He thought about it for a minute — the money sounded good.

But apparently, *they* were not laughing. They were dead serious. Maybe he considered it just for a second. (Laughs)

But, no, of course, he wasn't going to go through with it.

Do you think others have gone through such things like this?

I'm sure. I have no doubt.

Do you have a look that you can pass for different nationalities?

Yeah, I would probably say so.

Your Girlfriend for Camels?

Joseph "Giuseppe" Spada

Luxor, Egypt, 1984. I am Italian; I'm Sicilian. I was living in Geneva, Switzerland. I was working in a hospital and I was ready for a break. I asked for a leave of absence, which they wouldn't give me, so I quit. I had saved up about the equivalent of $3,000 U.S., and so, it was all about traveling and how long I could stretch out that money.

But, in those days, that was a pretty good amount of money compared to today, huh? It stretched more.

Yeah, yeah, it was good; I mean during those days, some of the hotels that I stayed in Egypt were only like 75 cents a night! You'd sleep in the hallway, and so, the money could really go a long way.

Egyptian Men

I did some traveling in Egypt. I remember this one time that was particularly interesting when I traveled down there for about two months. So, I had gone up and down Egypt, and so, I pretty well knew Egypt inside and out by that time.

I had met some local people near Luxor, which is the Valley of the King's area. My then girlfriend and I had arranged for her to come down and visit me. The short of it is that essentially she came down and she met me, and it was kind of an adventure trying to find each other at first, but we finally did find one another. And so, we stayed in this hotel that I was already staying in.

I remember this one time where she was in the room, and I had gone out for a little while to run an errand or do something,

When I came back these two local guys were in there, and they were really after her. It wasn't a very private kind of a situation there; it was a small hotel and things where you know you would walk in and out of places, and they were there, and they were really interested in her. So, after a while, I was just kind of having to fend them off, literally.

But then, these men and I talked a little later. They basically wanted to offer me five camels for her.

Now, I have heard of this sort of thing before. So, are you treating this as a joke? How are you treating it then?

No, not at all. I was like, "Forget it! You are not getting the girl!"

But, it was just interesting to know their perceptions of how they saw that white women were essentially very easy to get.

Was she blonde?

No, no. She was dark with dark hair and dark skin. She was also a little on the tall side. She was French from the south of France. So, she had that air about her. She was really good looking.

It was just interesting to see how they thought that they could just go to bed with her, just like that, and that if they offered me enough for her, I would just simply let her go — that we would exchange her, and that I would just take the camels and then do whatever with them. I would just sell the camels or keep them. To these Egyptians, camels are prized possessions. So, this wasn't just some hasty, haphazard glib offer; they were dead serious.

Were you concerned about these guys? Were they potentially dangerous?

I think they could have been, but I wasn't really too worried about it. You know, they were just young guys, probably in their early 20s. And it seems to be more about their culture, per se, rather than if they were really going to go through with it or not. I think that to these two Egyptians, the attitudes that they had towards women were pretty strong and pretty possessive and very machoistic in some way.

What did they think about European girls in particular?

To them, Western women were whores, no less.

That's right, and that's part of the problem. Do you know that white slavery in North Africa is or was a problem in North Africa at that time?

No, I didn't know that, but it certainly had that energy about it. I mean, that they wanted her. It wasn't because they liked her or because they cared about her or because they thought she was nice; it was that she was an object to them, and they were going to use her for whatever purpose or to whatever extent they do use women.

So, they were absolutely serious?

Absolutely. No question about it.

Did you leave that hotel?

Yeah, we left. We didn't want to hang out too long there after that.

I was kind of pissed, because one of the guys was really aggressive towards her, and he really wanted to make out with her, you know.

And she, all the while, was trying to kind of go with the flow and be nice, and minimize it all — that sort of thing. But when I saw this going on, I kind of got all riled up, like, "Hey you, you move off of her!"

This was not very pleasant for us there anymore, so we left.

Italian Men

Let me ask you this. I have met a lot of American women who have had problems in Italy, you know, like having to do with Italian men's attitudes towards northern European and American women.

So, you know, you being from Italy, do you know a little bit about this? They don't treat these foreign girls like they treat their sisters or their mothers or their aunts, do they? What is that attitude?

The attitude is that these Italian guys are really hot for sex and they really are very physical, and so, they go for it — they're not shy. They just go for it. And it's difficult for the woman to know what to do.

Now, the Italian girls over there know better what to do, so they're not quite as bothered.

What do they do? What do the Italian women do?

They do several things: They avoid eye contact. They don't respond. They keep walking. And they ignore it. The ignoring is the biggest thing.

I mean, if you look back, if you start to feel flattered, if you respond — and I mean, just even make eye contact — they're going to go, "Okay, now is my chance!"

And they're going to start digging a little further. And it then makes it more and more difficult for the woman to pull out of it afterwards.

This is great! You're a great source to talk to about this stuff. And I appreciate that. But, tell me this: how come you are different from them then?

Well, I'm different now. I wasn't always. But the thing is, you know, it's not, of course, all of them — all Italian men.

I'd say, at a deeper level many of them are not like that at all. Because they've grown up with the culture that they are mommies' boys, so really it's kind of funny, because it puts out that image. But underneath, it's kind of the opposite; really, they're just these same little boys after all.

Like I say, they don't treat their sisters the same way as they treat these Scandinavian girls coming down.

Absolutely not.

It's interesting because a lot of girls do travel there to hook up with guys!

So, there's certainly some truth to some of the stereotypes, huh?

There's some truth to the myth. And I've seen it myself. Especially if you go to Rome and maybe even Naples, but at least to Rome and south of there, a lot of women do go there if they're lonesome, single and divorced, or whatever, just to have a good time.

Sold to the Highest Bidder?

Charlotte Byrne

Tangier, Morocco, 1970. I was traveling through Europe and ended up in Morocco, planning to go further down in Africa. But Morocco kind of stopped me right in my tracks.

Why was that?

Well, I had many adventures in Morocco and I was traveling there alone. I was a young woman alone in Morocco. And that's one tall order!

Oh wow, that's a pretty powerful statement because Morocco can be scary, huh?

Well, at first I was very naïve and unaware. (Laughs) I was just having a good time.

The first thing I was told when I arrived off the ferry to Tangier was that I could not stay in the Casbah by myself because that would be too dangerous.

So, I went to stay at a hotel by the beach where the tourists typically stay. On the second, day I was there, I went out on a tour with an elderly couple, the tour guide, and myself. We went to see some of the caves that were in the area.

And when I came back, the tour guide said to me, "Well, why don't you come with me. I'm going to go up into the mountains, and we can have some coffee there, and we can look at the place where the Mediterranean and the Atlantic Ocean join."

And I said, "Well, that would be very cool, so, yes, let's go do that."

So, off we went in a taxi up into the mountains, and we did indeed stop at several different cafes.

As a sidebar to the story for a second, why was it so dangerous for a young girl to stay in the Casbah?

It was because women in that society don't have a lot of freedom, and they're either in the homes of their fathers or in the homes of their husbands. And they do wear veils and the full covering, depending on their personal tastes, but they just don't go out onto the streets without at least a veil on or without being accompanied by a man.

Okay, so why would that be dangerous for you, a foreigner?

Because I would have been seen as someone who was 'available' to maybe being treated as a man would care to treat me, however they would care to do so. So, women at that time were more like property. They were sort of like cattle in that sense — owned as property. Maybe the word "chattel," as in property, would be a better choice of words.

I was totally unaware that there was that much of a difference between the two societies, namely, that of the U.S. and that of Morocco. And so, naturally, I would never have thought of myself as possibly being cattle or chattel.

However, by the time I left Morocco I understood that that just might be so, according to someone else's perceptions.

At any rate, I never really left Tangier during this visit to Morocco. Shortly thereafter, I left Morocco for Europe.

So, you're now stopping at these cafes going up towards the mountains.

Yes. We're sitting in the cafes, and the tour guide and the taxi cab driver are now communing with one another, and now are beginning to slap each other on their backs and joke around, undoubtedly saying in Arabic the equivalent of such stuff as, "Oh, my buddy, buddy," and whatnot.

And, of course, I'm just sitting there and am picking up absolutely nothing at all about the ensuing discourse and what's really going on. I don't understand what they're saying. And I am making no assumptions at all about what may or may not have transpired between the two of them under these circumstances.

After a while, when we're up in the mountains, I say to my tour guide, "Well, I have someone I have to meet; I need to go back to Tangier."

So, my tour guide now says to me, "Well, okay, but on the way back we need to stop off at our taxi driver's apartment for a moment."

So, I say, "Fine, okay."

And we leave. Off we go to the apartment. The three of us enter the apartment together. And there, now the tour guide says to me, "Well, I'm going to go out and get a coke or something."

I say, "Well, okay."

And, no sooner than he leaves, the cab driver grabs me. He just *GRABS* me!

What goes through your mind then?

Well, it's something like this: *I don't want to be here; I REALLY don't want to be here.* So, I struggle with him and manage to break away and get into the bathroom and lock the door.

You were scared, huh?

Yes, of course, I was. I was terrified! And I was also very seriously concerned for myself, for my safety.

After I got in the bathroom and locked the door, I must have stayed there for, what must have seemed like an eternity — I don't know how long, maybe half an hour, forty-five minutes or so. But then, good news! Through the door, I hear him snoring. *It's time to make my escape*, I am thinking.

So, I sneak out of the bathroom as quietly and carefully as I possibly can, which is just across from the entrance door, and I just about manage to get my hand on the doorknob.

And suddenly, the cab driver jumps up and grabs me from behind. However, I manage to get the door open maybe four inches or so. And outside the door is someone standing there in one of those typical Moroccan robes that they wear there, called *djellabas.* These are those common woolen robes with brown and white stripes on them that every man in Morocco wears.

As soon as I see that other person, I feel the taxi driver's hands suddenly release me and I just bolt out of there. I have NO idea who it is standing there in that robe, and I could not care less; I am right out that door instantly. It is now dark outside, and I am definitely in a part of Tangier that I do not know at all.

What was that like?

That was scary. That was really scary. And the streets of Tangier were scary. And I was doubly scared as well because I had no idea of what was going to happen next. But, I did know by that time, of course, that I wasn't very safe as a solo female wandering alone by herself around the streets of Tangier at night in the dark.

I decide my best bet is to head towards the beach and try to find my hotel. At least, if I can find *ANY* hotel at all, that would be a lot better than ambling along in the dark in a very indubitably questionable and very scary area of Tangier.

I'm walking down the street looking as focused and on purpose as I possibly can because I really don't know where I was going. And wouldn't you know it — that very same cab driver now drives right up behind me. And he's yelling and screaming at me, and gesturing, "Why don't you get just right back in the cab?" and stuff like that. And silly me, I get into his cab. Where is my head at?

Why in the world would you get right back in that cab with that very same driver who only minutes before was about to rape you?

Because I figure that that was safer than walking the streets as terrified as I was. So, I get in the cab and he drives me down towards the beach.

On the way, he stops a policeman and starts screaming and yelling at the policeman and pointing to me at the same time.

The only word that I can just barely make out was "*dirham,*" which is the money in Morocco. So, at first, I thought that he was complaining to the cop that I owed him a taxi fare. My God, what else could it possibly be? I had not the least idea. Would he / could he even dare attempt to pull off some sort of a taxicab fare scam on me?

And, as I am sitting in the back of the cab, suddenly all the pieces fall right into place. I'm now saying to myself, *Gosh dang it — I have just been sold!* My thoughts are now reverberating back and forth in my mind: *How can this possibly be?*

Then the thought strikes me: The tour guide has SOLD me to the cab driver! He *SOLD* me! Can you believe it?

And the cab driver was upset (and perhaps rightly so, according to *his* way of thinking) because he didn't get what he bought that he thought he had paid for, meaning *ME!* In other words, the cab driver was scammed into buying me and now thought he owned me! That it was as if I was his property, his cattle or his chattel. And he didn't get his money's worth! Or he didn't get his money *AT ALL!* And that, therefore, he was cheated!

Apparently, he was unsuccessful in trying to make his case to the cop. And so, he then drove me back to the hotel and simply left me there.

So, what do you think the cop said or did?

Well, I can't be sure at all. The cop was speaking to him in Arabic, which I could not, of course, understand. The cop was probably not buying it at all and just said something to the effect, "Oh, just take her back to her hotel," and motioned to him to just do that.

So, the tour guide sold you to the taxi driver! And the taxi driver, in turn, then tried to rape you in his apartment, thinking that he actually 'owned' you — that you were his. And you escaped. He found you again and decided that he owned you and complained to the policeman.

Yep. I would say that about sums it up!

And you had no idea, really, what it was all about, and slowly, but surely, you just began to figure it all out. I thought at first, myself, that he was trying to scam you for the taxi fare.

No, no no. Not at all!

Okay, so he then took you back to your hotel, dropped you off, and just left?

Yes, that's it exactly.

And then I got changed and I went to go try and meet this person I was supposed to meet earlier. And on my way there, the floodgates opened, and I just started crying. It was all too much for me.

And so, what my big lesson after all that was that you really do need to trust your instincts and act upon them.

In the first instance, I actually did get the message that something funny was going on, but I did not respond to that. I just went along with the weird program and went back to the taxi driver's apartment, which was very stupid of me.

The second instance was when he came back after me in the taxi after I had run away. I really couldn't figure out why I felt like I ought to get back in his car, except that I was really scared where I was. And it certainly seemed that it was the lesser of two evils at the time. It was like choosing between the devil you know and the devil you don't know!

All is well that ends well, I guess. My dear, you just skirted white slavery, you know.

Well, now you really fully understand the dangers of Morocco of that era, huh?

Sold (Out) to the Arabs?

Jerry R. DiMento

In Kabul I picked up a Texan girl. She wanted to travel with us because she was scared to go to the Muslim countries alone. We told her sure, but neither of us liked her from the start. She was a nag.

She came along with us. Our next stop was Teheran. On the route to the Far East, there are four big cities, Istanbul, Teheran, Kabul, and New Delhi, where you get cleaned up after traveling everywhere in between.

I was running low on money, but I had just enough to get to Naples, where my relatives would take care of me. My friend left us in Teheran. The girl and I caught a bus to Istanbul. This girl was really getting on my nerves. I really had to get rid of her some way. But I wasn't just going to leave her; that wouldn't be right.

I had planned to hitchhike overland through Yugoslavia and head down to Italy. But she persuaded me that the boat from Athens to Brindisi in Italy was only $10, real cheap.

So, we took a boat from Trabzon in the north of Turkey on the Black Sea to Istanbul. It took two days and two nights to get there. The cost was amazingly low, only $2.50! You couldn't beat that!

The Turks were very attracted to her. They kept asking me if she was *MY* woman. I kept saying no; she was up for grabs. The Turkish guys were treating me royally; they were feeding me like a king, just because she was with me, and I certainly wasn't making any claims on her.

We got off the boat in Istanbul. It's a hole. It's funny; I just could not wait to get to Istanbul! All I could think of were all the good things that I'd heard about the place. But as soon as I got there, I couldn't wait to get out of there.

From Istanbul, we had to hitchhike to Athens. It took us 17 rides just to get out of Turkey!

I had heard rumors that they hassle you crossing over into Greece on foot. But, you could enter Greece if you could show that you had $100 in cash on you. So, one of the reasons I let her stay on with me was because she had $400. When we got to the border she just slid me $100. And that was okay.

When you hitchhike you live free. If you smoke cigarettes you never have to buy them, because people are always offering them to you. There's always food in the trucks, and they are always feeding you. You never go hungry hitchhiking.

We got to Alexandropoulos. Two Jordanians in a Mercedes-Benz pulled up. Their car was filled with food and fruit and everything. We got in. And, no sooner that girl was out of sight later on, for some reason, they said, "Can we have her tonight?"

I said, "Sure," because we desperately needed the ride. They were on their way to Athens.

All day long we stopped at really good restaurants and they fed us. But at Thessaloniki, I began to feel guilty about the deal I made with the Jordanians. I got her aside and said to her, "Look, I told these guys that you were theirs!"

The car came to a red light and stopped. We suddenly grabbed our packs and literally dove out of the car! Of course, the Jordanians were quite upset by this but drove on. I mean, what could they do. They were rich people. They owned a refrigerator company. They weren't hurting. So, no problem.

I found out later that the boat to Italy actually cost $30, not the $10 that she told me it would cost. That was finally the last straw. I told her to go fuck herself and get lost. And that was the end of that.

I was desperate for money. So, I even gave blood in Athens! It gave me $22, not quite enough. So, I hitchhiked all the way across Greece to Patras on the west coast. The boat cost maybe $20 to go to Italy, instead of the $30 price to leave from Athens.

I was thinking, *The clothes I'm wearing — the shirt's got all holes in it; the pants are all raggedly. I feel like shit.*

I just had to get to Italy to meet up with my relatives. Meanwhile, I had joined up with another traveling companion. It took us two days to go the

80 miles. We had spent only $2 on food. We slept out. In Greece, it's easy to sleep out, because there are so many unfinished houses you can sleep in. It was easy to find a half finished house, go inside, put out the sleeping bag and be sheltered from the wind. It was pretty cold by then; it was fall.

The next day we ended up by having to jump on a bus, which left us like a couple dollars short for the boat tickets.

My traveling companion met some French girls who were willing to pay his way but not mine. Maybe they didn't like Americans; I don't know. Maybe they just didn't like me. Or maybe they didn't like filthy Americans, like me.

I was a dollar short and walking around trying to think of what to do. A Greek guy just happened to come up to me. He was walking his dog. He looked at me and said, "You need anything? You look like you are in trouble."

I said, "Yeah, I need just one dollar for the boat!"

He gave me the dollar! I was just walking around. I wasn't asking for nothing from nobody. I was looking for a job. And he just gave me the dollar. I got on the boat. Maybe it was the way I looked. He saw the clothes. I had a long beard. I was skinny like a stick.

On the boat the French girls turned out to be friendly. They gave me some food. Landed in Brindisi at 6 PM that night. All's well that ends well, I guess.

It's funny; the things you may be driven to do, like 'selling out' the girl to the Jordanians, in exchange for that critical ride and free food. I'm glad that I at least maintained some semblance of self-respect in regard to her.

The Train Station Epiphany

Stacey Vickery

A small town in France, 2003. Well, I was so tired of traveling for 34 hours straight on trains. I was coming back to Spain from Lille, France, which is like at the very top of France, almost to Belgium. This was quite a trip, and I ended up falling asleep in a little train station in a tiny French town not far from the Spanish border.

France

I must have eventually dozed off on this one bench because a security kind of guy kept kicking me periodically on this great bench, which was not a particularly comfortable place, to begin with. The guard kept kicking me, seemingly all night. Finally, it's like 6 o'clock the morning or whatever, and the guy is gone.

My falling asleep on this bench, I realized later, was probably not the best idea in the world, because I woke up and there's a man standing and staring right across from me.

Well, first I look over and there's this big bag sitting right next to my head on this bench, and I'm thinking, *What is that?*

It wasn't there before. And I look at this man standing there just looking at me very intently.

And, I look right back at him, just, you know, looking at him like, "And what on earth do you want with me?"

And that feeling was like, "I'm not gonna let you harm me!"

I'm looking at the bag, and I notice it's probably been placed there as some form of intimidation, leaving me thinking to myself, *Maybe it's a bomb or something?*

Suddenly, I have this thought that is as plain as day to me — this sudden realization that, *I have as much power that that man has!*

344

And, you know, I ended up just sitting there, which kind of scared him, even. I think maybe because I was putting out such a mental shield like, "You can't hurt me."

What was in the bag?

I didn't look in the bag; it wasn't my property. Just his personal stuff, I imagine.

That was an adventure.

Why was the other one kicking you?

Probably because he didn't want me to fall asleep, thinking some weird man might put a bag next to my head, and who might stare at me all night! (Laughs)

Were you scared at all?

I was a little scared, but I think that's what brought on my sudden realization and my power to be like, "Well, you can't hurt me!"

I think it was the fear in me that triggered in me my thought that, *I don't need to be scared.*

Is that like changing it into an adventure?

Yes, basically. I believe that we can make anything in life into an adventure, even though we do fear things, but that the moment that we fear — the moment we become the victim, that is the moment we _ARE_ the victims.

So, you have a choice: you either bow your head down and look like a victim, and that's when the predators are gonna get you. Or, better, you can decide *NOT* to be the victim. That is the instant I hold my head up high.

Spain

Now, being a single woman traveling by yourself through Spain... It's a Latin culture. These guys always come on to girls.

They're very horny.

Okay, so how did you deal with that?

The first day I was in Spain all I knew of Spanish was a pathetic *"Ola!"* (Hello!)

Since then, I've had a lot of men coming up to me and talking to me, and it wasn't the words that I could tell they were being sexual, but the way that they spoke to me. And I'd just look at them — and go "hmm" — and then just smile and did not give in to their sexual energy. I didn't want to look particularly sexy; I didn't want to be sexual, because the way I want to attract people was more, you know, I wanted to get to know people.

And in Spain, I really wanted to get to know the people; I wanted to speak with them. And the only way to learn and speak with the people is I wound up speaking with a lot of men in bars at night. And, of course, they were coming on to me, and I'd sort of go, "Hmm," and I'd just keep talking with them.

Did this work?

It worked; but in some ways it didn't. I never had much in the way of problems, really. The people in Spain are very respectful people, you know.

But they look at an American and they say of a white American woman traveling in Spain, "Oh, she puts out."

They think that if you're an American girl, you're a "Baywatch babe."

And, I've had people attack me verbally. I remember one of the first sentences I learned to say in Spanish was, *"Yo soy an individual,"* which means, "I am an individual," because they'd verbally attack Americans.

They'd say, "What are you doing to the world?"

I'd say in response, "It's not _ME_ that's doing it! I am an individual."

Did that work?

Yes.

I lived in a town called Oviedo for the majority of the time in northern Spain near the Basque area.

And those boys that initially attacked me verbally, I ended up becoming buddies with them, because they were just like, "Yeah, you're okay!" (Whatever the Spanish equivalent is.)

So, I ended up feeling like I really showed some people in a foreign country that Americans aren't like they all presume.

So, what is your advice to other girls or women traveling when these men come on to them?

I tell them, "Hold your head up high, and even if you don't understand a word they're saying... it's all about the way you present yourself. It's all too easy for American women to try to use their sexuality to their advantage You need to be careful about doing this.

So, if you want to meet people and really get to know people anywhere in the world, even if you speak the language, the best thing to do is to not bring out that sexuality. That's exactly what they are trying to bring out in us, especially in foreign countries, and you learn to fight against that, without doing so in a mean way. It's best to have an attitude of, "Well, I'm not really feeling like giving you that satisfaction."

And so, how about couching all this in terms of the victim idea that you were telling me before? How do you keep from becoming the victim with these predator people?

It is so easy. All it is, is holding your head up high, and at times you might even feel like you're a snob, because your nose is pointing towards the sky. But you know what? That is your best defense against anybody on this planet. I think they end up being maybe not scared of you, but they know not to mess with you.

I have power! You have power! Hold power within yourself and keep that in you, because they're going to try to steal it away from you.

I've I seen way too many people try to take my power away or diminish it in order feel more powerful themselves. But, you know, if you put your head up high and you walk strong, there's no way that people can take that from you.

I just think it's great you're doing something like this! (Writing on this.)

Two Mini-Strategies that Paid Off

Kelly LaRose

———————◆———————

Paris, France, the late 1970s. Have you ever had any scary moments?

Yeah, a couple of times that were scary at first.

What happened?

Well, a couple of times I had been followed by guys from the Paris Metro.

The first time, for instance, one day this guy was following me from the Metro. I was going back to my place.

I didn't want to make it very obvious, however, that I was scared of him and that I was trying to escape from him. So, this one time, I didn't make it very obvious that I was running from him. So, I purposely did not run right in front of him, so that he did not actually see that I was, in fact, doing so. As soon as I turned the corner, out of his view, then I ran like hell.

Why didn't you run in front of him?

So that it did not obviously become more like a chase, you know, like triggering in a cat the natural hunting and chase instinct. At first, I made it seem that he was only just barely aware that I knew he was following me. I just didn't want to make it too obvious.

Did you finally make your escape?

Yeah.

The second time, I actually confronted the guy by purposely making a scene in public. I was sort of hiding from him at first, and then when I saw him coming up and looking for me, I first made sure that there were other people immediately around me. And then I yelled out in my poor French for all to hear something to the effect, "Why are you following me?"

He then seemed taken aback by that and blurted out that he wanted to 'buy me a drink' (or something like that).

I then shouted in plain view of everyone, "Look, I don't like it; I don't want you following me, and; I don't want a drink!" And then I added, *"GO!"*

I think by my gestures and shouting I made it all quite clear and embarrassed him.

And then I watched him slink back to the Metro before I quickly walked off.

That took a lot of courage to do that, don't you think?

Yeah.

Two Tested Strategies:

These are two really good strategies if you can possibly do them:

1) Try not to be too obvious by running directly in front of or away from someone, if possible, but then, as soon as you can — as soon as the coast is clear — then just bolt.

2) To confront someone when there are other people around in order to create a public scene and make it very obvious that you are being bothered or menaced by him, you know, so they won't likely do anything right in the public view, that's a very good thing.

Where did you learn all this? It's your own savvy, huh?

Uh-huh.

Travel Tip #9:
Do Various and Sundry Acts!

Michael Brein

A variety of miscellaneous behavioral acts are likely to foster your safety and security in an unknown or potentially unpleasant situation.

Rule #1 Act Like You Belong!

Always do your best to appear "in place." If you appear to be a regular who knows what he or she is doing, that communicates confidence. No creep or pervert wants to bother with someone who appears to be cued in, and ergo, knows what is going on and what is happening.

It is the exceptions that attract the criminals. Separating the sheep from the goats, so-to-speak, has always been the law of the jungle. Predators always try to separate the easiest prey from the herd.

If you look like you belong, if you look like the 'normal,' you won't likely be spotted as the best and easiest prey. Though this is not always easy to carry off, it certainly is a plus factor working towards your continued safety and security.

Rule #2 Walk Tall!

Exude confidence as best as possible. Not 'over'-confidence, but the notion that you have a firm grip on things. Standing tall, walking confidently, steadily, and ignoring unwanted advances, and neither heeding nor paying attention to overt acts or calls, as best as one can do, will suggest that you are not to be messed with.

Rule #3 Act Like You Are in Control!

Never, _EVER_ appear as a struggling victim in distress. Never give cues that you are the victim. Nothing broadcasts more to a predator than that you are someone NOT in control. Thieves and predators of all kinds are essentially cowards.

If you seem 'easy' in any way, whatsoever, you will attract creeps of all kinds that are on the prowl in search of easy victims or easy prey.

Appearing to be in distress, appearing to be out of control, or appearing distracted in any way, i.e., looking at a map, staring into a book, or engulfed in your technology devices is a clear indication that you are not paying attention to what is going on right around you.

Since, these are all, in a way, distractions that detract from your paying attention, you are, in their minds, "easy pickings."

Rule #4 Seek Others Out Immediately!

Finally, when alone while being followed, harassed or otherwise undesirably being sought out, try to seek the presence or company of others as quickly as possible. There's nothing like the presence of others to dissuade the cowardly acts of predators. Whether simply a couple or a larger crowd, nothing works better than creating a public 'scene' that hardly ever fails to send an unwanted marauder off packing.

The author discovered in Spain and witnessed several times (even when possibly one of these events pertained to HIMSELF), that as soon as a crowd spotted a pickpocket in the vicinity, whether on a Metro or in a square, they would all begin to chime in and chant out loud in unison as a group, *"Ladrone! Ladrone!"* (Thief! Thief!), which immediately served to send the would-be pickpockets scurrying off.

Rule #5 Seek Out Safe Havens!

If other people are not immediately available, seek out some sort of a safe haven, where a pursuer would not likely follow you. For example, run into a nearby building, like a bank, a post office, a hotel, a church, or even a café — a very public place — where it would be obvious what is happening, and where it would be very easy for you to create a public scene. Cowards, bullies, and others who would do you harm will very likely back off in such situations. And then you can plan out your options for continuing to where you are going.

Travel Tip #10:
Manage Your Fear!

Michael Brein

———◆———

Try to manage your fear rather than let your fear manage you. Unrestrained, rampant fear leads to blind panic. And panic appears to be the complete absence of rationality — the complete failure to be able to deal with any possible options to safe and secure outcomes in any meaningful, realistic and rational way.

Thus, panic would seem to be the rather randomized, unrealistic, and ineffective way of dealing with fearful situations that can and do arise from time to time in travel in any meaningful, constructive and potentially effective way.

However, in the absence of total and complete panic, any options that do remain, however limited they may be, do at least seem to offer some possibilities. And where there are possibilities, there is still hope.

One attitude that seems to be described by some travelers who have experienced fear in their travels is their apparent ability to muster or manifest on some occasions some kinds of — for lack of any other better term — inner personal strengths that have helped them overcome some dangerous situations.

Almost analogous to the famous saying, "the only thing we have to fear is fear itself!" by Franklin D. Roosevelt, many travelers have personally evolved the notion that being fearful of having "bad attitudes" is what makes you the potential 'victim,' and is what creates in you the psychological personal space that somehow 'attracts' to you or enables in some way the predators and dangers; and. therefore, the potential for bad things happening to you is increased.

An oft-stated popular corollary to that is that if you, therefore, maintain a good, positive, upbeat, confident and non-fearful outward attitude

352

and demeanor, you will not, therefore, attract the negativity and danger. In other words, by having or enabling these "positive" attitudes and demeanor you are less likely to attract to you and experience or suffer the consequences of perceived dangers.

Whether this is reality or truth is basically open to question. This book has provided plenty of examples that, despite what people do in their travels, sometimes these adages do appear to hold true, and sometimes they do not.

The basic rule, no matter in which direction you lean, is to, nevertheless, leave all your options open, and the more options to escaping potentially dangerous or harmful situations, the better.

The more personal degrees of freedom of choices that travelers enable themselves to have, the more and the better their options are for avoiding being in harms' way.

Abiding by the *"Travel Tips"* offered in this book as well as those offered by other travel writers can certainly not hurt and can only be viewed as positive and constructive.

It has been my opinion that the best way to maximize the potential benefits of travel and to improve on the odds of safe and secure travel for the solo woman traveler as well as anyone else, is to learn from the experiences and wisdom of other travelers. And this is what I have sought to provide in this book, *Travel Tales: Women Alone.*

Travel Tip # 11:
Trust No One!

Michael Brein

One popular theme that has emerged from the famous TV and movie series, The X-Files, is the notion that you dare not, for your own good, trust anyone, ergo the mantra, "Trust No One." For a solo woman traveling, unfortunately, this often holds too true to be good.

The single most pressing psychological question that every solo woman traveler, or any other traveler, for that matter, ought to at least ask themselves is, *how do I know I can trust someone?*

Given the nearly 100 accounts in this book of women traveling alone, the single most overriding factor for their getting into the trouble in the first place is due to their failure to carefully assess enough who to and who not to trust.

By far, that women get themselves into difficult situations is mostly attributable to their trusting someone too easily, too quickly, or in many cases, trusting the wrong people totally, whereas if they had been even a little more astute enough or wary enough, they may not have trusted so easily so quickly. And they, therefore, might have saved themselves the grief, the harassments, and the assaults that they have suffered.

Indeed, what many women travelers fail to realize is that thieves, pickpockets, creeps, and perverts of all varieties often know, understand, recognize, and anticipate all too well the tendencies of troubled, anxious or scared women travelers to let their guards down too easily, because their anxieties or fears overwhelm them to the point that they do not evaluate carefully enough the intentions of strangers and too readily and eagerly fall into a trap, whereby they become easy and willing victims. Needless to say, neediness anticipates carelessness.

I've asked women travelers many times, "How do you know who you can trust?"

I've even heard some women say, "I am trusting of others, because I, myself, trust others!" I trust, so, therefore, I expect others to be trustworthy as well.

Unfortunately, nothing could be further from the truth, where there are bad people vis-à-vis good people. Young, naive, and relatively inexperienced travelers need to understand and know full well that just because they, themselves, are of high moral character, good-willed, and possess many of the good and wonderful traits and characteristics that we seek and honor in other good people everywhere, not everyone is like them!

That's a tough life lesson to learn. It is an age-old conundrum for anyone to duly consider: why he or she tends to trust people, whereas perhaps they should not.

It is for the lack of due diligence or good common sense that some of these women featured in this book got themselves into trouble.

Now, it is always a good idea if you can modulate your tendency to have to trust or rely on others, whom you encounter in travel and do not know very well, with options that give you ways out if need be.

Unfortunately for some women in this book, they found themselves getting deeper and deeper into situations that they could not back themselves out of. Instead of choosing immediately to extricate themselves, they opted for *"the devil you know, rather than the devil you don't know."*

In other words, the alternatives, like finding themselves in scary, dangerous and seedy areas, seemed more frightening to them than staying in and hoping to cope with the ominous situations that they were in.

I'm reminded of the old Russian proverb, which became the mantra of the Reagan administration in dealing with the Soviets: *trust but verify*! It's damned well nice if and when you can do that, but it is not always the case that you can do so!

Yes, it's good to trust others in travel, when you *can*, if they've earned your trust somewhat, but only do so, if and only if, you have sufficient escape options.

It is often, if not mostly always the case, that women in these instances are purposely and surreptitiously manipulated into situations where they have decreasing choices, and where, sadly, escape is ultimately the least viable option!

So, how do you know who you can trust?

This book has provided many examples of the really good cues that some travelers have sadly noticed, realized or learned too late — many, even, recalled after the fact, of dangerous and horrible encounters.

We have seen many examples throughout these pages of intuitions and cues that have saved the day for some solo women travelers.

In the end, it is for all of us to determine for ourselves if and when we can trust and rely on others and to what extent we can and should do so. These are constantly changing life lessons that we must all do our best to learn and continually apply to our travel lives as well as our ordinary more mundane home existences.

Hopefully, the ample examples of sexual harassment and assault of women travelers provided in this book, and how women have coped with these pernicious travel situations have given us all good grist for the mill.

The New #MeToo of Travel

Michael Brein

According to *Wikipedia:* The #MeToo (or Me Too) movement is a relatively new phenomenon created to refer to a growing presence and voice of many women who are finally coming forward as having been prior silent victims of the widespread prevalence of sexual harassment, assault, and abuse among women, particularly in the entertainment industry and other workplaces.

Increasing vocal public revelations by women, many who are relatively famous, who have heretofore been silent victims of such behaviors, are becoming the new rallying cry — indeed, the new norm — that is encouraging more and more women to come forward with their own accounts of similar sexual abuses.

The evident widespread occurrence of such sexual misconduct is coming more and more into the public eye by the growing admissions by many women, including many public figures and stars, that they too have been victims.

And this makes it easier, indeed, for more and more women to come forward, themselves, with their own personal accounts of sexual harassment and assaults, due to the growing momentum of public awareness of the extent and magnitude of such sexual abuses.

As this book *Travel Tales: Women Alone* amply demonstrates, there is indeed the equivalent prevalence of sexual harassment and assault within the context of domestic and foreign travel as well.

Indeed, we are hearing more and more about it as a result of the growing #MeToo phenomenon emerging in the United States and spreading worldwide. Undoubtedly, sexual harassment and assault have also been rampant among women travelers probably since time immemorial.

Moving forward, women will have more opportunity to give vent to and air out in the open, the demeaning and disgusting sexual abuses that many have suffered and continue to suffer in their travels today.

While many women travelers have come forward in this book to tell about their own harrowing sexual harassment and assault experiences, the voices of many more women sadly still remain as of yet unheard.

For it has been the unfortunate norm in society, particularly in the past, essentially to remain silent. Women have been accustomed to bearing the brunt and suffering silently with such degrading behaviors, simply because they did not believe that much of anything would or could likely come of it.

But now, it seems that times are finally a changing. Not only are women speaking out — rather, they are *SHOUTING* out, *"Me Too!"* — because doing so now makes a difference!

Sadly, though, the sexual assaults and abuses we have heard of recently in the context of travel merely represent more the tip of a vast social iceberg.

It has been one of the purposes of this book to begin to make the sufferings of women travelers better known. And, hopefully, by doing so, the world can now become a better and safer place for all travelers, especially for women.

Now, the momentum is growing; women travelers are shouting out *"Me Too!"* — and the world is finally listening and paying more attention. And change is beginning to take place, at least, initially, because more people not only are listening now, but they are also speaking out!

Groped on a Plane!

Michael Brein

———◦———

Recently, women have been coming forward to let others know what has happened to them in hotels, on metros, on trains and elsewhere in their travels. And, in the news, these days, some women travelers have also become even more vocal about such sexual abuses that they have suffered as passengers on airplanes — on *AIRPLANES*, no less!

Recent Cases in Point

Whereas the airplane environment has often heretofore been considered to be a fairly sacrosanct space, it is now coming to light that such an attitude can only be termed as being more naive than anything else!

If you are a woman unfortunate enough to have been groped on an airplane by a man seated next to you, what can you do? What should you do? What is the airline's responsibility to protect you and to ensure that your rights are protected? These are all very good questions.

Unfortunately, occurrences of these assaults, though probably not particularly rare in the past, are slowly coming to light in the modern era, when women are speaking out more about their rights and abuse by fellow passengers.

The current #MeToo movement unfolding in the United States and spreading worldwide is, no doubt, fueling the tendency for women to be angered by these abuses and to seek recompense and satisfaction not only for the abuses committed by these sexual predators but also to make sure that the airlines themselves begin to take responsibility for dealing with these affronts in a satisfactory manner.

The good news is that recently at least one major world airline, Air India, has already taken steps to institute women-only seating sections on their aircraft in order to help curtail the incidences of sexual harassment and abuse on their flights.

It was fairly widely reported in the news media as recently as 2018 by the India Times, CNN, the Washington Post, the Seattle Times, and other media, what happened to at least three female airline passengers. These revelations, which appear below, are merely the tip of a vast iceberg.

Thanks to the media, in conjunction with the emerging #MeToo phenomenon, more sexual assault incidents that many women travelers are suffering as passengers on airplanes are coming to light.

Fortunately, when such matters do finally become more widely and publicly known, there is a good chance that positive change will take place.

Groped on a Plane #1

Pam Ross

Somewhere over the Pacific Ocean, 1986. I was once "felt up" on a United Airlines flight from Honolulu to Los Angeles. I was seated in the window seat and two men were in the center and aisle seats of my row.

I don't remember being traumatized by it. I just remember waking up and realizing what was happening and stood up in my window seat. Although not possible to stand up fully straight, I faced outward towards the aisle, pushed the call button and just waited for the flight attendant to appear.

I never spoke to the man in the seat next to me or even looked at him but just stood waiting. When the flight attendant came by, I told her what had happened; everyone was looking at me; it was the middle of the night, and I spoke in a loud voice.

They reseated me in first class, moved the guy to the window from the center seat, and that was it. I did not complain to the airline; they handled the situation effectively and efficiently. They seemed to know exactly what they were doing.

In retrospect, how do you feel about it all?

I did not feel violated, only angry that someone would try something like that. Yes, I did want everyone around me to know what this person had done; that's why I spoke loud enough for everyone around me to hear.

He put up no resistance. He was around 40, was not drinking, and I never spoke to him.

I, at that time, had never heard of this happening. I do not have a particular take on the flight attendant, however. She was very businesslike and professional, did not accuse him, and did not expect me to remain in that seat.

When we landed in LA the pilot made an announcement, something like, "Please remain in your seats; there has been an incident on the flight, and LAPD will be boarding the flight to remove a passenger."

After I had been reseated, the flight attendant gave me paper and pen and asked me to write out a statement and give my contact phone number. I was later contacted by a California district attorney who asked if I wanted to file charges. I did not. United Airlines had acted appropriately; the perpetrator had been exposed and life went on.

Groped on a Plane #2

Unknown

According to the *India Times,* an Indian man was arrested for allegedly groping a woman multiple times on a flight from Delhi to Mumbai. The alleged offender was seated next to a woman, who just happened to be a lawyer, when, according to police, he touched this woman with his hand and his leg.

She asked him to sit up properly, but he touched her yet again, this time with one of his arms. The woman complained to one of the flight attendants, whereupon they assigned her to another seat. But no sooner had she arose to move to that seat, the man asked her, "You do not like to be touched?"

Simply unbelievable!

Police were alerted by the airline captain, and when the airplane arrived at the gate in Mumbai, the offender was removed from the plane and promptly arrested in accordance with the Indian penal code.

Groped on a Plane #3

'A.D.'

According to CNN, the Seattle Times and other media outlets, a woman, who we shall refer to as A.D., claims that she was sexually assaulted by a fellow passenger in the air during a 10-hour flight to Europe from Seattle to Amsterdam. A.D. says she was seated in a window seat when the passenger right next to her aggressed her several times.

Says A.D., "I suddenly felt a hand in my crotch, and without even thinking I swatted and yelled, 'No!'" And then, again, "As I was starting to get away, he grabbed me again. I hit him again, and then, as I was going to leave, he went to block me and grab me as I was trying to get away out of the seat."

All told, the man, according to A.D., touched her three times in all.

Statistics do not appear to be relatively common, but one source reports that inflight sexual assaults, according to the FBI, increased by some 60-70 percent over the last few years. There is no doubt that inflight sexual aggressions are underreported, probably due to victims' reticence to report them. So, more than likely, many more of these sorts of assaults do occur. Assaults, even of young children, too, are sometimes reported.

Unfortunately, it appears that the airlines are not doing nearly enough to deal with the men doing these sexual assaults. While, no doubt, some victims are possibly litigating these matters on their own, we can expect more legal cases to emerge as the #MeToo phenomenon gathers steam.

One flight attendant says that the airlines are not doing nearly enough to keep passengers and their children safe. She adds, "In my years as a flight attendant, I have never been trained on what to do if I encounter a sexual assault on the plane. That simply has got to change."

A.D. maintains that the flight attendants on her plane did not do nearly enough to help her.

As for the alleged assailant, he simply walked off the airplane once it landed and that was the end of it.

Says A.D., "He changed seats, and he wasn't in his original seat," adding, "He walked off the plane. I don't know where he went and we've never been able to figure out who he was."

She says no report was ever filed even after she complained to several crewmembers that she had been assaulted, and no one interviewed the passenger or got his identification.

"Their response to me was, 'We're sorry for any inconvenience. It's unfortunate when one person's behavior affects another. Here are 10,000 miles,'" Furthermore, they said, "We actually have no record of any incident on your flight, so this matter is closed."

And that was A.D.'s problem on her flight: that they failed to create such a report either out of an unwillingness to do so or out of negligence.

Her airline told her that they were disheartened by the events that she had described to them, adding — unsurprisingly, of course: they could be expected to say this — that they take all reports of sexual assaults very seriously along with the safety of all passengers and crew.

So, what do experts say that you can do to protect yourself from sexual assaults on airplanes? They say that you should stay alert and let flight attendants know as soon as possible. Also, try to book a seat on an aisle, because sitting by the window restricts your freedom of movement leaving you in a more vulnerable position.

Says A.D., "Absolutely find a crewmember on the flight that can help you. Let them know what happened, inform the pilot, inform the ground crew and make sure a report is filed."

Groped on a Plane #4

'K.C.'

K.C. was seated on a short flight from Newark to Buffalo. Within just minutes of taking off, a drunken male passenger sitting next to her began groping and harassing her and another female passenger in the same row, grabbing K.C. repeatedly despite her demanding for him to stop.

"He grabbed my upper thigh, like in the crotch area, and he grabbed it pretty forcefully," K.C. said.

The man stopped touching her after she left her seat and raced to the back of the plane to tell a flight attendant what was happening. K.C. adds that when she told the flight crewmembers what the man had done, she didn't feel that she was taken at all seriously. When she refused to sit back down next to the aggressor, they then began to get the picture.

According to K.C., "I felt like no one, no one that was supposed to be in charge, could handle the situation. I kept on feeling, and I continue now, as I'm like filing these reports, to feel like I'm the one who is doing something wrong, and I'm not being protected."

As a last resort, K.C. was reseated immediately behind the man who was harassing her. The airline said that was because there were limited seats available on that flight.

Again, the man, K.C. said, didn't stop touching her even after she relocated. "This man continued," she said. "He should have been restrained so he couldn't continue to do this. And just continuing to touch and stare just made me feel completely helpless and horrible. It was terrifying."

Again, that particular airline said that the airline has "Zero tolerance for this type of behavior."

Furthermore, "Our pilot requested that local law enforcement meet the aircraft on arrival."

When that flight arrived at the gate, police were already waiting and took the man off the airplane. He was later charged with disorderly conduct.

Men Alone:
Men on Men

Michael Brein

———◉———

As a final chapter, I would be remiss if I did not address sexual harassment and assault of men traveling alone, too — so-called "men on men." It happens to men traveling alone, but apparently not nearly to the extent that women are sexually harassed and assaulted in their travels.

Here are several accounts of incidents of such sexual harassment from interviews I have conducted over the years with male travelers.

The reader will note the similarities to what has happened to some women travelers, particularly when hitchhiking and in train stations.

It stands to good reason and almost goes without saying, that men traveling alone would be wise to pay heed to the occurrences and outcomes of sexual harassments and assaults involving women presented in this book.

Two Incidents

Hanno Huppe

Dijon, France, the 1980s.
Hitchhiking
How did this happen? Tell the story from the beginning.

I was hitchhiking. I just came out of the youth hostel and tried to find a car to hitchhike with.

A man stopped and asked me, "Where do you want to go?"

I said, "I want to go in the direction of Lyon."

He said, "Yes, get in."

I wasn't in the car for very long, maybe for only five minutes or so.

Every time he shifted gears, he'd put his hand on my knee.

He actually put his hand on your knee? What did you do?

Yes. I'd jerk my knee away. But he continued to do it further.

I said, "No. It's better I leave the car."

And fortunately he stopped the car and let me out, but he wasn't very nice about it.

The Train Station
Paris, France. Another time was in Paris at the Montparnasse train station. Maybe it was around 10 PM in the evening. In Paris the youth hostels are very expensive, so I thought I'd sleep anywhere I could.

I left my luggage at the station there. My plan was to leave Paris the next day. But anyhow, I was looking at my map in the meantime to see where I would go next in Paris that night.

It was at that point that I met this guy. I don't remember exactly how this happened. Maybe he saw me looking at my map and started a conversation with me.

I talked to him briefly. He said he had two children and a woman with him for the holidays, and he invited me to sleep at his place.

369

So, I said, "Okay," and went with him.

We had a very good conversation at his place. We drank a lot of wine and whiskey, and so on.

I slept without incident. But about 6:00 AM in the morning he came to where I was lying on the couch. He was nude and wanted to come onto the couch with me to make love with me, and so on.

I said, "No!"

I got my clothes on as fast as I could.

And he was shouting, "No! Stay! Stay!"

I said, "No, I don't want to."

No way was I going to stay there. I left the house as quickly as I could. Thankfully, I wasn't forced in any way to stay. I could, of course, have left any time I wanted to. There was no force involved.

Needless to say, it was only he and I at the apartment. There were no other people: no children and no woman that he was supposedly traveling with. It was all an apparent ruse. I think he was at the train station 'trolling!'

The Christian Prison

John McComas

M eknes, Morocco, the late 1980s. Another Moroccan experience happened to me in Meknes, in the old city, in the *medina* (market). It was the middle of the day when basically everybody takes a nap or goes and eats or rests because it's really, really hot. So, there were very few people around. I was still hopping around and looking at things and exploring the area.

Meknes has an old subterranean Christian prison. It was a prison in which the Arabs, during the time that the Arabs and the Christians were fighting in the Mediterranean, would put their captured Christian prisoners. There may have been other prisons, but this was a very, very large one.

I went to take a look at this prison. It was very, very quiet, but there were a few young Moroccans hanging around the prison area while I was there. I was by myself. They approached me in a typical way that young Moroccans will with their four, five or six languages in which they are fluent in order to find out which language you speak, so they know which language to communicate with you in.

So, they approach me and I do, in fact, talk to them, because I am interested in going down into the prison. As I descend towards the prison, I see that there is a metal bar gate at the entrance, which you have to pass through. You go down these steps, pass through this metal bar entrance gate, and you're in the prison.

It's just basically a huge cavern, or several huge caverns, supported by pillars. There is almost no light. There are just occasional little holes where you get a beam of light going through. A little light, but basically fairly dark, but you can still see the places where they have the metal links in the wall to which they would chain people to.

I walk around there a bit and just take a fairly quick look in there. Again, as you spend time in Morocco, you can cue into things that people say and the way that people behave. So, one of the questions that comes up is, "Am I traveling by myself?"

I say, "Yes."

The next question is, "Where's your wife?" or, "Do you have a wife?"

I say, "No, I don't."

Now, this is usually a lead to homosexual or gay advances. Homosexuality for pay, and, sure enough, it is. I see this coming, and there are three of these young Moroccan guys down in this prison with me, and there's nobody else around. It's really isolated. This is the middle of the day, and there's not going to be anybody else around for a couple of more hours.

I am thinking that this is not a very comfortable situation at all for me to be in, in terms of what seems is now the tone of the conversation, the way the conversation seems to be heading.

So, I sort of start wandering, making my way in the direction back towards the exit out of this place.

I decide that I don't really want to be down in this isolated prison with these guys hanging around me. This prison is actually outside somewhat of the town, a bit isolated, so there's not really a lot of traffic running past.

One of the Moroccans says to me, "Do you want a blow job?" (Or several other kinds of unsavory options that are apparently available to me.)

He continues, "If you just drop your pants or something, I could fuck you off here and it won't cost you very much, just five *dirham* (Moroccan money)," whatever that is; it's not that much, really.

I say, "No, no, that's all right."

"Why not? Why not? Is there anything wrong with it?"

"If that's what you're into, there's nothing wrong. That's okay, but I'm not interested in that, and I don't do that kind of thing."

"But everybody does that. Why? What's wrong with that? Why don't you want to do that? There's nothing wrong in that. You should do it. How about four dirham?"

"No, I'm not interested."

" Three?"

"No, I'm not interested."

"There's nothing wrong with it. We can just do it right here. We can do it really quickly. Just a few minutes."

"No, that's okay."

I'm making my way back, working my way while this conversation is going on, no longer interested in the prison, back to the gate, and, hopefully, outside and away from these guys.

Just as we get to the gate, the one guy that's making all these propositions to me, who's the oldest guy there and the biggest guy there, darts quickly right past me up the steps to the gate. Of the three Moroccans with me, two of them are fairly young, I'd say, maybe 15 or 16; the older guy is maybe 18 or 19.

They try to go by me, but I realize what's going on at this point, and so I block the steps, but I cannot catch the other guy in time before he can get to the gate. He gets to the gate first. He then closes and locks the gate, trapping not only me but his two colleagues as well.

I am really angry and I am scared at this point because I am not going to let these guys go by me, but I also don't like being cornered, especially when there's nobody else around.

Now the guy outside the gate starts saying, "If you want to get out, you have to pay me some money."

I say, "I'm not going to pay you any money."

He says, "Then you're not going to get out!"

I say, "If I don't get out, then these guys aren't getting out, either."

I'm being really brave, but I'm sure that if they really want to get out, they both can easily run right over me, especially since there're two of them and only one of me. This is the stand I decide to take, though, and, as my only bargaining chip, I need to keep these guys inside with me.

So, the three of us are locked inside together and this guy is outside. It's a 'Mexican standoff,' sort of, at least for the moment.

A fourth guy now shows up outside the gate, another fairly young guy. I start getting really angry because now this fourth guy basically starts taunting me. I cannot really remember precisely what he is saying, but it is just the way he is saying things.

"Well, we don't ever have to let you out, you know. If you don't pay us money, we're never going to let you out. We don't care. You can just stay here as long as you want to."

I am getting really angry, but at the same time, I am trying not to show it. So, I sit down on the step that's right next to gate — the gate actually opens in — so that the gate has to open into my back, and I am thereby preventing it from opening.

I figure I'm not going to move. If the gate opens, I'm going to be the first one out of the gate. If the gate doesn't open, then nobody else is going to go by it, either.

I say, "Okay, I'm in no hurry. I don't have any place to go. I can sit here."

I guess, ultimately, I am thinking, *In two or three or four hours, somebody is bound to eventually come by and open the gate for me.* So, I'm not really all that worried.

The guy keeps saying, "Give me 10 dirham (Moroccan money), and I'll let you out. Let's not hassle this. Only 10 dirham, and I'll let you out, and you can go free. Why don't you just give me the money, and I'll let you out and then there'll be no problem? You can just go out and go and no problem at all."

I stand my ground and say, "No."

So, we sit there, and five minutes pass; then another 10 minutes pass, and now the guys who are locked in with me start talking to the other guys in Arabic. It's pretty clear these guys are not at all happy just sitting in there, either.

Finally, the guy starts to open the gate, and I immediately stand up, put both my elbows out and block the path of the others, because I am going to make sure that I'm the first one out the gate.

The gate opens, and, in fact, I am the first one out the gate. I get out of the gate and now I'm really incensed, but there's really nothing that I can do. That's the frustrating thing. There's absolutely nothing I can do.

You think, *Well, I could go to the police,* but it's really sort of ridiculous to think about doing that kind of thing. It's just the feeling of frustration that you are so angry that these guys could do something like this to you. And you have basically no control over it at all. So, you just really seethe.

I walk up the steps to the ground level, and now the guy who locked me in in the first place, who was the largest guy there, runs up after me going, "Hey, wait, wait, wait. I'm the caretaker here. I'm the caretaker here. I opened the place up for you. I showed you around. Aren't you going to give me some money? Aren't you going to give me a tip for showing you around?"

And I blew up. I turned to him and said, "Are you kidding me? Give you some money? You're lucky I don't report you to the police."

And I stomped off.

This is one example of Moroccan scams that can happen to you, among con games and rip-offs. This one was the "prisoner scam," or whatever you want to call it. But in its own way, it was at least sexual harassment if not potentially sexual assault.

Travel Tip #12:
Be the Good Traveler!

Michael Brein

For women (and men) *tourists*, good, better, and best *travelers*, *adventurers*, and *explorers* — in that order — all become increasingly more involved with, experienced with, and knowledgeable of the peoples, languages, and cultures that they visit in their travels.

There appears to be a direct correlation between the degree to which you are experienced as a *traveler* and the degree of safety and security that you will enjoy in your travels. The more experienced you are as a traveler, the safer and more secure you will likely be, and the fewer sexual hassles and assaults you as a woman solo traveler will likely have to suffer.

Thus, it stands to reason, that the 'better' the traveler you become, the safer you'll tend to be.

Thus, there are basically three types of travelers that fit along a continuum: the *tourist*, the *traveler* and the *adventurer*. And you can go even one step further, the *explorer!* For most of us, becoming a seasoned traveler is more than enough.

This continuum represents the degree of involvement and depth to which people engage with and understand the subtleties of the cultures they are visiting.

To become the best traveler you can be, and therefore the *safest* traveler as well, you should morph from being a simple mere *tourist* — don't be satisfied with being only a superficial tourist — to being a *traveler,* and even better yet, maybe even evolve into a *true adventurer,* and hence, the best traveler you can be!

The more you travel, and the more you become involved in new cultures, the more you learn and the fuller and more rewarding your travel experiences will become.

And, a corollary to this is the more experienced, and hence, better a traveler you are, the safer you will be as well. The two go hand in hand.

The first stage is the *tourist*, in which people are essentially only passive visitors, becoming only superficially involved with the cultures they are visiting. They neither particularly understand much of the depth of the peoples and cultures of the countries they are visiting, nor do they have an appreciation of the languages and subtleties of the cultures.

The less involved you are in a country overseas, the less you know, as well, about how to be safe and secure there.

So, what are the differences between a *tourist*, a *traveler*, and an *adventurer*? There are no hard and fast rules. However, one relatively simple way to look at it is to think of it in terms of differences in the degree of involvement one has with the people, language, and the culture of the country one is visiting.

Of course, being a tourist or a seasoned traveler is neither a good or bad thing, in and of itself. Naturally, there are times when you are interested in only being a relatively passive visitor, who is only superficially involved in the country you are just briefly visiting or passing through. Thus, you are a mere *tourist* or a *visitor*. By any standard, you are a travel *lightweight*, so-to-speak. And that's all right.

By becoming a more seasoned *traveler* or *adventurer*, however, you are now becoming more of a travel *heavyweight*. And over time, as you gain the benefits of travel, and as you gain more and more travel experience and confidence, you evolve into the second stage, the *traveler*.

The *traveler* begins to realize and appreciate the things in travel that are the most beneficial, exciting and rewarding and develops a deeper understanding and connection with the new cultures and people that he or she is visiting. Probably the most rewarding experiences are the people connections that you make. The more experienced you are as a traveler, the easier it is to understand, appreciate and relate to the locals, and the deeper your personal connections are likely to be.

Your involvement with the cultures you are visiting goes to a deeper level, whereby you better understand the more subtle differences between home cultures and those of the countries you are visiting.

If your purpose for traveling is to reap more genuine experiences with people, you will, of course, want to interact with them more, perhaps get to know them a little better, and maybe even participate or involve yourself more with them.

You need to, in effect, *immerse* yourself more in the foreign or host culture. If you are staying for a relatively long period of time, although you are, technically, still a *traveler* to there, you are residing there for a while — maybe, say, as a Peace Corps Volunteer.

The ultimate stage for anyone who devotes a life of travel is to become an *adventurer*. The adventurer may speak two or more languages and understands better the subtleties and nuances of the peoples and cultures they are visiting. And they may, thus, understand and appreciate more both the verbal and the non-verbal aspects of the language and communication, as well as the subtlety of gestures, spatial behaviors, and the like.

The adventurers, for all their immersion in the new host culture, undoubtedly reap the most benefits out of their travel experiences and understand and adapt much better to the subtle nuances of safety and security in their host environments.

So, they likely tend to be safer and more secure in their travels and suffer fewer sexual harassments and assaults, mainly because they essentially know what they are doing.

How this translates to the solo woman traveler is this: the better you understand the people, in general, and their cultures, in particular, and the more you can relate to them, appreciate them and understand them, the more you'll know, as well, how to better survive and overcome possible sexual hassles and dangers that you may be exposed to.

It goes without saying that the more experienced you are in your travels, the more you have gone the distance from being a mere *tourist*, only superficially involved in the new cultures being visited, through to becoming a seasoned, experienced and knowledgeable *traveler*, to the ultimate of maybe becoming a *true adventurer* — one who is just about as comfortable in any exotic culture you can think of as you are at home!

And, that, in essence, is what I mean by becoming a better traveler.

A corollary to this is: from the seasoned *traveler* to the *true adventurer*, by virtue of a lifetime of travel, not only do the most experienced travelers understand exotic cultures better — like the backs of their hands — they also understand their *OWN* cultures even better as well!

Now, here's the rub: If you know your own culture better, then you can then appreciate a new culture even more. You can perceive the very subtle differences between cultures all the more, and you are now more aware of subtle differences that exist in new places that those only superficially involved with travel can only hope to get a glimmer of.

And how does this translate into travel life? Seasoned travelers or adventurers also have a better idea of what to do and what not to do, and, thus, how to be safer and more secure.

Thus, by becoming more of a *traveler* than a *tourist*, — hence a *better* traveler — according to the Abraham Maslow 'Needs' hierarchy that virtually every beginning college student learns in Psychology 101, you are learning from travel the deeper experience of 'living' and 'experiencing' a culture instead of just touring, surviving, and meeting only the most basic of your travel needs.

If you aim to fulfill your higher order goals and needs in life through travel, rather than just satisfying the most basic, simple and routine ones — you will 'live' your travel-life to the fullest rather than just survive.

Safety and physiological needs are the most basic of human needs. Love, belonging, self-esteem, and self-actualization are all higher-order human needs, that if one fulfills them during travel, the overall human experience that results is far more rewarding.

The more successful you are as a *traveler*, vis-à-vis as a *tourist*, you are now a *good* traveler; you'll reap all the higher-order benefits that come from that, and you'll surely enjoy a more safe and secure travel experience.

Happy safe and secure travels!

Don't miss out!

Click the button below and you can sign up to receive emails whenever Michael Brein publishes a new book. There's no charge and no obligation.

https://books2read.com/r/B-A-KKFF-UIMQ

BOOKS 2 READ

Connecting independent readers to independent writers.

Did you love *Travel Tales: Women Alone — The #MeToo of Travel!*? Then you should read *Travel Tales: Michael's Own Best 150* by Michael Brein!

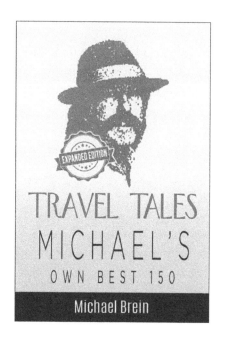

THIS SERIES

Over the last few decades, I've interviewed nearly 2,000 world travelers and adventurers. I am weaving the best of their nearly 10,000 fantastic travel tales into a psychology of travel as revealed by these very telling stories.

These are travelers I've encountered on planes, trains, buses, ships, tours, safaris, and in campgrounds, cafes, and pubs.

These courageous travelers have freely shared their most personal travel experiences, some good and wonderful and others even horrific and life-threatening, which I, in turn, get to share with you now through my *True Travel Tales* series.

Expect upwards of 100 ebooks covering many different countries and travel themes as well.

THIS BOOK

Travel Tales: Michael's Own Best 150, is Volume 2 of the *True Travel Tales* series which is the expanded *full* collection of the best of all my own personal travel stories in my rich, varied and adventurous travel life that has taken me to more than 125 countries.

My travel tales include a selection of my best, worst, funniest, and truly most horrible travel experiences, that, by virtue of their emotional impact upon me at the time, whether positive or negative, have now become my most memorable and interesting travel stories today.

From my unique perspective of being the world's first and probably *only* travel psychologist, I think you'll find my own travel experiences riveting, informative, funny, and entertaining. Please enjoy!

While some people say that some of my stories are riotous, others say that I should be kept locked up at home and not allowed to travel anywhere!

These events, as unbelievable as some of them may seem to be, really did happen to me! Read on!

Note: The 150 travel stories included in this book are divided into three parts. The first part includes my *own* personal 25 top travel stories in their entirety that make up Volume 1 in this series, *Travel Tales: Michael's Top 25.* The second and third parts contain an additional 125 of my *own* personal best travel stories.

So, if you are obtaining this *full* expanded Volume 2, *Travel Tales: Michael's Best 150,* please note that it also includes the *lite* version, Volume 1, *Travel Tales: Michael's Top 25,* in its entirety in Part 1 (Parts 2 and 3 include 125 more of my *own* personal best travel stories.)

DISCLAIMER

Please be forewarned that some stories in the *True Travel Tales* series may be graphic, unpleasant, and disturbing.

This series is generally aimed towards a more mature adult audience, yet, no doubt, some material ought to be communicated in a clear and responsible manner to younger and relatively inexperienced and naive travelers, who could benefit by knowing how to travel more safely and securely.

The author does not necessarily agree with opinions expressed by contributors.

Finally, no story in the series is meant to depict any country, people, culture or religion in a negative light. Good and bad things can and do happen anywhere and to anyone.

Note: Some stories may appear in more than one ebook in the *True Travel Tales* series, depending on the subject matter and countries covered. Read more at www.michaelbrein.com.

Also by Michael Brein

True Travel Tales
Travel Tales: Michael's Own Top 25
Travel Tales: Michael's Own Best 150
Travel Tales: Women Alone — The #MeToo of Travel!

Watch for more at www.michaelbrein.com.

About the Author

Michael Brein, also known as the *Travel Psychologist,* is an author, lecturer, travel storyteller, adventurer, and publisher of travel books and guides. He regularly appears in newspapers, magazines, blogs, and Internet radio programs on the psychology of travel.

Michael is the first person to coin the term 'travel psychology.' Through his doctoral studies, work and life experiences, and extensive world travels, he has become the world's first and maybe only travel psychologist.

His travel guide series, *Michael Brein's Travel Guides to Sightseeing by Public Transportation,* shows travelers how to sightsee the top 50 visitor attractions in the world's most popular cities easily and cheaply by public transportation.

Michael also publishes his *True Travel Tales* series, a collection of ebooks of the best of 10,000 travel stories shared with him from interviews with nearly 2,000 world travelers and adventurers that Michael has encountered in his own extensive travels around the world.

Michael Brein resides on Bainbridge Island, Washington.

Read more at www.michaelbrein.com.

About the Publisher

Michael Brein owns *Michael Brein Books,* the publishing arm of his *True Travel Tales* series and *Michael' Brein's Travel Guides to Sightseeing by Public Transportation* series.

The *True Travel Tales* series is based upon Michael's interviews with nearly 2,000 world travelers and adventurers over the last four decades of Michael's extensive travels around the world.

Michael has gathered about 10,000 travel tales shared with him by these courageous travelers, which he, in turn, shares the best of these travel stories with you in his *True Travel Tales* series.

Expect upwards of 100 *True Travel Tales* books to be published soon in this series

Michael also publishes the world's first travel guide series to sightseeing the world's most popular cities by publich transportation. In his 13 travel guides in this series, Michael shows you how to go exactly to the top 50 visitor attractions in each city using their public transportation systems.